The Price of Peace

and Other Stories

The Price of Peace
and Other Stories

By
Mary R. Zook

Rod and Staff Publishers, Inc.
Crockett, Kentucky 41413

Code no. 75-4-96

Foreword

Teenagers will read! As publishers, we have a burden to publish only that which encourages youth and instructs them in a happy, faithful Christian life. We believe this collection of true stories will be a source of edification to those who read it. Many have found them helpful already.

The stories have been published a number of years ago in *The Christian Example*. They are based on actual happenings, but the names and places have been changed and some details reconstructed. Care has been exercised to avoid changing the consequences of man's choices.

We are concerned that the imperfections in the lives of the characters in these true stories are not considered by our readers as acceptable conduct. In some cases the story itself presents those imperfections so the reader can see them for what they really are. In other cases the main character faced problems because the home or church setting were not what they should have been. Some publisher's notes have been added to help teenage readers to understand this and to prepare a good foundation for their own homes and churches in those matters.

May the Lord bless the stories that they may be an aid in building strong Christian character and faith in God.

The Publishers

Contents

The Price of Peace

Harold walked slowly to the house, wiping perspiration from his forehead. He had surely got stuck on that deal. Duke was the stubbornest mule he had ever seen. How would he ever get that field plowed with such an obstinate beast? He had very nearly lost his patience with Duke this morning. It was high time to get the crops out. Harold could not well afford to lose a crop now. The depression had just begun; and, having little to start with and a growing family of five, Harold had to make every day count. The rains had held up the planting for a long time—now this. Just when he most needed good help, he would have to be swindled by such a bargain. Fifty dollars for a mule was a large sum of money those days—fifty dollars for a no-good mule!

About a week ago Harold had gone to the sale, hoping to find a good mule for a reasonable price. Faithful old Floss was not able to pull the plow alone. Duke had certainly put on a good show working in a team with another good mule. Yes, it was true that Duke could put on the best show anyone could ask, but that was about all there was to it. The first half hour's work was well done, but then he was no more good than a dog. Duke just would not pull. He would hold back and kick. He would not budge. Coaxing, whipping, or bribing with grain were all to no avail after Duke decided to stop. Nothing could make him go.

After about an hour of frustration, trying to conquer his stubborn mule, Harold finally admitted defeat. "I cannot afford another mule. I cannot get along with Floss alone." Harold wondered, "What can I do? How can I ever make ends meet?" Things had gone very hard the past several months. "Fifty dollars thrown away—fifty dollars which could have been used for so many other things, things badly needed by the family." And yet the mule was needed, too. If only he had known that mule.

The following morning, a beautiful spring day, Harold decided to try again. While he was on the way to the barn, he wondered, "Will things go better today? Will that stubborn mule ever be conquered and make a good teamworker with Floss?" Every day for a week he had hoped. Every day had been the same trying story.

"Come, Duke. Good boy." He patted the mule's head, giving him good breakfast. "There now; do your best for me today," Harold begged. After finishing all his morning chores, Harold returned to the mules, gently placed the collar around their necks, and led them out to the field. Duke seemed willing and energetic. He kept in step beautifully, threw his shoulders into the harness, and pulled with all his might. He was surely doing his share of the work. There was never an act of ill humor shown until the beginning of the fourth round. Suddenly Duke stopped for no apparent reason. When encouraged to go, he rared back. Harold insisted; Duke kicked. It was no use. Harold unhitched the team and led Duke back to the barn. Would he never win? Must he lose his fifty dollars? How would an honest farmer ever be able to provide a living for his family?

Harold worried. He tried again the next day. As usual, the first half hour was going very nicely. Harold hoped for the best. As he neared the end of the third round, Harold noticed Mr. White standing at the end of the row. He wondered, "If I stop now, will Duke ever start again this morning?"

"Good morning," he greeted his neighbor in a friendly

manner, pulling up to a stop at the end of the row. "How are you?"

"Oh, I'm very well," Mr. White answered. "I've just been watching your team. Sure looks like they work together well. That mule is a real worker, isn't he?" Mr. White asked, walking around to get a better look at Duke.

Harold opened his mouth to tell the faults of his stubborn mule when Mr. White again began to praise the efforts that the mule had been putting out. "He is the kind I need. Sure wish I could get hold of a couple of good ones like that," he remarked, casting a quick glance at Harold.

"Ah—yes, he was really working hard, wasn't he?" Harold replied.

"Certainly was!" Mr. White agreed. "Say, Harold, you wouldn't consider selling that mule, would you?" the other farmer asked a bit overanxiously.

This was more than Harold expected. "Ah, yes," Harold hesitated. "Ah, yes, yes, I would consider it. I just hadn't thought of it before, but I would consider it."

Mr. White spoke quickly. "I'll give you fifty dollars cash for him," he offered easily.

"Fifty dollars!" Harold could hardly believe his ears. How glad he would be to have his fifty dollars back! At least he could buy some groceries and a few things very badly needed—maybe even a better mule for a better price, maybe one that would work more than a half hour a day. "Fifty dollars," he repeated. "Yes, I think I'll sell him. Money comes hard these days, you know!"

"Yes," Mr. White concluded, "so do mules that are any good!"

The deal was made. Mr. White came back that same afternoon with the cash and got his mule. He seemed very pleased with the bargain he had made.

Harold was not quite so pleased. Oh, yes, he was mighty glad to be rid of his no-good mule and felt himself very fortunate to have gotten his money back. He never expected to get half that much out of that mule. He just was no good. But—something else was bothering Harold. Had he made an honest deal? Had he been fair? Was his part in this transaction Christian? Harold wondered. He reasoned, "Mr. White set his own price. He saw the mule work. I did not brag on his work or try to make a sharp bargain. The man simply offered me so much for my mule and I accepted. Could that be wrong?" Still the conscience of this honest man would not be satisfied.

"I did need the money so badly," Harold concluded. "A man has to provide for his family."

"But not at the expense of honesty," his warning conscience probed. "God will provide. Your duty is to honor His Word.

"But he made the deal," Harold reasoned. "I wasn't trying to push my loss onto another. I had no intention to hide the faults of the mule and try to sell him at a good price. After all, that's what I paid for him, too, not knowing his lazy characteristics."

" 'As ye would that men should do to you. . . .' "

"I know. I know. But what is a man going to do?"

" 'Do ye also to them likewise.' "

Harold ceased his argument, appalled that he had dared to contend with God. Had God not plainly spoken through His Word—and Harold had resisted? "Yes, I should have told Mr. White the mule is no good. His good appearance would last only a short time. Then nothing would induce him to work. I should have, but I needed the money so badly. How can I provide for the children?"

"God will provide," the still small voice consoled. " 'My God shall supply all your need according to his riches in glory by Christ Jesus.' "

Finally, after a long period of indecision, Harold could no longer rest without doing something to clear his guilty conscience. His reasoning that the bargain was not his, but Mr. White's would no longer ease the heavy load he had borne since the day Duke left his farm.

In desperation, Harold finally laid out the problem before his loving heavenly Father. In humble contrition he knelt at the cross to have his load removed. He was willing now, at any cost, to have his conscience cleared.

"Father, what will You have me to do?" he prayed. "You understand my circumstances. You know my needs and how hard it is to provide for a family these days. You know what I have done and what I need to do."

After submitting his will wholly to God's will, it all became very plain to Harold what he needed to do. There was only one way: Do unto others as you would have them do to you. Harold closed his prayer. Peace ruled in his soul. He arose and went about his duties, trusting in Him for all things, spiritual and material.

Harold went to visit Mr. White, wondering what his reaction would be and wondering how he had felt about the deal. He had not seen Mr. White since he had left with the stubborn mule. Had he been able to do anything with him?

Harold entered the gate. Walking up through the yard, he wondered, "What kind of impression have I made on this man? What does he think of my Christianity now? Will he be angry and hard to talk to?" How Harold regretted now that he had allowed the temptation to overcome him! Praying that this incident would not bring reproach on the Name of Christ and His church, the humbled man started across the porch steps.

"Good morning, neighbor," Mr. White greeted him warmly. "Come on inside." Harold stepped into the kitchen, greatly encouraged by the friendliness of the man he had wronged. While he hesitated to mention the incident of the stubborn mule, Mr. White continued to chat in a friendly way.

"Mr. White," Harold began at last, "I came over to talk to you about the mule I sold you."

"Oh, yes," Mr. White replied.

"Are you having any trouble with that mule?"

Mr. White chuckled. "Trouble? Well, not anymore."

"You don't mean you got him trained?" Harold asked in surprise.

"No, not exactly. I finally gave it up as hopeless."

"Mr. White, I have felt very bad about that deal. I knew when I sold you the mule that he wasn't going to be any good. I needed money very badly and yielded to the temptation to get it in this way when I had a chance. I realize I should have told you about the faults of the mule the day you saw him working there in the field. I knew you wouldn't buy him if I did. I have decided to do one of two things. Either I will give you back all your money and take the mule back; or, if you want to keep the mule and see what you can do with him, I will give you back half the price you paid. The mule was never worth fifty dollars."

Mr. White listened quietly until Harold had finished. "No, the mule certainly was not worth fifty dollars. I had him only a few days before I realized that. But he surely was putting on a good show of what he could do the day I stopped by your field."

"Yes," Harold agreed, "that was the way he always worked—a half hour, then he was done. I knew when you asked about him that he wasn't what you were looking for."

"Well, after a week or so I realized I could not afford to spend my time with him so I sold him for fifty dollars!"

Harold was surprised. "You got fifty out of him?"

"Yes, just as you did. A few days later the man brought him back and I gave him his money back."

"I see," Harold replied. "So you were still stuck with the mule."

"Yes, and I decided not to try again to get a good price for a no-good mule and sold him cheap just to be rid of him. I sold him for twenty-five dollars."

Harold reached into his pocket and pulled out two tens and a five.

"Here is your other twenty-five."

"No, no," Mr. White insisted, "I don't want your money. You were stuck with him, too."

"No, I cannot do that, Mr. White. I sold the mule for a good price knowing that he was no good. Regardless of what I paid, I was not fair in the deal. If I had told you about him, you know you never would have bought him. I will be satisfied only if you take the money." Laying the twenty-five dollars on the kitchen table, Harold assured his neighbor that this was what he wanted to do. Mr. White, expressing his appreciation for this attitude and honest effort to do right, placed the money in his pocket.

"I would never have expected you to do this, Harold. You are a neighbor I will always know that I can trust," Mr. White held out his hand and shook Harold's heartily.

Harold left with a feeling of deep satisfaction, knowing he had gained a friendship of far more value than twenty-five dollars. And now his mind and heart were at peace. The price of peace had been very small in comparison with the heavy load he had borne a long time.

A Tormenting Memory

"Marvin," called a worried mother. "Marvin Dale."

The evening was calm. The night air was beginning to feel chilly. "Mar-vin Da-a-a-le!" she called again before going in and closing the kitchen door.

"Where could he be?" She was sure he had left the house, without even a sweater, about an hour ago. "It's so unlike Marvin not to answer when I call," his mother worried. "He has been so different lately. It's ever since we came West," she mused. "Can it be he's not happy here? Possibly leaving his old friends in the East meant more to Marvin than we realized."

Someone was coming across the porch, "Must be Papa."

"O Papa, has Marvin been in the barn with you?"

"No. Anyway not since he finished his chores about an hour ago. I thought he came in."

"He did, only for a minute. I think he went back out without any wraps on. Have you noticed he acts—well—different, lately? He seems dissatisfied."

"Yes, Mama, I've noticed. I wish he would stop chumming with that Baker boy."

"Andy?"

"Yes, I think he has a bad influence on our son." The tired father slumped into a chair by the kitchen table.

"Well?" Mother began setting dishes of steaming food on the table.

16

"I've talked to the boy about it several times. But—," Marvin Senior dropped his head into his cupped hands, resting on the table. "It's like he says; there just isn't anyone else his age here. Most of the boys at church are at least two or three years younger or else a lot older."

"I wouldn't be surprised Andy is eighteen."

"I know, but he sure seems to have taken a liking to him. I don't like it. But like I say, I've talked to him about it and—well, Mama, we'll just have to pray about it."

"Yes," she agreed, brushing a tear from her eyes as she walked once more to the back porch.

"Marvin!" It was almost dark now. "Where can he be? Shall we go ahead and eat?"

"I don't like to," Papa answered sadly, "but maybe we'd better."

"Papa, he didn't go exploring again, did he?" she asked anxiously.

"No, I've forbidden him to do that again since the day he and Andy were lost for almost half an hour in that cave over at Black Gap. I'd have thought he wouldn't want to go anymore after the scare he got that day."

"It is so dangerous. I don't know why he enjoys exploring so much, especially a dark, unexplored cave." Mother shuddered. "I am so afraid he's going to get himself into trouble. Why, it's just a miracle they ever found their way out of that last cave."

"I know. God has been good to us, Mama. Marvin has always been an obedient boy, and very respectful, until recently. We can commit him to God and try, by His help, to guide the dear boy."

*　　*　　*　　*　　*　　*　　*　　*　　*　　*　　*　　*

The night air was chilly and damp. The clouds were hanging low. A tall, strong youth walked across the Flat Rock Bridge. He shivered. Marvin quickened his step, not to reach home faster, but to keep warm. He should have worn a sweater. But then, Mama would have asked where he was going. He could not risk that, not tonight. Of course, she would not have approved of his going to Bakers during supper time, or any other time for that matter.

"I don't know what is wrong with Papa and Mama lately." He shivered again. He was cold. He trembled. "Well, maybe they don't like me to be with Andy. What of it! There is no one else. I have to have someone my age. Why do my folks have to be so old-fashioned?" Marvin could not keep his teeth from chattering. "They are trying to keep me a baby. Andy says he wouldn't put up with it. I won't, either!" Marvin had never shivered so hard. He trembled till it hurt.

"I don't know what's got into me. It's not that cold." He broke into a full run. At the end of the lane he stopped to get his breath. Marvin was sweating, still his teeth chattered. "I think it's time I show them I'm an adult. Sixteen years old and they don't think I can take care of myself. I'll have to prove to them that I can." Marvin trembled as he neared the house. What would he tell Papa? There would have to be some explanation for being out at this hour.

The kitchen light was still on, but Mother was finished in the kitchen. Marvin walked across the porch.

"Well, I won't tell them where I was, nor what we planned for tomorrow. If they don't know, they won't worry. I can take care of myself." He entered the kitchen. The house was very quiet. Marvin tiptoed across the kitchen floor, through the living room and peeped into the open bedroom door. There were both of his parents on their knees. A wave of guilt swept over him. "Of course, I will not tell them a lie. Of course, I will not go exploring with Andy tomorrow again," he decided, quickly changing his mind.

18

"Dear good Mama and Papa. How can I treat them as I have?"

"But what will Andy say? 'Goody, goody boy. Can't do anything without asking Mama.' " Marvin could just hear him hoot.

Oh, how would he ever face Andy? What excuse would he give him? Marvin walked back to the kitchen. He pulled out a chair and sat down.

"Good evening, Son; ready for supper?" There in the doorway stood his sweet mother, smiling so lovingly at him.

Marvin was not ready to face her yet. The struggle inside was too great.

"No, Mom. I'm not hungry. I think I'll go to bed." Great beads of perspiration stood out on his neck and forehead.

"Aren't you feeling well?" her sweet voice broke the silence.

"Yes, Don't worry, Mother, dear. Good-night." Marvin turned and went upstairs. "Why? Oh, why do I have to have such good parents? Other boys' mothers aren't forever worrying about what their sons are doing, and where they are going, and how they are feeling." He dropped into his big chair with a groan.

"I'd be glad to give up that exploring trip we have planned for tomorrow if it wasn't for what Andy would say. But I know him. I'd never hear the end of it. And it's just as well Mama and Papa learn now as ever that I'm old enough to take care of myself."

The troubled boy kicked off his shoes. "I'd better get to bed." He shivered. "I'll be sick next. That would be a good excuse to stay home." Marvin rolled and tossed most of the night. He was miserable. If only his parents were not so particular about him. "If only Papa hadn't forbidden me to go exploring with Andy again. But then, how long is a grown boy supposed to have to listen to his father? After all Papa just doesn't understand."

On Saturday when Marvin awoke, the sun was shining. It was a very beautiful day. He felt better. He'd go on the exploring trip.

Surely there could not be anything very wrong with that. If his parents did not know, they would not worry.

At two-thirty, the boys met at Flat Rock Bridge.

"Did you tell them where you are going today?" Andy asked.

"Naw, I decided not to worry them," Marvin answered hesitantly.

"Good for you!" the older boy responded with a slap across Marvin's shoulders. "One of these days those old fogies are going to realize their little boy has grown up." He laughed.

Marvin tried to chuckle, too—a dry, halfhearted chuckle. What right had Andy to talk so disrespectfully about his parents? The boys started out toward Black Gap. This time they had a lantern and lots of chalk to mark their trail—everything they could need! They would not take another chance like they did last week.

"Whew! I was scared for a while there," Andy recalled. "I really began to wonder if we'd ever get out. Some of those caves go back in there an awful long way."

"You're not the only one who was scared. If it would have been another minute before we saw daylight, I think I'd have died. That was terrible."

"I don't see yet how we got lost like that. I sure want a better look at that place."

"Yes, me, too," Marvin added with little enthusiasm. Somehow he felt a little jittery today. Perhaps it was just because his parents did not know about it. Maybe because his conscience was bothering him. And maybe some unseen and unheeded power was warning him of danger.

"Say, boy, you don't sound very enthusiastic. Not scared to try it with a light, are you?"

"No, not a bit." Marvin tried desperately to hide the anxiety he felt.

"Well, here we are." Andy lit the lantern. He handed Marvin

several pieces of chalk. "Now make marks like this, about every so far apart," he instructed. "You mark that side wall and I'll mark this one. See, we can't have any trouble finding this."

"Sure," Marvin answered, squeezing through a narrow passage behind Andy. "Yes, I remember this . . . then we walk about six steps and turn sharp left."

"Say, Marv, look what I see," Andy exclaimed, holding the lantern higher. "Here's where we made the mistake last time when we went to come out. See, there is another hall leading off to the right. Here's where we missed the narrow pass leading to the entrance."

"Yes." Marvin was marking his wall well. He noticed that Andy, in his excitement, had forgotten his chalk.

"Andy, do you see that?"

"What?"

"Why, over here behind you, there is a straight drop off, about ten feet, I'd say. Be careful!"

Andy's foot slipped. Bang! The lantern hit the rocks overhead, bringing down a shower of dust and rock.

"Say, that was close!" Andy regained his footing. "If I had slipped another yard, I'd be down there now. You know, we ought to have brought a rope."

"I had no idea how dangerous this place was when we were here last week," Marvin said weakly. "Do you think we should go any farther in this direction?"

"Let's go on a little farther," Andy urged.

Marvin wished Andy would not be so daring, but he would not let him know. How he wished he were out of here!

"Marv! I don't see what kept us from falling to our death last week, with no light, in a place like this."

"It surely must have been God watching over us," Marvin thought, but aloud he said nothing. "I sure wish Mama knew where we are now. Maybe she would be praying," Marvin thought. He felt very uneasy.

"Marv, hold the light a minute. I want to see if we can get through here. Look! There's a large room over there."

"O Andy, don't try it!" Marvin begged. "That looks too deep. I'm afraid we couldn't get back up out of there."

"Naw, it isn't that deep." Andy stuck his head and shoulders through. "I'm going to try it," he said decidedly.

"This is such a narrow ledge we're on." Marvin was worried.

Andy sat down with his legs dangling on the other side. "My feet won't reach the floor. Here, take my hand; I'm going to jump."

"Andy!" Marvin screamed as he saw his friend slipping. He grabbed for Andy's outstretched hand. "Oh, oh!" Marvin's head hit the wall. A large rock fell, knocking the lantern out of his hand. "Andy! Help!"

"Marv! Marv! What's wrong?" Andy was excited now. "Marv, help me! I'm just hanging here. My feet won't reach the floor. Marvin! I'm afraid to jump. Help me back up."

"Splash!" Marvin hit the water on the other side of the ledge. "Marvin!"

"Andy! O Andy, where are you? I—I f-fell," Marvin gasped. "Andy, there is water over here." Marvin beat his arms wildly, trying to stay up.

"Where's the light?" Andy shouted frantically.

"I—don't—know," Marvin sputtered.

"Marvin, help me, I can hardly hold on!"

Marvin was gasping for breath. He had gotten a big mouthful of water in that first splash. Oh, how he wished he had been obedient to his dear parents! How glad he was that he had learned to swim last summer!

"Andy!" he called when he could talk. "Hang on. Don't jump; there may be water there, too. I'll get out of here as soon as I can find anything to get a hold of. The rock is so slippery. I can't get up." His voice sounded strange and hollow, echoing back from the dark rocks.

Marvin was panting. "Oh, why did I come? Why didn't I tell Mama and Papa? If I could just find that light! Oh, if I ever get out of here, I'll never forget this experience. I'll appreciate my parents' advice more. Oh, if I ever—" but he somehow felt he never would.

The next few minutes seemed like an eternity to the two stranded boys; one hanging onto a narrow, slippery rock, the other in a deep pool, with steep slippery sides, and in absolute darkness!

"Andy! Are you still there?"

"Yes." There was anxiety in his voice.

"Hang on a little longer. I'll soon be there," Marvin called. But to himself, he said, "O Andy! We never should have done this. We're lost! No one will ever find us. If only I had told Papa, he might come here looking for us. The chalk marks might lead to our rescue." His conscience smote him. "It's my fault. He'll never know where to look."

The water was cold. Marvin shivered. His heavy clothes were weighing him down. How much longer could he hold out?

"Oh, if only I were right with the Lord!" Marvin trembled. He remembered well the day he had received the Lord Jesus Christ. He remembered his first acquaintance with the Bakers, the first hike, the first cave they explored together. He remembered his grieved parents the numerous times he disobeyed. Oh, the agony these thoughts brought now!

"O God, help us," he breathed. "God, forgive me. Oh, it's so dark! O God, save us. Don't let Andy lose his hold till he gets help." All the time Marvin was working feverishly, trying to find a place in the wall where he could get up.

"Marv!"

Oh, was Andy falling? He sounded so far away.

23

"Marv, Marv!"

"Marvin!" Was that Andy calling? The voice sounded so unnatural. "Marvin, you knew all the time you were doing wrong. Why didn't you tell your parents about your plans today? It's too late now!" Marvin struggled desperately to keep his head up. It seemed as though some powerful force were pulling him down.

"Marvin, answer me!"

"Marvin Dale!" Who was that calling? "Marvin Dale! Don't you see how much better it would have been to obey your parents? Remember your baptismal vows? Remember how you used to love and obey God?"

Oh, the tormenting memory of all these things! How different things were now! How different things would be again if—"I never knew a person could remember so much in so short a time." Marvin was almost beside himself with fear.

"Marvin, O Marvin! Where are you? Can't you hear me?" Something struck Marvin's hand. He grabbed it.

"The lantern! Andy, the lantern!"

"O Marvin, why didn't you answer me?"

"Andy!"

"Marv, where are you? I'm back up on the ledge. I don't know how far I am from you."

Marvin was worn out. He could not stay up much longer.

"Marvin. Hang onto that lantern! Stay along this side of the rock." Andy shouted these directions frantically, hastily slipping out of his jacket. He rescued the matchbox, then swung the jacket over the edge of the rock on which he was sitting.

"Marv, you sound like you're getting farther away. Come this way!"

"I—I—can't." Marvin gasped painfully. How long had he been swimming? Hours? Days? "Help, Andy, help me!"

"Marv, I'm coming. Stay still. Hang onto the lantern."

Andy slid along cautiously. He stretched out flat on the rock and threw out the jacket, keeping a tight grip on one sleeve.

Splash! This time it hit the water!

"Marv! Marv! Do you hear me?"

"Yes." The drowning boy answered weakly, breathlessly.

Andy slid along, dragging the jacket. It splashed along in the water.

"Andy, I've—I've got it! I've got it! Help! Pull!"

"Steady now, Marvin, don't lose that lantern. That's it, keep on. We'll make it."

A new ray of hope gave Marvin extra strength, and soon he found himself lying on the narrow ledge beside Andy.

"God, I thank You," his heart cried out. "I'll keep my promise."

He wanted to weep. How he wanted to be safe at home. He wanted to tell his parents how sorry he was for causing them so much grief. Now it was easy to see that they were not just old-fashioned or too strict. It was easy to see their reasons for having some rules and restrictions.

Aloud he said, "Thanks, Andy. I had almost given up." Marvin choked and coughed.

"Are you all right?" Andy struck a match.

"Oh, what a bright light! Andy, let's get out of here."

"You don't have to say that twice. Say, doesn't that white chalk line look good?"

Marvin shivered. His teeth chattered. He was anxious to be home.

*   *   *   *   *   *   *   *   *   *   *   *

"Marvin Dale!" his mother met him at the gate. She had seen him staggering up the lane, dripping. His father stepped onto the porch, holding the door open for Mother and Son.

"Mama! Papa!" Marvin broke down and cried. "I . . . I'll

have . . . to get warm . . . and dry. Then I want to talk to you."

The sympathetic mother threw her arm lovingly around her son, who she felt sure had learned another lesson the hard way.

"Mama, I'm sorry. Forgive me," he cried.

What rejoicing there was when Marvin related his miraculous deliverance; especially the deliverance from his selfish desires! Now he was ready really to live for the Lord!

The Plea and the Promise

"Oh! Oh!" gasped John, clutching his chest. "Oh, this pain!" His heart seemed to be standing still; his breath was coming in short, painful gasps. His large, strong-looking arms felt weak and helpless.

"Oh, if only—if only this pain would leave for a minute. Oh, for a minute to be able to think clearly." The middle-aged gentleman groaned.

John Andrews lay helpless, his broad shoulders heaving, his big, brawny arms clutching at his chest. There seemed to be no way to get air into his lungs.

The suffocating feeling was only intensified by every move of his body as the rescue workers carefully lifted the two-hundred-pound body onto the stretcher.

"Anna, Anna!" he gasped, trying to raise up on his elbow.

"Lie still, Mr. Andrews. Keep calm till we can get you over to the hospital." These orders came to the sick man as faint, uncertain sounds through a fog. The men standing around the stretcher were only shadows—dark shadows pressing so close that he was being suffocated.

"What—what's wrong?" John asked weakly. Again he clutched at his chest. His fingers were stiff. His brain felt numb. All he felt was the heavy, heavy fog hanging over him. Then all was black.

* * * * * * * * * * * *

"Anna, Anna! Oh, I'm afraid. . . ."

"Be still, Mr. Andrews. You must keep very quiet for a while."

John tried desperately to open his eyes to see where the soft, quiet voice was coming from.

"Is Anna here?" he asked, scarcely able to form the words. John tried to move, but he was unable even to wiggle his toes.

"Your wife was here," the nurse explained, "but she has gone to rest awhile. She'll be back again this evening."

"But I . . . must . . . see her—now," the sick man stammered. His breathing was becoming more difficult. "I must . . . ," John gasped for breath. The color left his face. He felt himself sinking again into the deep, dense fog. What was the nurse saying? Oh, if he could only make her understand.

A few minutes passed. He felt her fingers feeling for his pulse.

"Nurse!" he cried, almost frightening himself by the sound of his voice. "Nurse, she's my wife. I . . . I'm dying!"

A needle pricked his arm. "Don't . . . please . . . wait," he panted, his heart throbbing violently now. "Nurse, I'm not ready to die. I want . . . I want . . . to be able to think." His lips still moved but he uttered no sound.

"Don't get yourself all excited, Mr. Andrews. It's the worst thing you can do."

The thick darkness again settled over his brain. Frantically John fought to shake it off.

"Oh, for another chance," he thought, "another chance to be able to think clearly! God, please, O God, please don't let me die now. Give me another opportunity and I'll serve You as long as I live. Just don't let me die now. I'm not ready to die!"

The nurse, standing by his bed, heard only the word "die" mumbled several times by the sick man. She could make out nothing else as she gazed intently at the deathly white face, drawn and twisted as if in anguish.

The medicine began to take effect and her patient calmed down. She felt his pulse again. Satisfied that he would be all right, she sat down across the room where she could watch him closely.

All that night John Andrews lay still and senseless. On the third day he roused again for a few minutes.

"Nurse, are you here?"

"Yes, Mr. Andrews. Can I do something for you?"

"Are you a Christian?" he asked.

"No, I guess I'm not," she stammered. "You settle down now and rest awhile," she changed the subject, "then I'll let you talk to your wife. She's been here most of the time for three days and nights now. She is anxious to talk to you. You rest a few minutes, all right?"

"But, nurse, I'm not ready to die. Can't you tell me how to become a Christian? My wife isn't saved. Don't you know someone who is—someone who could tell me how to become a Christian?"

The pain again stabbed his heart, leaving him weak and his thoughts fuzzy and confused.

"Mr. Andrews, you'll have to be quiet or I'll have to give you another hypodermic. This excitement is working against you."

"Please, quick . . . call a minister . . . someone!" The suffering man struggled for breath. "I'm dying . . . not ready . . . God, have mercy."

When her patient again lapsed into unconsciousness, the nurse, disturbed by his urgent request, went to the telephone.

"Hello, Mrs. Andrews. Yes, this is your husband's nurse. Yes, all right, just a little confused. Could you come over? He's been talking quite a lot, though what he says is not rational. It may help him to think more clearly if you talk to him. All right.

29

Good-bye."

"John, John," Anna whispered softly. She did not wish to wake him if he was asleep.

"What?" the sick man groaned, moving his head slightly. "Anna! Anna, are you . . . you ready?"

"Were you resting well?" she asked, evading his question. "Did you know you slept most of three days now? Can't you wake up and talk to me a little? Can you see me, John?"

"Yes, but you look so far—far away. Anna, I'm not ready . . . to die. Do you know anyone . . . ?"

While he worked his mouth, his breath came in short, painful, catchy gasps. Anna spoke, "John, you are going to get well. You will soon be better, then we'll talk about that. All right?

"Look, John, do you see the flowers your mother sent?"

"I've got to do something . . . quick. . . . Anna, I'm not going to be here much longer. Please . . . I'm not ready. . . . I . . . I'm lost. I . . ."

"John, John, don't! You're getting yourself all worked up. Please, John."

"Nurse, Nurse!" Mrs. Andrews called. "Hurry, my husband is choking. Do something for him, quick."

"Just keep calm, Mrs. Andrews," the nurse said softly as she hurried into the room with a hypodermic. "We'll give him some medicine to help him calm down. Has he been carrying on again?"

"Yes," Anna sobbed, "he's afraid he is dying." She covered her face with her hands and wept uncontrollably.

"You'd better step outside, Mrs. Andrews," the nurse suggested sympathetically. "We'll call you when he feels better."

"No! No!" gasped the choking man. "I . . . I . . . don't want it. Please, Anna, don't let her. . . . I want to . . . think, to think. Not ready! God, help. . . ."

"Now, Mr. Andrews, just calm down. You'll soon feel better.

This will help you to rest."

He felt himself sinking—sinking into unconsciousness. "God, don't let me die. If You will show me the way, I'll serve You. If only I can get well long enough to find someone to help me."

Several days passed before John's condition began to improve. His life seemed to hang in a balance; sometimes swaying toward death, then back again toward life. On the seventh day after his heart attack first occurred, he began to show marked improvement. Until now, he had been kept under sedatives most of the time to keep him calm.

"Anna, how long have I been here?" John asked when he awoke Thursday morning.

Anna got up and walked closer to the bed. His voice sounded more natural, less strained than before.

"How are you feeling, John?" she asked tenderly. "This is your seventh day. Do you feel rested?"

"Oh, I feel like a weight has lifted off my chest. I can breathe without difficulty," he whispered. "It's such a relief. I believe I'm going to get well." Slowly the smile began to cloud over. His brow furrowed. "But, Anna," he began, "I've been doing some serious thinking. You know, if I had died, I'd be in hell now. It scares me to think of it. I'm not ready to die. But, Anna, by God's help, I'm going to get ready before anything like this happens again. It was all so sudden."

Completely exhausted from speaking so long, John closed his eyes and drew several deep breaths. "I tell you, Anna, it's good to be alive, after an experience like that. God has been merciful."

All this time Anna shifted nervously from one foot to the other. John had a new urgency and determination about this. Always before he had seemed perfectly satisfied to be a good moral man. Would this notion continue after he was well? Or would he forget it? Possibly it was just his condition that caused him to talk this way.

"John, the doctor says you'll soon be home. You're more fortunate than lots of men your age after having a heart attack."

"Yes, I believe God answered my prayer," John answered.

Anna's face clouded. Why could he not talk of something else?

"As soon as I'm out of here, I want to find a minister who can help me. And, Anna, tomorrow bring my Bible along in. I think I'll soon be able to read a little."

"Well, have you two had a nice chat?" a smiling nurse inquired from the open doorway. "We'd better not make it too long. You know, Mr. Andrews is still very weak."

Hesitantly Anna kissed her husband "good-bye." "It seemed like an awfully short visit," she said, starting toward the door.

"Don't forget my Bible," he reminded her.

John drew a deep breath, and thanked God for it. "Soon I'll be home, and I'll serve You," he promised. "You heard and answered my plea."

Ten days after his heart attack, John Andrews was at home, feeling well and almost as strong as before, just a little older.

Though he was no longer able to work, he had very little boresome leisure time. Anna did many things to pass the time pleasantly for him.

"John, have you forgotten your promise?" asked a quiet voice one night as he lay sleepless on his bed.

Startled, John sat up and rubbed his eyes. "What was that? Indeed I had almost forgotten!"

"John! Are you all right?" His wife reached for the light. "Is your heart . . . ?"

"Yes, yes, Anna. Don't worry. It's just . . . ," his voice drifted off into nothingness. Somehow it seemed harder to talk about his soul's need now than it had when he thought he was dying.

"It's what?" She waited patiently, rubbing her hand over his damp forehead. "Why John, you're trembling! I'm going to call the doctor." Anna reached for the telephone.

"No, Anna, don't." Gently he took the receiver from her hand and laid it back in its cradle.

"Lie down, Anna, and turn off the light."

Reluctantly, she obeyed.

"John, are you sure you're all right?"

"Yes."

"Why were you getting up?"

"I must have been half asleep. I thought someone had spoken to me."

"Oh?"

"Anna, you know I haven't seen a minister yet about becoming a Christian. I'm not sure I can understand all about it by myself."

"Why don't you get some sleep now and we'll talk about it tomorrow, all right?"

"Yes," John answered, and rolled over.

"How long do you plan to put it off?" the voice asked again. It seemed to be pleading for immediate action.

"I'll do something about it soon," John promised.

"But suppose you don't have many more opportunities?"

"I'm stronger now," John argued. "My heart seems to be working normally."

"God heard your plea. Why don't you keep your promise now?"

"I will soon, but not now. Not now!"

"Remember how you felt?"

"Yes, yes! I'll do something about it soon." John reached for his capsule to help him rest. Anna stirred. Very slowly and quietly he took the capsule.

He must not worry her again. John slept.

Days passed quietly for the Andrews. John grew stronger. He was again bright and cheerful. The strained and anxious look left his eyes. Life was almost back to normal again at the end of one month. John began to do light household chores.

One Monday morning he stood by the kitchen sink, washing dishes when suddenly, like a swift and deadly arrow, a pain struck through his heart that numbed every nerve and muscle in his body. His head struck the sink, then the floor. For one moment all the experiences of his past month flooded through his brain in jumbled confusion. All his previous terror, with more added, stared him in the face like a hideous monster before whom he was completely helpless.

Minutes later Anna screamed when she entered the kitchen. She dashed to the phone. The numbers blurred. With trembling fingers she dialed "0."

"Operator—call Southside Hospital—quick. Get Doctor Green on the line."

While she talked to Doctor Green, her eyes glued to her husband on the floor, she heard the same gurgling, choking sound she had heard in the hospital a few weeks before.

"O John, the ambulance will soon be here. John, can't you open your eyes? Please, John, please try to talk to me." Kneeling by her husband, Anna heard the screaming of the siren and knew help was near.

For a few days, unconsciousness obliterated the painful memories of John's neglect.

On Wednesday evening as Anna entered the hospital room, John opened his eyes. He glanced about, his eyes dark with fear. His face twitched nervously. He moved his lips.

"John, are you awake?" Anna asked, pushing her face as close to his as possible. The oxygen tent was between them.

"John, do you hear me?"

His lips moved again. John groaned painfully and tried to push the tent back.

"Don't, John," his wife begged. "You need this to help you breathe."

Now John was working frantically with the tent, "Help, h-e-l-p!" he moaned, the words scarcely audible. "I . . . I'm dying. . . . O God, . . . not ready . . . I'm going . . . I'm . . ."

Quickly the nurse rushed in with some medicine to help her patient rest.

"No!" he screamed, his voice getting louder. "I'm not . . . ready."

"Be quiet," the nurse ordered calmly and pushed the needle into the skin. "This will help you feel better."

"But, I'm dying! Wait!" he begged. "Someone tell me how to . . . be saved. I'm going to hell! Can't . . . someone . . . help me? I'm dying . . . not ready." A look of horror crossed his face as the sick man struggled desperately to raise his large body from the bed. He gasped painfully for breath and slumped onto his pillow.

"Doctor Green. Doctor Green," the nurse called. She felt for the patient's pulse. Seemingly there was none.

The doctor entered the quiet room.

The nurse looked up, troubled. "I'm afraid he has overexerted his heart," she said. "He became all excited again, then collapsed."

Doctor Green stayed by the bed, working rapidly over the dying man. "If he could only stay quiet, he'd have a good chance of recovering," he spoke anxiously.

John groaned, his eyelids fluttered. "Please help," his parched lips carefully formed the words.

"Another hypodermic, please," the doctor ordered. "We must

keep him under."

Soon John was again unconscious as his life hung in a balance. For days the deathlike atmosphere hung over the room.

Finally, his heart became stronger and he was allowed to awake from his long, sound sleep.

When he awoke one Sunday morning, Anna was not there. A nurse was nearby. His mind was clear. "Nurse," he called.

Immediately she was by the bed. "Yes?" she answered cheerfully. "How are you feeling?"

"The pain in my chest is gone," he responded with a smile. "But my breathing still comes with much difficulty."

She nodded, pleased that he was able to talk this much, rationally, at least.

"I want you to call a minister for me," were his next words. John's breath began coming in short gasps. He coughed.

"Mr. Andrews, I'm sure you understand you've been a very sick man. You will need all the rest you can get."

"But," he interrupted, "I must . . ." another coughing fit seized him, leaving him very weak.

"Mr. Andrews, now don't become excited. I'll call a minister for you."

"It's very important! I made . . . a promise to God," he paused. "I'm going to keep it," he finished determinedly.

"All right, I'll go now. You rest awhile."

John nodded. His eyes were closed and his lips moving.

When John awoke on Sunday evening, an elderly gentleman was seated by his bed. The stranger sat with bowed head, a small black book clasped in his hands, which rested on his knees. His eyes were closed. John looked intently at the peaceful, contented expression of the older man.

The sick man lay very still, trying to recollect where he was and why. Who could the stranger be?

Then he saw the Bible clasped in the minister's hands. The

memory of his request came back and with it a recollection of his soul's need. John groaned.

The minister rose. "Mr. Andrews," he spoke softly, "I'm James Newton. I understand you're looking for someone who can tell you how to get right with God. Do you feel like talking now?"

"Yes," John answered. "Sir, do you think God will save my soul? I've rejected Him so long. But, oh, I don't want to face death again without Him! Mister, I thought I was going to die. I wasn't ready." He paused, breathing deeply. "I promised God I'd serve Him and I mean to do it, only I don't know how to begin."

Brother Newton turned to several Scriptures in his worn Bible, carefully explaining to John the way of salvation. With the aid of the Spirit, the honest seeker quickly grasped the truth. The Word was real to him. John saw himself a sinner, hopelessly lost outside of Jesus Christ. He opened his heart to Jesus, completely trusting in His redeeming blood. John surrendered his will wholly to his Lord.

Peace flooded his soul. "The Lord has graciously granted my plea," he cried. "Oh, I do want to be faithful to Him."

From that hour John began keeping his promise, as his physical strength allowed.

His nurses and visitors often heard the simple story of salvation from the overflowing heart of "a sinner saved by grace." Joy and peace were sweet to the weary man, now resting confidently and trustingly.

His body began to mend rapidly and physical strength returned.

"The Lord blessed me with two heart attacks," John Andrews often said to his loved ones. "But don't put off your salvation," he warned. "Suppose I had died the first time. You never know when your time may come to go. Get ready now."

Melvin's Trial

"Son, what have you decided to do?" the elderly gray-haired man asked in a shaking voice. He walked around the log on which the young man had been sitting for some time, and seated himself beside him.

Melvin breathed a deep sigh. He shook his head and remained silent.

The older man's chin trembled slightly. A sad look crossed his face. He did not press the young man for an answer.

The mutual feeling between father and son could be felt and did not need to be spoken. In fact, no words could have expressed the feeling of either at the moment.

The struggle was too great and the trial too severe to be discussed until Melvin was able to gain control of the emotions he felt.

Both men sat with bowed heads and bent shoulders. Occasionally a deep sigh escaped the young man's lips.

"Father," he said at last, his voice clear and steady, though filled with emotion, "it is not that I'm afraid to die, or ashamed to confess Christ. It is not that I want an easy road. And yet . . . this has been a hard decision to make. I have all confidence in God. I believe I'd be ready to live or die for Him. And yet . . . the flesh shrinks.

"Father, by God's help, I'll be a faithful Christian until I die, no matter what this decision costs me."

Again the older man's chin trembled. "I knew. I knew that would be your answer, but I had to hear you say it." His voice faltered. "Melvin, I've been looking for your call to come for weeks. Many men have been drafted. I always knew your turn must come soon. You were twenty a few weeks ago. This country has called you to give your service. But, Son, always remember, God has also called you. His call is the most important call you'll ever hear. Tomorrow you must appear to give your answer to the officers. Someday you will have to appear to answer before God."

"Yes, Father," Melvin answered with the assurance of having made a right decision.

Melvin was personally acquainted with young men who had suffered trials of cruel mockings and persecution, and some had even bravely faced death rather than give up their belief in the Word of God. They would not take up arms. They had stood firm and true to the end. Even now some of his dearest friends were in prison, not ten miles away. But he had not seen them for months, not because he would not have liked to, but because they were allowed no company.

Melvin was also acquainted with some young men who, rather than bearing the hardships of the conscientious objector, obeyed their government rather than rendering obedience to God. He knew from the first what his answer would be. And yet, when the time came, it was not an easy decision to make. There was much to face. So much hinged on his answer. Father and Mother were becoming old. All the other children were married and far from home. How could his parents get along without him? Would they ever see him again, after he left to appear before the draft board on Wednesday afternoon?

Many doubts and fears haunted the mind of the young man that Tuesday night. But his hope was anchored in the solid rock, Christ Jesus; and he remained firm and true to God.

On Wednesday morning Melvin tried to be cheerful, and

assured his parents that his hope was in God.

"God will be with me, and with you, until we meet again." He bade them "good-bye" and set out on foot down the country road, not knowing whether he would ever see his loved ones again in this life. The walk to the courthouse was about ten miles. He could easily make that before late afternoon.

Melvin was the only conscientious objector to appear that Wednesday afternoon. His trial was cruel and heartless.

"There is no other way," he was told by the officers. "You have no choice."

"I will serve my country in any way which does not conflict with God's Word and will for us," he boldly replied.

For several hours a number of officers tried to convince, persuade, or force him to sacrifice his beliefs for their way.

Melvin remained firm. His convictions were well grounded in the Word of God.

"You will be sent to prison," an officer informed him.

"Yes," Melvin answered calmly. "I will go."

"And stay until you are willing to submit to authority," another officer cried.

"I cannot submit to any authority adverse to God's authority," he answered unwaveringly.

"You'll learn what you can do after spending several weeks on bread and water with nothing other than concrete under and above you," the officer sneered.

"I will do whatever you ask of me as long as it does not conflict with God's Word," Melvin answered again.

"Well, suppose we ask you to get in the firing line?" an officer probed.

"As I said, I will do anything you ask of me if it does not conflict with God's Word," the young man answered wearily.

"Do you know what the firing line is?"

"No, I'm not sure that I do."

"I'll explain; then maybe you will change you mind."

"I will not change my mind about disobedience to God," Melvin declared firmly. "I will obey God."

"Then come with me," the officer shouted. "I'll show you what I mean."

Melvin was led out into a dark hall. There, standing alone for several minutes, a calmness and peace engulfed him. The trial had been strenuous, but his heart was free and quiet. Melvin waited. A door opened.

"This way, young man," a gruff voice called.

Melvin followed. Outside he could see only about twenty feet; a huge brick wall cut off all other vision. Four young men stood facing the wall. None moved.

"What can this mean?" Melvin wondered. His heart throbbed; he felt troubled. Melvin stood gazing a full minute at the backs of the young men before the other man spoke.

"Do you know any of these young men?"

"Yes," Melvin faltered, "I think I know the last three. The first one I don't know."

"Who are the last three?"

"John Yoder, James Miller, and Roy Brunk."

"You are right. Now, this is the firing line."

For the first time Melvin noticed the large gun the man held.

"These young men, foolish as you have been, will not give up their beliefs of right or wrong. You may take your place at the end of that line; or you may submit to our orders and take up arms against the enemies of our country. The decision is yours."

The man held the gun steadily on the men by the wall. His finger was on the trigger.

Without a moment's hesitation, Melvin said, "I will not take up arms," and walked to the end of the line.

All was deathly quiet for a moment. Hundreds of thoughts rushed through the young man's mind.

41

Suddenly a shot rang out. Melvin trembled, the hair on his arms seemed to stand straight up. He would not give up now. "Jesus died for me," he repeated softly. "I'll die for Him."

"Will any of the rest of you change your minds now?" a voice rang out. No one stirred.

"I'm coming right on down the line," the voice boomed out again.

Another shot rent the air. "He must have started at the other end of the line," Melvin reasoned. "That first boy—I wonder who he was.

"John Yoder, he was next . . ." The third shot split the silence.

"James was next." A lump swelled in Melvin's throat and he longed to throw his arms around his old friends and comfort them. There was a long silence. Only Roy remained between him and death.

"O Father, Mother, don't grieve for me when you hear this. I'm ready to go. Thank God for His mercy and for His plan of salvation."

The fourth shot sounded. Melvin scarcely paid any attention. What difference did it make how one died? All the difference was in being ready to die. He waited and waited. The expected fifth shot never came. Finally there were voices behind him. Melvin listened. He wondered, "What can this mean?"

"They won't give up," one voice said. "There's no use; they aren't afraid to die."

"We'll have to try some other means to convince them," the second voice answered. "This is enough for today. Bring them on in."

"Boys, come on inside," a stern voice ordered. Melvin slowly turned around, dreading the sight which he feared would meet his eyes. He felt weak and dazed. What had taken place? What did it mean?

Melvin turned toward the wall. "Boys!" he exclaimed, almost under his breath. To his amazement he saw four boys standing calm and composed before the brick wall.

"Come on in," the voice commanded. The mock trial was over.

*   *   *   *   *   *   *   *   *   *   *   *

Now, years later, Melvin is a happy Christian man, serving his God faithfully. And his God has never forsaken him. Praise the Lord!

"He That Overcometh"

The sun had already disappeared behind Big Mountain. Laura walked restlessly from one room to the other, casting anxious glances down the valley road.

"Why is Bill so late?" she repeated occasionally. Her tone plainly showed the irritation she felt.

"Is Papa late?" questioned three-year-old William. "Is something wrong?"

"No, no, Son," the anxious mother hurriedly assured the young child. "It's all right. Sometimes Papa just has to work a little late, you know." Quickly Laura walked over to the crib and took the cooing one-year-old up in her arms. Pressing Susan to herself, she buried her face in the child's hair, trying to brush the anxious tears from her eyes before William noticed them. "Oh, I just must hide my feelings better for the children's sake," she scolded herself.

Laura had never before felt this nervous and fearful. She had always been a most cheerful and dutiful young mother. Now, in a few weeks' time, there was a drastic change taking place in her disposition. This, of course, was felt by the children.

Bill and Laura's home had been a happy Christian home since their wedding day, and new joy was added with the birth of each child. Laura had scarcely known a worry or care until the day she heard the dreadful news. "The United States is facing a serious crisis, which will probably end in war!"

"War!" The first time she heard it, Laura could hardly believe there would really be war involving the United States.

As the rumors of war continued to flood the valley, Laura felt more and more uneasy. Of course, she had heard of wars before, but they were usually across the ocean. Then Laura had been younger, too. She had always trusted in God for her protection. But now it was different. There were the children. "What if—" Laura shuddered. She could not bear to think of what would happen to dear, brave William, and sweet, innocent little Susan if something happened to her and Bill.

Day after day the tension mounted. The crisis became more and more serious. Laura began losing sleep, spending a large portion of the night worrying about the children's safety. What if she and Bill should be taken and the children left? Would they ever hear the sweet story of salvation? Would they ever know the love and sweetness of a home? Would their physical needs be supplied? On and on rambled her troubled thoughts till Laura could not bear to lie in bed, so she would walk the floor, still weeping and wringing her hands. It seemed she could think of nothing but the war and the children.

After three or four weeks of living under strain and tension because of the threat of war, Laura's entire personality seemed greatly changed. She was extremely nervous and tense.

One Monday afternoon, Laura wearily dragged the ironing board from the closet. Her head throbbed. There were dark circles under her eyes. She set up the ironing board in the front room, scarcely noticing the children playing gleefully on the floor. Slowly and laboriously she ironed one piece after another, noticing neither the collar she scorched nor the sleeve she missed. War, war, war, kept ringing through her mind. Broken homes, crippled people, missing people, homeless children, orphans! Laura could stand it no longer. Rushing into her bedroom, the burdened young mother burst into tears. Dropping to her knees, she poured out her heart to God.

"Father," she cried, "we are so helpless, and I am so afraid. I have always trusted in Thy loving care. Help me to trust in Thee now. Father, I want to commit the children into thy care just now, knowing that only Thou canst care for them and protect them, and knowing that Thou dost love them even more than we do. O Father, if it is Thy will that Bill and I should be taken from our children at this young and tender age, I pray that Thou wilt provide some means for them to hear the good news of salvation."

After committing her cares to the all-loving and all-wise heavenly Father, Laura asked yet one more petition. "Father, just show me a portion from Thy Word that will help me through this trying time." As Laura rose to her feet, the tears ceased to flow. A great peace and calm flooded her soul in a way she had never before experienced. Her one thought now was that everything is in the hands of God.

Returning to the front room, Laura found the children still stacking blocks. They had not missed her. Quietly she stepped over and unplugged the iron. Picking up her Bible on the table, the pages fell open to a portion in the Book of Revelation. Her heart seemed nearly bursting with praise and adoration to God for the new peace she had found through trusting in Him. She faced the Word of God with the anticipation of receiving a special message direct to her from God.

The portion of Scripture she read was Revelation 21:7, 8: "He that overcometh shall inherit all things; and I will be his God, and he shall be my son. But the fearful, and un-believing, . . . shall have their part in the lake which burneth with fire and brimstone: which is the second death."

"Fearful!" she thought to herself. "That was certainly me. How strange that such a horror and dread could get hold of me this way, when God is my Father: the almighty God rules the whole universe!

"Yes, Lord," she humbly confessed, "I was fearful. I thank Thee for the atonement that Jesus made for me, and I thank Thee for the wonderful peace Thou hast given."

Laura arose and went about her duties with a new song in her heart. God had promised to be her God. She could surely trust Him with their precious treasures, the children.

True Riches

Early that bright October morning, just as the sun began to tint the eastern horizon with a golden-pinkish glow, Marlene arose and began to hurry around, thinking of all the things she planned to do that day. There was no time to lose, she knew, if she was going to have her share of the cleaning, the ironing, and the mending done, and be ready by noon for her visit in some of the mountain homes with Pastor Weaver and his wife. Unacquainted as yet with most of the mountain people, Marlene looked forward with joyful anticipation to this opportunity to meet some of her neighbors. Since arriving at the mission home a few weeks ago, where Marlene had decided to spend a year, she had been hoping for an opportunity like this.

Now the day had come when she would get into their homes and see what they were like and how the mountain folks lived.

Upon arrival Marlene's first impression was that the people of this community were very poor.

As they entered the small mountain community, she began to exclaim over and over, "Surely no one lives in that shack!" or "Look at all those children; they surely can't all be from that small house!"

The pastor answered, "Yes, Marlene, that is the way our people live. They don't know anything about living like some of the folks from our large congregations back home. Our people are poor, financially."

Then, looking way up a hollow and pointing to the left, he said, "You see that house up there; those people are rich, very rich."

Looking in every direction, the bewildered girl asked, "Where, Brother Weaver? Which house? Surely you don't mean that one?" she asked, looking in the direction he was still pointing. She saw only a poor shack resembling all the others she had seen as they neared the mission home.

"Yes, that's the one," he replied. "Old Mr. and Mrs. Miller live there, happy and contented. I want you to get into their home soon, Marlene. You see, they have only a few things in this world but a wealth of treasures spiritually and everlasting life."

"Yes," agreed the sober girl, "they are truly rich." But the poverty she was seeing now was different from what Marlene had been used to.

She had never considered her family rich, but now as a picture of her comfortable home several hundred miles away flashed through her mind in comparison with these homes, there was quite a difference.

Then had come the first week or so of getting adjusted to life in the mission home with the other young people and the pastor and his wife, who were like parents to the group of young people who had come to help with the work in the mountains. Marlene had enjoyed it all very much.

"Marlene," called Sister Weaver shortly after twelve o'clock, "are you going with us today? John and I are ready to go now."

Very soon, Marlene, beaming with anticipation, joined the Weavers in the jeep and they were off for an afternoon in the mountains.

Passing the Miller home, Brother Weaver said, "We'll stop there a little on the way home if it isn't too late."

Awed by the beauty of the surroundings, Marlene took it all in, wondering how anything this rough and rugged could be so beautiful and majestic as these rocks and mountains were.

Seeing the very evident need in the community, Marlene wished there were more she could do to help. How her heart ached for the little ones in large families who apparently had scarcely enough to exist!

She continued her reflections as they neared a small log cabin where Brother Weaver was pulling up to stop.

"Is the spiritual need here as great," she wondered, "as the financial need? If so," she continued, "I can understand why the Weavers were willing to bury their lives in these mountains."

Approaching the porch, Brother Weaver said softly, "Frank Caldwell and his son live here alone. Mrs. Caldwell died about sixty years ago when Jim was only a few weeks old."

Marlene shuddered as they walked across the uneven boards on the porch, wondering whether she might go down through if she stepped at the wrong place.

A mumbling could be heard from the inside, which stopped abruptly when the pastor knocked at the door. Slowly the door opened. In the darkness of the room Marlene could faintly see the form of someone lying on the bed in the corner.

"Howdy, Preacher, what can I do for you?" came the surly voice of the man at the door.

"Good evening, Jim," the pastor greeted him with a smile. "Just thought we'd drop in for a while. How is your father today?"

Jim, shrugging his shoulders and stepping aside so that they could enter, pointed toward the cot on which the old man was lying. "He's there. Speak to him if you wish, Preacher, but he's awfully out of patience today."

"Patience, huh," snorted the man in the corner. "I guess that boy's about as mean as they get, if he is my son. Hasn't got a bit of decent respect for his old father."

Marlene, trembling, stepped closer to Sister Weaver in the

dark room. Unhappiness and hate seemed to reign in this home.

All was quiet a moment. Then the pastor spoke, "Mr. Caldwell, have you and your son been considering the question I left with you on my last visit?"

Jim fidgeted uneasily and fumbled with the door knob. The others, too, remained standing, since the cot, the stove, and one rickety chair seemed to be the only pieces of furniture in the small room. After a slight pause the pastor repeated his question, looking from one man to the other.

"Yes, Preacher," the older man finally spoke. "But, you see, that stuff ain't for us. Religion's all right for your kind but it's too late for us to change our way of life now. Your religion ain't been in these parts till recent years; it's too new for me." Then, sinking back into his pillow, the old man relaxed the arm on which he had been leaning.

"No, Mr. Caldwell, this religion we profess isn't new. The same God who created this universe is the One to whom we owe our lives today. The God who created these mountains and streams is the God we serve. He it was that sent His only Son to die so that we need not continue to live in darkness."

Then turning to the younger Mr. Caldwell, the pastor continued, with loving concern in his voice, "Won't you acknowledge Jesus Christ as your only means of salvation? Jim, you know the Scriptures; you know that unless your heart is changed nothing but more darkness and suffering is ahead for you. Won't you decide today?

"We have no promise of the future, Jim, and even if we did, why live any longer in darkness and fear when you could be enjoying peace and joy now?"

Shifting restlessly from one foot to the other, Jim opened the door and stepped out onto the porch, where, from the sound of his footsteps, they knew he was pacing back and forth, back and forth, evidently pondering the heart-searching questions he had been asked.

Feeling very helpless in this situation, the small group inside silently breathed a prayer for these two hardened souls in darkness.

Turning again to the sick man on the cot, the pastor pleaded earnestly with him to come to Jesus and be rid of his load of sin. But, though he seemed deeply under conviction, Mr. Caldwell would not yield.

With heavy hearts the Weavers again got into the jeep and started down the mountain.

"What a dark, dark home—no peace, no joy, no hope! We must pray earnestly for them, that the Spirit will work mightily with them while there is yet time for repentance," sighed Sister Weaver, wiping the tears from her eyes.

Marlene, sitting quietly in the back seat, replied, "I've never seen anything so sad. They have practically nothing here, and nothing to look forward to."

Presently the jeep was stopping again and the girl, not used to such scenes of darkness, shrank back in her seat, wishing she would not need to go in.

"Come, Marlene," Sister Weaver was saying softly, "you'll enjoy this visit."

Climbing slowly from the jeep, Marlene looked toward the house, which was much like the one they had just left—only two small rooms, a few small windows, one door, and a rickety porch. She stepped cautiously onto the uneven boards and, glancing about, was surprised to see several potted plants blooming. Then, as if to add to her surprise and pleasure, a sweet voice burst forth in singing melodiously an old familiar hymn.

In answer to the pastor's knock, the music faded and a pleasant old lady appeared at the door.

"Oh, do come in, come in, Brother Weaver. I'm so glad you've come and brought your wife and the girl. Is she the new one who just arrived?''

"Yes, this is Marlene.''

"Marlene, this is Sally and Ed Miller,'' said Sister Weaver, drawing the girl inside.

"Here, Sister Weaver, take this chair,'' said Ed, arising and walking shakily to the bed across the room. Sally soon brought the only other chair from the kitchen for Marlene, then seated herself on the bed beside her husband and the pastor.

Marlene glanced about. A stove, some kind of large old crate evidently used for a table, and the two chairs and bed were all the furniture she could see from where she sat.

As she sat thinking of the poverty of this home, her thoughts were interrupted by the conversation of the other four.

"Yes,'' Mr. Miller was saying, "God has abundantly blessed us. I've been able to get around and help myself quite well.''

"And I, too, have been exceptionally well,'' Sally added. "And Sarah, you and John should have seen my garden, prettiest beans and tomatoes you ever saw. God surely has been good to us.''

"We were able to sell that pig we raised, and get a few winter clothes,'' put in her husband.

And so the conversation went on through the afternoon, the Millers praising God for His goodness!

Marlene marveled at the radiance and contentment evident in this home.

Before leaving, they sang a few hymns together and all bowed reverently in prayer to thank and praise God for His loving care over them and to pray for the souls in darkness about them. As they arose to leave, Mrs. Miller squeezed Marlene's hand and gave her a warm invitation to come often. The girl knew she had begun a friendship here that would be a blessing to her.

The drive back to the Weaver home was a pleasant one. All were quiet, each one thinking his own thoughts.

"Marlene," the pastor asked, "did you enjoy the afternoon?"

"Yes, very much," she replied, and then added, "especially our last visit. The difference in those two homes is as different as day and night."

"That's right," agreed the pastor, "and what would you say the difference is? From the first appearance, weren't the homes nearly alike? Did one have many more earthly possessions than the other?"

"No," answered the thoughtful girl, slowly. "The whole difference was the presence or absence of Jesus."

"Very true," the pastor replied, pleased with her answer, "and that's why we're here, to bring the Gospel and enlighten other homes. Would to God all the folks back home could make the wonderful discovery you've made this afternoon."

Marlene resolved to get into as many homes as possible with the good news of salvation.

The Lord Will Provide

Grace walked listlessly about the house. There were bottles on the sofa, toys on the floor, and a stack of diapers in the pail that needed washing. The kitchen sink was full of dirty dishes. What did it matter? David would not be coming home this evening. Not often did anyone ever see Grace Well's home in this condition. In fact, it just did not get this way. But now—just two and a half years after their happy marriage—the house looked just as Grace felt—as if the world could not go on! Never had she felt this way before. But who cared now? David would never again come whistling home at five-o'clock. What was there to live for? What mattered now? Oh, yes, there was little Lucy—the charming joy of their home until this time—now even she seemed to add to the burden. How could one young woman alone care for a one-year-old child and earn a living at the same time? David would never again bring in the groceries, or say, "I'll rock the baby till you get supper on." No, things were different now. But worst of all, David was no longer here to take a father's responsibility in the home.

It was just one week after the funeral. David's death had come as a sudden shock. He had left the house, whistling, last Tuesday morning without the slightest thought of never again entering happily through those doors. One hour later she had gotten the word. "David was crushed beneath a heavy steel beam at the mill where he worked."

The realization of all it meant did not fully dawn on her then. But now—the funeral was past—her friends had all gone back home, and Grace was alone in the house with the baby. Now what? There was no nice bank account to count on. No, there was not even enough money in the house to buy a month's supply of milk for Lucy!

Grace had never had a job. There had always been plenty to do at home, which she cheerfully did until she married David. For two and a half years now she had kept house spotlessly for David. A year ago Lucy had joined them, adding to the responsibilities and joys of the already happy home.

"Now what?" Over and over the question came to her. "How can I take a job? What could I do? What would I do with Lucy?" Grace could not bear the thought of someone else raising and training her child—their child. She and David spent hours planning and praying much about the responsibility of bringing this child into the world and raising it for God. They were determined to work together and, with God's help, train her in the ways of the Lord.

Now she was left to face the responsibility alone—and with no support! How could it be done?

Grace Wells was near despair that Friday evening when a faint knock was heard on the door. She was tempted not to answer. A wave of shame and remorse swept over her. The baby was asleep in the crib with a dirty face and hands. She had not washed her after taking her up from crawling on the floor. Lucy had cried herself to sleep while her mother walked listlessly about from room to room, indulging in her self-pity and fighting the growing bitterness within.

Casting a horrified glance about the disorderly room, Grace decided, "I just cannot let anyone in now!"

Just as the knocking ceased and a soft footstep was heard descending the steps, Lucy cried out, still grouchy because of the lack of love and attention she had always been used to. Lucy generally awoke cooing and smiling—but not today. She was as cross and disagreeable as she had been before her short nap. Quickly Grace pushed the almost-empty bottle into her mouth, hushing the outcry, but not in time. Now the caller knew someone was at home and decided to try again. The knock, though soft, was persistent. With the air of "what difference does it make anyway," Grace walked toward the door, kicking several toys out of her path.

"Come in," she said feebly with a wan smile, scarcely noticing or caring who the visitor would prove to be. Grace stepped aside to allow Sister Gains to enter. "Good evening, Grace. How are you getting along?" Sister Gains met her with a hearty smile.

"Oh, I don't know," Grace sighed, "I think we just can't get along!"

"Oh, you must not talk that way, Sister Wells. Remember, you still have a heavenly father who loves and cares for His children. Dire circumstances make no difference to His bountiful supply. He will provide for you. All your needs shall be supplied if you only look to him."

"How?" asked Grace despondently. "How is a mother with a one-year-old going to earn a living and take care of a baby? It is impossible—impossible!" Grace burst into sobs.

"Sister Wells, of course it is hard, but you know the company will take care of your financial needs, don't you?"

"The company?"

"Yes." Sister Gains went on, encouraged with the apparent interest Grace had shown. "The mill has a plan to provide for the widows of all their men who are hurt on the job. You would only have to apply for your widow's pension."

"But," Grace replied doubtfully, "I don't believe in that kind of support. It is not Scriptural and our church does not approve of such things. Didn't that very thing come up in the discussion several months ago and we decided that the brethren and sisters in the church should not apply for such help?"

"But, Grace, don't you see it is the only thing you can do? Of course you will apply for your widow's pension. You will receive $75 a month. This isn't very much but it will surely help. You will not be entirely without support. You should apply immediately so that you will not miss a check. I will be glad to go in with you tomorrow morning to make your application if you would like. I know you will not have any trouble getting it."

"Oh, I just don't know what to say," Grace looked troubled. "If only David could help me decide."

"As I see it there is nothing to decide. You must have the monthly check. You cannot get along without it. There is only one thing to do—in your case the check is a necessity."

"But, Sister Gains," Grace protested, "you just told me the loving heavenly Father will provide for us. Now must I take things in my own hands and see that my needs are supplied in a way that may be displeasing to Him?"

"But, Sister Wells, what makes you so sure this would be displeasing to Him?" her visitor continued her persuasion. "Of course I said God will provide, but perhaps this is the way He will do it. Don't you see how He is supplying your needs already by the company check? You must accept what you can get. The Lord helps those who help themselves! You cannot turn this down."

Grace Wells sat thoughtfully for a while. "Sister Gains, I will have to have time to think about it first and to pray about it. I cannot say just now what I will do. Please do not ask me to decide by tomorrow morning. If I decide to go in I will call you. I would be very happy to have you accompany me if I go; but it has always been my conviction that we should not ask for such help, but that the Lord will provide our needs without going to the world and its means for help. I want more time to think and pray about this."

"Sister Wells, I cannot understand you." The older sister shook her head. "You dare not turn down this offer. Don't you realize you have to have it? You cannot get along without it. Of course friends will help you, but that is not like the regular check that you can count on." Sister Gains was almost growing impatient. "You wouldn't want to put your child in a home somewhere to be taken care of, would you?" she asked as a last thrust toward persuading her neighbor to see the necessity of following her plan.

"Oh, no!" Grace cried, again bursting into sobs. She sat silently for some time before replying again. "I guess I will have to do it. I do not want someone else to raise my little girl. I want to take care of her myself. I guess I will have to take the pension. But—oh, is it right?"

A half hour later Sister Gains left with a promise that she would be back in the morning at nine o'clock to assist Grace with her business in town. They would go directly to the mill and apply for the check and Grace would have that at least toward her support and for the child. "I will bring my oldest daughter along to stay with Lucy so that you won't be burdened with her. Just trust in the Lord, Dear, and He will provide for His children," she assured her weeping friend as she left. "See how He is already supplying the financial need!"

For a long time Grace stood gazing absently at the sinking sun. Had she done the right thing? After all, there was Lucy to consider. Grace wanted to be the one to raise her child, but if she did it at the cost of displeasing her Lord, what had she gained? Would she then be able to bring her to love the Lord and His commands? As the shades of dusk gathered about her, Grace dropped to her knees right there on the porch. At last she poured out her heart to her Father in heaven, who inclines His ear to those who cry to Him. There she sought His perfect will and His aid in her great need. Realizing at last that her only hope was to trust in Him and obey at any cost, she willingly laid on the altar all her own will and selfishness. Now with nothing in the way, she looked to Him in complete confidence and assurance. He would provide!

"And I do not believe it will be by means of worldly organizations," she mused. "I want my Lucy to grow up trusting in God, not in pensions the world gives." She was firmly convinced that it would not be right to ask for this help from the world, so that settled the matter. There would be no trip to town tomorrow morning with Sister Gains—no monthly check of seventy-five dollars. Not once did she even consider the possibility of such a means of aid again. Her hope was in God and she was at rest. She would look to Him to guide her to whatever means of support she should have. With a deep settled peace in her soul, Grace rose from her knees in the darkness after committing her beloved daughter to the care of the kind heavenly Father, to supply for her what was best materially and spiritually. She entered the house with a lighter heart than she had known for days.

One sweeping glance about the disorderly room told Grace that it was high time to change her careless attitude that she had allowed the past few days. Lucy, who was now contentedly playing with her empty bottle, looked up and cooed, smiling happily at her mother.

"Lucy, dear, it's time for some cereal, isn't it?" Lucy clapped her chubby hands. Grace walked on past the crib. "While she is happy I suppose I could clean up a bit," she decided. "It is going to be different from here on, my child," she spoke softly. "We are going to stop this worrying and just look to God. He will provide!"

In a matter of minutes the living room was a different looking place. All the toys had been removed from the floor, bottles from the sofa and the chair covers straightened. Talking to Lucy as she worked, Grace flew about the house with a new enthusiasm. The world would go on—Lucy would grow up—the Lord would provide!—someway. But how? Grace did not know. But this she knew. She had resolved to be true and faithful to Him, and joy and peace again were hers. This is the way David would want her to carry on. Forty-five minutes had so transformed the cozy home that Grace felt cheerful and relaxed as she took Lucy in her arms and sat down at the clean kitchen table. Dishes had all been put away and the floor swept. With real joy and satisfaction she fed the eager baby bite after bite of the warm cereal with applesauce, amid her pleasant cooing and gurgling.

Another knock was heard on the door. This time Grace turned to answer with a smile of satisfaction. She quickly wiped the baby's mouth, glad that she had just put a clean white dress on her. Her home was no longer anything to be ashamed of and she longed for fellowship. The knock was a welcome interruption.

"Good evening, Brother and Sister Smucker. Do come in," she greeted the minister and his wife warmly. She stepped aside to welcome her guests. "God bless you, Sister. It's good to see you looking so well." The minister stepped over to the sofa and was seated beside his wife. Grace took the rocker with Lucy in her lap. Very relaxed and at ease, they all enjoyed a good visit. "Well, how are things going?" Brother Smucker asked presently.

"We are getting along well," she replied. "Many friends have been so kind to us, and helpful. Of course, nothing can take David's place. He is missed so much," she added, with unbidden tears coming to her eyes. "But God is so faithful to supply all our needs and His presence is precious to us."

"I am so happy for this testimony from you," the pastor replied earnestly. "We want to be a help to you whenever we can. I hope you will always be free to come to us with any problem or anytime that we can aid you in any way." Reaching into his pocket, he pulled out a small folded piece of paper. "I would like to ask you one more question, if I may be very personal."

"Surely. I will be happy to answer if I can," Grace replied, wondering.

"We realize that David does not have a large bank account laid up for you. And we appreciate the way you and your husband have worked together and laid up treasures in heaven to await you there, rather than laying them up here. I was wondering if you have any means of support now for yourself and the child."

Grace took a deep breath. "I am sure the Lord will provide somehow. He has given me this assurance, but I do not know how He will provide," was her simple answer, with no trace of worry or anxiety.

Brother Smucker walked across the room and laid the folded paper in her hand. When she began to unfold it, he asked her to wait until they were gone.

"God bless you. Keep trusting in Him. 'He will not fail thee, nor forsake thee. . . . ' " the pastor quoted, walking toward the door.

"God bless you, dear Sister," his wife spoke softly, greeting her warmly again before leaving.

Grace watched them leave before turning her attention again to the folded paper in her hand. "What could it be?" She opened one fold and then another till the little paper laid out flat in the palm of her hand.

"Dear Sister Grace," she read, "we, your brothers and sisters in the Lord, wish to help you in whatever small way we can. We have each decided how much we can help financially each month so that you will have something regular that you can count on." Below, the heads of nine families had signed their names, pledging to pay ten dollars a month each—nine families—nine tens—ninety dollars a month! Grace's hand trembled as she held up the paper to look again. Could it be true—ninety dollars a month! Tears of joy flowed freely. "The Lord surely does provide and even better than the world—if we just trust in Him!" She dropped to her knees again. "Thank You, Father! Only by trusting in Thee completely could I have learned this precious lesson. Thank You, Lord!"

The Price Is Paid

Sarah snapped on the light. She picked up her Bible and began leafing through it. She glanced at the clock. "Eleven-thirty," she sighed wearily. She turned some more pages, not sure for what she was looking. She read a few verses here, a few there, then turned the page and scanned a few more lines. Nothing made sense. She rambled on, her mind scarcely on the printed words before her. She had rolled and tossed restlessly in bed for more than two hours. Finally she had given up trying to sleep; and, thinking that reading awhile might put her mind at rest, she sat thus on the edge of the bed with the precious Book before her. Sarah had not taken time to acquaint herself with God's Word for a long time now.

The tired girl laid the Bible aside, her brow furrowed in deep thought. She turned off the light but remained sitting on the bed, facing the window. The soft moonlight, the twinkling stars, and the quiet, still night calmed her.

"How peaceful everything looks! I've enjoyed a pleasant day at school and spent a happy evening with my family. Why should I be so restless?"

Soberly she tried to analyze the cause for her restlessness.

"I'm not unhappy," she argued with herself. "It's just that I always have this vague feeling of uneasiness when I'm alone and quiet. I have every reason to be perfectly happy—a good Christian home, a pleasant school, and lots of friends." She went on

64

counting her blessings. "I can't understand myself. Why should I be restless and unhappy? I should be sleeping soundly, peacefully."

Sarah leaned back on her pillow, trying to relax. "What is it I'm longing for?" she questioned her own heart, honestly seeking an answer.

"It seems I'm always searching for something. I don't know what. Why can't I be satisfied and content? Why this restlessness, akin to fear? It's certainly no earthly comfort I lack. I have good Christian parents. I have joined the church and always try to be faithful to it. What could cause this uneasiness I always feel?" Sarah remembered the joy and peace she had felt a few years ago when she had received Christ as her personal Savior. She had confessed all her sin, confessed Christ as Lord, and yielded her life wholly to Him. He had taken all her fear and given peace. Her heart had been at rest for some time. What had happened that this old restlessness and fear again stole into her heart? Sarah could not think of one unconfessed sin in her life.

Awakening rather late on Sunday morning, Sarah felt relaxed and cheerful, scarcely remembering her struggle a few hours earlier.

In this way the weeks and months passed. The apparently happy girl was troubled. This secret longing was always nagging her, especially in the quiet hours as she grew older. Sarah began to search more earnestly for a calm serenity that would not give way to restlessness, uneasiness, and even fearfulness.

"I've joined the church; I've confessed my sins. Why would I not be prepared to meet the Lord and to spend eternity with Him?" she reasoned. "Still, I cannot face the thought of Christ's coming or of death without fear and dread."

About this time, Sarah came across a book on Christian victory in the church library. Immediately she thought, "Now here will surely be what I need." She checked out the book and could hardly wait to begin reading it.

On Sunday afternoon Sarah slipped upstairs to her room, closed the door, and settled down with her book. She was expecting a great need in her life to be filled.

Very much enthused, she read on and on. This wonderful message of victory through Christ thrilled her soul. Many Bible verses were used. "The book is good," she thought. "The writer must have been inspired of God to be able to portray the Christian experience in this way."

By the time her mother called for supper, Sarah was too much wrapped up in the book to be interested in anything else.

"I'm reading, Mother," she answered. "I don't believe I'll come down. I'm not hungry." She read on until time for the evening church service.

How light and happy Sarah felt that evening! The wonderful experiences of the writer seemed to become a reality in her own life. Sarah felt as if her feet were on the clouds. Quoting over and over again to herself favorite passages from the book, Sarah beamed brightly, experiencing the same emotions that the author seemed to feel.

On Sunday evening after church, Sarah went to her room.

"The secret to victory," Sarah breathed triumphantly, picking up the library book on her bed and laying it on the table. "At last I have found it!" She slipped into bed and fell asleep.

Sarah awoke with a start; she rolled over. "It must be almost morning," she sighed. The moon shone brightly into the window. Sarah looked at the clock. "Eleven o'clock." It must have stopped. But, no, it was running. "Oh, dear," she thought wearily, "why did I have to wake up now? I do hate to lie awake at night."

That wonderful emotional uplift she had experienced in the afternoon was no longer there. She felt depressed. "Why can I not enjoy the blessed experiences the writer speaks of in his book?" she wondered. "This afternoon, I really thought I had found what I've always longed for; but somehow, I don't feel the same anymore."

The old uneasiness crept over her, captivating every thought. For more than an hour Sarah rolled and tossed restlessly.

Finally, she got up, turned on the light, and reached for the wonderful book. Her Bible lay unnoticed beneath it. She tried reading awhile, but the words no longer held the wealth of meaning they seemed to have the first time she read them.

"What is wrong with my experience?" she sighed. "I don't feel the joy and peace that rightly belong to a child of God. Now, Sister Anna I'm sure has experienced the wonderful joy and sanctification this author speaks of in his book."

Sarah loved her Sunday school teacher dearly and often wished to be like her. How she envied her Christian experience! Thinking of her now, Sarah decided, "I will speak to her concerning my problem. Surely she will be able to help me. But what will she think of me? No doubt she thinks I've been enjoying victory. I hardly even know how to tell her what my problem is."

Sarah had become so distressed and perplexed by this continual feeling of uneasiness that she determined to seek help. "Sister Anna will understand, I'm sure; she is always sympathetic and willing to help us girls with any problem."

During that week, Sarah found the opportunity she was waiting for. She had gone to baby-sit for a neighbor while the parents were away from home. Just after the children were tucked in bed, there was a knock on the front door.

Sarah opened the door. "Why, Sister Anna, I'm so glad to see you. Do come in," she invited cordially.

"Oh, I had come over to talk to Mrs. Brown," Anna said, "but I don't have anything special to do this evening, so I may as well stop in awhile."

The two girls sat on the sofa, chatting pleasantly.

"Anna," Sarah finally began, "there is something I've been wanting to talk to you about. I hardly know how to tell you how I feel or what is bothering me." The room was quiet, save the ticking of the grandfather clock.

"What is it, Sarah?" Anna encouraged. "Just tell me in your own words. I'll try to understand." She paused a moment. Sarah's eyes looked troubled. The experienced Christian sensed that the girl was having a real struggle. Anna had not been entirely unaware of this before. She often saw the longing, faraway look in Sarah's eyes and was happy for the opportunity to help her. While she waited for Sarah to go on, she breathed a silent prayer for guidance.

"Oh," Sarah sighed, "I wish I hadn't started about it. What will she think of me?" She looked up to meet the loving eyes of her Sunday school teacher looking searchingly into hers.

"Sarah, is it some problem you have that you'd like to talk to me about? Why don't you just tell me about it? We all have problems, you know," Sister Anna spoke sympathetically.

"O Anna, you always seem so—ah, well, so happy and . . ." Sarah stopped abruptly, leaving her sentence unfinished.

Placing her hand on Sarah's shoulder, Anna asked, "And why shouldn't I be happy with such a wonderful Savior as we have?"

"But, Anna, that is what I wanted to talk to you about; I'm not happy. I'm afraid. I fear death and dread the second coming of Christ. Why shouldn't I be happy?—but I'm not!"

Sarah burst into tears.

Anna questioned. "Hasn't the Lord been good to you? Hasn't Jesus given His life for you?" She waited. "What more could you want? Have you accepted all that He freely offers?"

Sarah still did not speak.

"Sarah, is there any known sin in your life that you are unwilling to confess?" Anna asked pointedly. Sarah shook her head.

"Sarah, Satan often tempts us to doubt God's Word and all His precious promises," Anna said gravely. "I believe your trouble is a failure to trust God—to take Him at His Word."

"But, Anna, I've received Jesus as my personal Lord and Savior. I realized that I was a sinner, helpless, and only the blood of Jesus could save my soul. I confessed my sin—but, still I cannot get rid of this feeling of uneasiness. I have never had wonderful experiences and feelings that bring peace and assurance as so many other Christians have. I don't enjoy the blessed fellowship with Him that you often speak of. Oh, at first when I received Jesus into my heart, I felt sure I was a child of God. Old things had passed away and all things became new. But since then, I don't know what happened. I don't feel the same. What is wrong? Why—?"

"Sarah, you say that you received Jesus as your personal Lord and Savior. Do you really believe that God has forgiven your sins? Are you trusting in His Word with complete confidence that it is true? Or are you trusting in your feelings? Do you believe that God has accepted you as His own child?"

"Yes."

"And that He forgave your sins?"

"Yes."

"Sarah, wasn't that a wonderful experience, to become a child of God—to have your sins forgiven, which would have damned your soul? Wasn't that a wonderful feeling?"

"Why yes—yes, surely it was." Sarah looked thoughtfully at her friend. "Do you never fear and dread death?" she asked quite suddenly.

"Well, Sarah, human nature naturally shrinks from death. It is only natural that these bodies strive to live. But, to the child of God, death is only sleep—falling asleep to awake to life in heaven. Death no longer has a sting. It is only fear and uncertainty of the unknown, the great beyond after death that puts the terror and dread into the heart of the unbelieving. Now we know that Jesus has mercifully shown us what is beyond—the glorious life with Him. To this we look forward with joyful anticipation. God faithfully supplies grace for each circumstance we face. When our time comes to die, He will supply dying grace. Now we have no need of it. Now He supplies grace to live, to trust in Him."

"O Anna, that's all so wonderful. I wish I could be like you," Sarah exclaimed.

"No, no, Sarah! It's not me you want to be like. You must trust Jesus, and seek to be like Him," Anna explained.

Anna drew from her purse a small New Testament and said, "Here is the basis for your joy, peace, and assurance. This Word will take away your doubts and confusion. Read it. Make it your very own. Don't trust anything but this Word." As she leafed through this familiar Book, she pointed out many precious promises and verses to bring assurance and hope to the troubled soul.

It was growing late and Anna had to leave. The Browns would soon be at home.

"Sarah," she said in tender tones, "repent of your unbelief and failure to stand on the Word of God; and then, when you have confessed every sin and turned from them all, yield your life wholly to God. Then read the Word and cling to what it says. Don't allow anything but what God says to take away your peace and joy. Take God at His Word. He is faithful. Fellowship with Him daily. Study the Word of God."

Sister Anna went home. In a few minutes the Browns arrived.

Sarah was thoughtful as she prepared for bed that night.

"Study the Word of God. I surely have not been very well acquainted with His Word. Maybe—" Sarah picked up her Bible. "Maybe this is where I have failed." With great difficulty she found some of the precious passages Anna had read. "Beloved, now are we the sons of God." "If we confess our sins, *he is faithful* and just *to forgive* us our sins, *and to cleanse* us from all unrighteousness." "Him that cometh to me I will in no wise cast out." These verses with many others Sarah began to grasp and claim for her own. She had confessed and Jesus had promised to accept her. Would He not keep His promise? Surely He would!

Sarah knelt beside her bed. In a simple way she confessed her unbelief to the Lord. She now believed the Word. What did her feelings matter when the Word spoke. As the light dawned, the darkness and fear fled.

It was no longer the experiences of others she sought, but real fellowship with her Redeemer and Lord—to simply believe what He had said. What more could she want? He had paid the price for her redemption, sealing it with His own blood. He had promised to accept those who come to Him in faith; none would be cast out. "He has provided everything needful for my salvation. The price is paid! I accept this by faith."

With this her joy was complete. How blind she had been! The Word was alive and powerful in her once more. Once again old things passed away and all things became new.

"Who Can Find a Virtuous Woman?"

Lois and Mary had been studying together at the dining-room table for about an hour. Suddenly, Mary jumped to her feet. "Oh, I forgot I promised to call Mabel!" she exclaimed. Mary quickly went into the front room and was about to pick up the telephone when her father stopped her. "Mary," he called. "What are you doing?"

"Only making a phone call," she replied with noticeable irritation. She hesitated a moment, with her hand on the receiver.

"Mary, I'm sorry," her father went on slowly, "but you know that I have asked you not to make more than three phone calls in an evening, unless it is something of importance. There have been too many complaints about this line being busy all the time."

Mary turned to her father with a pout on her lips. "Please, just this once. I haven't called anyone for an hour. After all, we pay for this line."

"Right," her father agreed, "and so do five other parties. Each one would like to be able to use it sometimes. Mary, if I'm not mistaken, I heard you make at least four calls right after supper," he spoke sternly.

Without a word Mary walked back to the dining-room table. Father's word was final.

Trying to smother the rebellion that she dared not show,

Mary pulled out her chair. Lois was just finishing her last paper. Enviously, she watched her gather up all her books and papers. Lois placed her work neatly on the corner of the buffet, then took an easy chair in the living room between her father and mother. Mother was mending some of Father's old socks. Lois picked up a few from her mother's lap and began to help with a cheerful smile. "I've finished a little earlier than I thought I could," she remarked pleasantly. "This test week has been tough."

"Yes," her mother agreed, "I remember what test time used to be like."

Father soon joined the conversation. The evening passed pleasantly for the three in the front room.

From her chair in the dining room, Mary could see Lois's happy expression as she stitched away. "Such a boresome task—mending socks. Indeed, and with a smile. I'd throw them all away."

Mary's mind was not on her studies at all. Now Mother was trying to show Lois how to keep from having an uneven place where she started darning. Mary knew she would throw up her hands and quit. If there was anything she hated, it was to have to be told how to do something. She always did feel like telling Mother to just do it herself if she was not doing it good enough. Mary had not finished her English yet when Father called. "Come, Mary, it's nine o'clock. We want to have family worship now."

"But, Father, I haven't even opened my math book yet. I've got to have at least another hour!"

"I'll call you an hour early in the morning. Come now!" He replied with finality.

She had been very determined to stay up until she finished her work. The rest could go to bed. She was no longer a baby. She would stay up.

Her determination wilted. Slowly Mary got up and walked to

the front room. Father had conquered her again. She had been determined to win out just this once. But no one could balk long with Father looking at him like that. The loving concern he felt for his children could be seen in every feature on his face. His voice was firm, but tender. Never did he raise it in anger. "I know test time can get pretty rough," Mother sympathized, seeing Mary's distressed face. "But maybe with a good night's sleep, things will go better."

Mary sat on the sofa without a word.

Test time passed. Another school year came and went. Mary graduated. Lois still had one more year of high school when her mother suddenly became very ill. For weeks she lay helpless. Lois, with great tenderness, cared for her day and night. Father helped all he could. Only Mary never offered her assistance. She became more and more independent. Her days were occupied with earning what she could to buy the many things she wanted. Her evenings were spent in pleasure with her many friends.

Lois was satisfied to patch and mend old clothes. She enjoyed cooking and cleaning. The meals she prepared were simple but tasty. Mary became dissatisfied with the plain food they ate and the simple furnishings in the house. She complained about the extra burden it placed on them by having Mother sick. Each evening when she came home from work she fretted and fussed about all the little jobs that Lois had not found time to do.

"Father, I'll drop out of school this year. Maybe I can finish later," Lois offered.

"No," her father replied. "Mary also must learn to do her part." He had been quite perplexed as to how to deal with his oldest daughter in the past months. Mary was eighteen and felt she had no more need of her father's help or advice. "I will talk to your sister about it this evening," he told Lois. "Mother and I appreciate very much what you have done for us. Your untiring care of Mother has been a great comfort to me. You have done very well with the housekeeping and gardening. I have always appreciated the way you cook and plan meals. But Mary must learn, too. I have noticed that much good food is wasted when she does the cooking and meal planning. Yes, Mary must learn, too."

"I will be glad to skip next year if you can't work out something satisfactory," Lois replied. "Maybe I could finish then the next year. Mother seems to be improving slowly."

"Thank you, Lois," her father answered, "but I hope you won't need to do that."

After supper Mary excused herself, apologizing that she would not be able to help with the dishes. "I must hurry and get dressed," she explained.

"Mary, this is Thursday evening," her father's voice broke in just as she was about to leave the room. "I thought you usually go out on Wednesday and Friday evenings. I hope you're not going to add Thursday to that yet."

Mary paused, showing great displeasure.

"I wanted to talk to you. It seems a girl should spend enough time at home that her father would have the opportunity to talk to her once in a while." Her father addressed her with a warm smile.

"Father, is there any special reason you wanted me to stay tonight?" Mary asked. "I surely don't want to miss tomorrow evening. Now I could stay home this evening, if you really want me to. But tomorrow evening I'm going out with Ray. I hope you won't ask me to give that up."

"Ray?" her father replied. "I didn't know you were going with him. I thought it was James."

"O Father, that's been off six weeks. Why, he's no comparison to Ray. And Ray's father has money. I had no idea . . ."

"Take it easy," her father cut in. "It's not just money you're looking for, I trust."

"Of course not, but Ray is wonderful."

Lois had started to clear the table.

"Will you spend this evening at home?" her father asked.

"All right," Mary agreed halfheartedly, turning to help Lois with the hated task—dishwashing.

Father went into the front room to sit with Mother till the girls came to join them. Lois soon joined them with a stack of mending. She could get this out of the way while enjoying a pleasant evening with her parents.

It was almost an hour before Mary came into the living room with a book in her hand. Immediately she sat down and began reading.

"Girls," Father began. "Soon school will begin. Someone will need to stay at home with Mother."

Mary looked up. She had been afraid of this.

"Lois really should finish school this year."

"O Father," Mary began. "I've got such a good job."

Father looked disappointed.

"I will be glad to stay and wait to finish school later," Lois offered.

Nothing more was said at the time.

One week later, on a Friday evening shortly after Mary had left with Ray, a car drove up.

"Who's coming?" Father asked Lois, who was sitting near the front window.

"It looks like Ray's car. Yes, Ray and Mary are back. She must have forgotten something."

"Come on in and spend the evening," Father invited warmly when the front door opened. "We would love to be better acquainted with you, Ray."

Ray stepped inside, seemingly embarrassed. He had been in Mary's home only once before. Mary seemed embarrassed also. They sat side by side on the sofa. Neither spoke for some time.

Mary knew her parents were not heartily in favor of her going with Ray. That made it all the harder to tell them what she and Ray had planned to tell them tonight.

It had all happened so suddenly that she hardly knew how she felt about it herself. At least she would be relieved of her family responsibilities now.

On Thursday evening when she told Ray that her father was expecting her to give up her job to care for her mother, he had simply said, "Well, let's get married. That would settle it. I would provide for you like your father can't afford to. You wouldn't have near the drudgery of housework, just keeping house for me. We would eat out half the time, and we'd have a new house; there wouldn't be any cleaning to do. I'd never ask you to mend an old pair of socks. We'd throw them out and buy new ones.

"O Mary, will you marry me real soon—right away? Why wait when we know we want each other?" He had seemed very excited!

"Well, why not?" she had wondered, and so she promised.

Plans were made for an August wedding. Next school year she would have no responsibility at home. Lois would have to get along the best she could.

Now, sitting in the living room with Mother, Father, and Lois looking at her, Mary began to feel differently about it. She no longer felt quite so bold or resentful toward her family. Fidgeting uneasily, she cast several anxious glances at Ray. He had little to say, but to answer Father's questions. They had decided he should be the one to tell of their plans. Now, unable to find words to begin, he remained silent.

Finally, he spoke nervously. "We came here to tell you folks of some plans we've made for this summer."

"Yes," Father encouraged. "I'm always interested in the plans my daughters make." He was entirely unsuspecting of what was about to follow.

"Ah," Ray cleared his throat and began again. "Well—ah—we plan to be married in August." That was all.

"In August?" Father repeated. "Why, I believe it's August now."

Father looked at Mary. Mother raised up on her cot, looking searchingly at her oldest daughter. She had been too weak and sick to talk much to the girls lately. Certainly there must be some mistake.

Lois gasped. Why, it had been only about two months since Mary had quit going with James and they had been dating for almost a year before that. She could hardly believe that Mary would rush into marriage like this.

"Are you ready to go?" Ray asked, taking Mary's hand. Together they walked out of the room. They spent some time in Mary's room, then went out the back door and on out to the car. The three in the living room sat silently until the last sound of the motor died out.

"O Father, isn't there some way we could convince her to wait awhile?" Mother asked beseechingly.

"I don't know. I'll try," Father answered. "Mary isn't ready to settle down to family responsibilities."

"Why, she is hardly able to fix a meal. She doesn't like any kind of housework. And they have only been dating such a short while. I'm afraid she will be sorry. She doesn't know what she wants yet. She has been so impressed with the amount of money he seems to have. I wonder what kind of boy Ray is. We hardly even know him," Mother worried.

"I know, Mother. I'll try to get her to wait at least awhile and think it through. It's getting late. Maybe you and Lois should go to bed. I'll wait up for Mary and see if I can have a good talk with her tonight."

It was a subdued little group that gathered for worship that evening. Their minds were all with the missing member of the family. After Scripture reading and prayer, they went to bed.

Father waited. The hours drew out long until midnight. After midnight they were almost unbearable, watching and waiting. He grew weary. Finally, after committing her to God about three o'clock, he went to bed with a heavy, burdened heart.

"Father," he cried, "Mary's stubborn will has never been broken. Help us to know how to deal with her now. And forgive us where we have failed."

In the morning when they discovered that Mary had not yet arrived, they all became quite alarmed. Lois had rushed out of Mary's room calling, "Father, she has taken most of her clothes with her."

Father immediately walked to the phone. He dialed Ray's number.

"This is Mary's father. I was wondering if Ray is home this morning."

"He's not? Do you know where he is?"

"Not exactly? What do you mean? Do you have any idea?"

"What was that—in the Carolinas, you say?"

"Married? You mean already?"

"No, no, nothing at all. Yes, they told us they expected to be married in August. No date."

Mother and Lois sat waiting breathlessly.

"When will they be back?"

"Thank you."

Father hung up the receiver. A strange look had crossed his face.

"Father!" Mother exclaimed. "What . . ."

"They're married." Father wept. "They are so young. If only she had talked it over with us! Mary has always been such an unbroken girl. I should have put forth more effort to talk things over with her." Father expressed his grief.

Mother was weeping. Lois walked over to the cot and straightened the spread. There was nothing to say. Nothing could stop them now. The vows had been made.

"They are so young," Mother repeated, heartbroken.

For several days nothing was heard from the newly married couple. Then one day a letter came. It had been postmarked in South Carolina. Lois could hardly wait to get into the house to open it. Mother had seemed very weak again the past few days. Maybe a letter from Mary would do her good. With trembling fingers, Lois broke the seal, and read:

"Dear folks at home,

"We are enjoying our honeymoon in the Carolinas. The weather is lovely.

"We'll see you all soon. We bought the Oakland Farm. We plan to build a new house on it right away.

With lots of love,

Ray and Mary"

Mother lay quietly while Lois read. With a little sigh she lay back on the pillows. "The Oakland place—that is a nice farm. I'm glad they are not moving far away."

"I wonder what they'll do with that lovely old farmhouse. It was such a nice house, and well kept." Lois folded the short letter and placed it back in the envelope.

Mother continued to grow weaker. The doctor came out almost every day now. During the second week after Mary left, Mother had to be taken back to the hospital. Father and Lois tried to contact Ray and Mary, but were unable to locate them. On Sunday night Mother passed away. Neither Mary's father nor Ray's parents were able to contact them. For two more weeks nothing was heard from the young people. Mother was laid to rest.

Lois began to make preparations to go ahead and finish her schooling. The days and nights were lonesome. How she longed to hear from her sister! How shocked she would be when she heard of her mother's death!

Father wearily went about his tasks. If it had not been for his insistence, Lois would not have consented to finish school this year. She had felt, at first, that he would need her at home too badly. Of course, she could have come home on weekends, but he had insisted that it would be best for her to continue school, and he could manage somehow.

*   *   *   *   *   *   *   *   *   *   *   *

After leaving her home that Friday evening, when they told her parents of their plans to be married soon, Mary said, "Ray, I wish you would have told them we plan to get married this evening. I feel they should know."

"I know, Mary, I had planned to but . . ." Ray left the sentence unfinished.

"I hope they won't worry. I guess they'll find out sooner or later," Mary replied. "Anyway, let's forget it. We must hurry and get ready. At least I'm glad your parents know. My folks will call there when I don't come home. I just couldn't tell them, either."

Mary had always thought she'd have a fine wedding—a church wedding, of course—but now that would all have to be changed. "How late did you say the justice of the peace would be in down there in Wayne County? Are you sure we can make it tonight?"

Mary felt uneasy. She began to worry about everything. She wondered, after all, if she were doing right. At least she would be relieved of what everyone seemed to think was her duty at home. If she were married she would be free to do as she pleased. And there would always be plenty of money. And that was something that was always scarce at home.

They were married and got a luxurious motel. Life was easy now. It would all be a bed of roses. Mary was sure of that.

After spending about a week of leisurely sightseeing, Mary began to think more and more of home. She wondered about her mother. She wondered how they felt about her leaving. When she began to grow listless, Ray sensed that she was homesick and asked if she would like to shorten their honeymoon. She wanted to go on and spend the month traveling as they had planned. She was not exactly anxious to move into the big farmhouse until their new one was built.

"Why not write to your folks?" Ray suggested. So Mary wrote. It was a short letter. It seemed that there just was not anything to write. Mary felt estranged from her family because of the way she had left.

It was the first day of September when Ray and Mary arrived at home. They drove right out to the Oakland Farm and unpacked. Ray called his folks.

"Here, Mary, call your folks," he suggested.

"I can't. I wouldn't know what to say. Why don't you call and tell them we're back? See how they act," Mary begged.

While Ray dialed the number, Mary stayed near the phone. She was anxious to hear Father's voice, or Lois's. She was anxious to hear how Mother was getting along. The phone was ringing. Mary felt a lump in her throat that would not let her speak.

"Hello," Ray's voice sounded loud and clear.

"This is Ray speaking."

"Yes, we have just arrived."

"We're at the Oakland Farm. Mary told you we bought it, I believe."

"Yes, yes, that's right."

"We had a very nice trip. We want you all to come—what—what?"

Mary was listening breathlessly. Would her family take her

and Ray in as if nothing unusual had happened? She was sure they would. How kind Father had been! And Lois, how sweet and unselfish she had always been! Tears filled Mary's eyes. Poor, dear Mother. Mary hoped she would understand.

"When did she pass away?" Ray asked softly.

Mary was jolted into reality now. "Why, Ray!" A new fear filled Mary's heart as she leaned nearer the telephone Ray clutched so tightly that his knuckles turned white.

"Yes, we'll come over."

"I don't know. I'll ask her." Holding his hand over the mouthpiece, Ray asked, "Mary, do you want to talk to your father?"

Mary was weeping. Ray dropped the receiver. "Mary, did you hear?" he asked softly. She sobbed harder.

"What?"

"That your mother passed away about two weeks ago? They tried to reach you but could not find us."

Mary's heart was broken now. Tears flowed uncontrolled. Ray stood helplessly beside her. He knew how Mary must feel. Lifting the receiver again he said, "She will not talk now. This is quite a shock to her. We will come over a little later this evening if she feels able. We are very tired."

"Yes, I would be glad if you would do that. Maybe that would be better. You and Lois just come right on over. I believe she'd rather have it that way this time. Good-bye."

The shock was more than Mary was prepared for, though she knew her mother's condition was serious before she left. How could she face her father and Lois?

The evening was spent quietly.

"Could I come over this weekend and help you get settled?" Lois offered before leaving.

"O Lois, I'd be so glad if you would," Mary answered, half apologetically. "This huge old house hasn't been lived in for almost six months. Everything is so dusty, and the windows need washing. We don't have very much furniture yet, but want to do some shopping right away. You are such a good housekeeper, I'd be real glad if you would help me. I hope we won't have to stay in this big house long, but it will take a lot of work to get it present-able while we are here."

"All right. I'll come over Saturday morning," Lois said with a smile.

"Thank you," Mary returned, truly thankful for her younger sister.

Saturday morning found the two sisters working side by side, dusting, cleaning, and polishing. Mary was very quiet. She seemed almost ill. Lois's heart ached for her. She sensed her sister's grief and remorse for her hasty actions just before their mother passed away.

"Why don't you rest awhile?" Lois suggested in the middle of the afternoon. "You seem so tired, and really, I'm not tired at all. I can easily finish doing the floors, and then that is all, isn't it?"

"Yes, that is all I had planned to do, but I hate for you to do that. This is my responsibility. You have already helped me so much." Mary looked very weak and tired.

"I really want to help, Mary," Lois replied sincerely. "I wouldn't mind. You look so tired. You haven't rested up from your trip yet."

With tears streaming down her face, Mary dropped into the nearest chair.

"Go ahead," Lois urged. "I'll be finished here before long. Then sometime I want to hear all about your trip. You've seen so many interesting things, I'm sure. We've hardly had a chance to talk much yet."

Seeing her sister's willingness, Mary consented. She really was tired. Mary went into her bedroom and closed the door.

Cheerfully Lois finished cleaning and waxing the last three

floors.

Glancing at the clock, Lois noticed it was almost five-thirty. Surely Ray would soon be coming in for supper. Hesitantly, Lois opened a few cupboard doors. Should she? Lois was not sure. There was plenty there to cook. Finally, Lois decided to tiptoe in first and see whether Mary was sleeping. In the hall, she opened Mary's bedroom door softly. Mary was sound asleep. Quickly Lois returned to the kitchen. She peeled a few potatoes. While they cooked she made a little pan of gravy over some slices of canned ham she found on the shelf. There was a small bowl of corn in the refrigerator, too, that she would warm up, and there were plenty of fresh vegetables for a nice salad.

The door was flung open. Ray stepped inside. "Where's Mary?" he asked, looking about the room. "Say, you girls have really cleaned things up around here," he added cheerfully.

"Yes, we've done quite a lot of cleaning today," Lois agreed. "Mary is resting awhile. She was so tired."

"Yes, I know. I'm glad she could get a little rest. She's been quite upset since we heard about your mother. It was such a shock to her, you know, not being here and all when it happened."

Ray looked quite worn out himself. He had been working very hard, trying to get everything lined up on the farm. Ray was beginning to learn how expensive it is to provide for a wife and all the household needs.

Mary entered the kitchen from the dining-room doorway. "Oh, did I fall asleep? I thought I heard your voice," she said, walking over to her husband in the kitchen doorway.

"Yes, so I heard. I'm glad you did," he smiled. "Feeling better?" he asked lovingly.

"Yes, indeed," Mary answered, still looking a little dark under her eyes. "What do I smell?" Mary turned toward the stove where Lois was beginning to dip up the food. "Hummm! That smells delicious. Isn't this awful," Mary cried, "the first time you come to my home to treat you this way?"

"No, indeed it isn't," Lois replied readily. "Are you two ready to eat some supper?"

"Whew, supper the minute I walk in the door—and I'm starved." Ray started toward the bathroom to wash up, well pleased to have a cooked meal ready and waiting.

"Yes, I've been a poor excuse for a cook so far," Mary apologized, with a slight tinge of offense coloring her voice.

"No, Honey, I didn't mean that. You haven't had a chance to cook yet. We haven't been at home much. You've been wonderful. I was just extra hungry tonight and the food smelled so good."

Lois almost wished she had not started supper. Ray went on down the hall.

"We've been eating out most of the time in the evening," Mary explained.

Several months passed. Lois saw very little of her sister because her weekends at home were full with housekeeping for her father. She felt that her first obligation was there. Father tried hard to be cheerful and get along by himself, but Lois could sense that it was very hard for him sometimes. Her presence in the home from Friday evening until Monday morning did much to brighten it with that womanly touch. Her little acts of thoughtfulness lasted through the week to cheer him. Sometimes it was a fragrant arrangement of flowers; sometimes a favorite dish, nicely prepared and placed in the refrigerator.

After the first several months of married life, Ray began begging, "Mary, please try to have a hot supper ready when I come in from the barn." She began buying more and more prepared foods, increasing their grocery bill almost double. These prepared meals were usually of the types that were hard to use as leftovers, and often more than half was wasted.

"Mary," exclaimed Ray one evening when she was about to throw out three-fourths of a delicious beef potpie, "can't we eat that tomorrow evening?"

Mary looked hurt. "It wouldn't be good," she replied.

"But we can't afford to throw away that much good food," he pleaded. "Let's try it tomorrow."

With a sigh, Mary turned to the refrigerator and put the open dish on an empty shelf.

"Wouldn't it be better if it were covered?" he suggested.

"Yes, I suppose it would be better if I just quit and let you take care of things inside and out," she cried, slamming the refrigerator door!

"I'm sorry, Honey. I shouldn't have said anything. I know it must get tiresome to have three meals a day to fix, without having to warm things over, yet." Ray tried to cover the unpleasant incident. He had no idea that she would take it as an insult. "Let's go out to the Silver Cup for supper tomorrow evening," he suggested, hoping to make amends.

"Oh, let's," she exclaimed. "Really, it's been almost two weeks since we ate out anywhere, and I'm sure you men have no idea how dreadfully boring it is to cook three meals every day."

"Yes, yes, I'm sure it must be. We'll have to try to get out more." Ray got up from the table and began drying the dishes. "It is just that I've gotten so busy on the farm and sometimes I get in so late. I feel too tired to go anywhere. But then I suppose you're too tired to cook, too. I'll try to be more thoughtful after this, Honey."

"If only we could get in the new house soon! This house is more than I can handle alone. I never get through. There is always something that needs cleaning. I'm never caught up with my ironing anymore."

The last dishes were put away. Ray had started for the living room when Mary called, "Let's go shopping awhile this evening,

Dear. Just sitting here in this big old house is most depressing."

"I think we should be in our new house in about another month," Ray replied. "Everything takes so much time. I'm sorry you have to put up with this so long. I really thought the new one would be finished sooner," Ray finished almost despairingly. He could have reminded her of the many changes that she had insisted be made that were holding things up, and of all the latest gadgets and conveniences that she wanted to be added, which greatly increased the price. But he never mentioned those things.

"Shall we go shopping?" she asked again.

"Well, if we need anything," he replied. "We got groceries just two or three days ago, but . . ."

"We need just a few things. But if you don't want to . . . ," she finished in mock resignation, throwing her hands up as if in despair.

"I can't see how we could need anything. Didn't we spend almost forty dollars in the grocery store the last time we were there?"

Mary flung herself down on the kitchen chair. "I didn't say we were going to a grocery store. There are other places to shop." Mary's voice had risen to a sharp pitch.

With a weary sigh, Ray replied, "All right, Honey, get ready. We will go shopping. But, look, we can't keep up this extravagance forever. We aren't made of money."

"Money, money, money! That's all you seem to be able to think of. Every time I open my mouth, you think I want money. I haven't asked for a cent," Mary scolded. "I only wanted to go window shopping. But, no—you are too tired. Just skip it! I can just sit here in this house all day. You don't care. I'm your cook—your housekeeper. What else matters? Are we poor? Are we broke? No! But anyone would think so—you never have time for anything your wife enjoys." Mary burst into tears.

"Mary, please, don't do that," Ray pleaded helplessly.

"I'm sorry. Please, come on, let's go have some fun. I'll try to stop worrying about the money. It just seems like it takes so much to get started. After the house is built we will not be so tight. There are so many things to buy now. But let's forget it. Come." Pulling his handkerchief from his pocket, Ray wiped away her tears. "It's only eight o'clock. We have an hour before most of the stores close."

Mary dressed quickly. In his wife's absence, Ray sat down at the kitchen table with his checkbook before him. He shook his head. The balance was rapidly getting lower. He had determined to buy nothing on time. There had been plenty for building a nice home. But then there was the new bedroom suite, much more expensive than necessary; the dining room suite, with the extra tables and oversized china cabinet. The kitchen table and chairs also seemed unnecessary, especially such nice ones, when they had already paid a lot to furnish the dining room. There had been a host of other things.

"Ready, Dear?" Mary called cheerily.

Walking through the store, Mary found two lovely pieces of material. Ray paid for them, wondering whether she would ever get them used up with many other pieces lying at home. There were several other gadgets and trinkets she wanted. Ray was afraid to say "no," so they, too, were added. The cash-register tape showed an amazingly high figure. Ray put his billfold back into his pocket and pulled out his checkbook.

"Let's go over to Legum's furniture store yet," Mary suggested as they left Grant's at fifteen till nine. "I just want to show you the bedroom suite I looked at the other day."

"The eight-hundred-dollar one?" he asked skeptically. "I hope you only want to look at it." He laughed.

"All right, let's not start that again," she chided. "I said I want to show it to you. It's really a beauty. Someday we'll want another suite for the spare room, you know. What is a spare room for? Of course, we can at least wait till we move in."

"Sure," he agreed jovially. "I was only teasing."

They both entered the store. It was almost time to close. The store was empty except for one salesman.

"Good evening, young lady," he began. "Still interested in that bedroom suite?"

Mary blushed. She turned away from Ray and pretended to be inspecting the suite more closely.

"You're her husband, I suppose," the salesman turned to Ray.

"Yes, sir. We are only looking around," Ray explained.

"Look, your wife wants that suite. You'll do yourself a favor to buy it for her." Mary walked on around the other side of the bed, touching the smooth, rich wood lovingly. Could the salesman possibly convince him if she could not.

"We really don't have the money now. Maybe after the crops are all harvested," Ray explained.

"Maybe by that time the price will go up," the salesman continued to put on pressure. "You know, we have an easy credit plan that lets you buy anything you really want."

"No, we'd better not now," Ray insisted. Mary looked disappointed.

"What kind of terms?" she asked.

"Any kind you want," the salesman replied eagerly. "Long range; low monthly payments; the add-on credit plan; pay nothing till the first of the year. . . ." The salesman's voice boomed on, explaining each plan in detail.

"I like the add-on credit plan best," Mary suggested. "Then we could always just keep on making the regular monthly payments." The salesman was filling out papers.

"We'd better go," Ray suggested uneasily. "We're holding him up. See, it's past store hours."

"Never mind," the salesman replied. "We don't mind staying

in late for a customer's convenience." He went on writing. "Shall we deliver it in the morning or wait till you get in the new house?" he asked slyly.

Mary looked at Ray. He was shifting from one foot to the other. "It wouldn't cost us much now," she coaxed, "and the little each month—why, we'd hardly feel that. But, of course, if you don't like it. . . ." Mary raised her eyes hopefully.

"Just sign your name right here. I fixed it up so the first payment won't come due until the end of next month. That'll give you more time." The salesman pushed the paper over the chest to Ray. Numbly he picked up the pen and with trembling fingers signed his obligation to pay this bill.

"I believe we'd rather wait to have it delivered until we get in the new house," she beamed. "Oh, I can hardly wait! Ray, you're a dear."

The salesman smiled proudly. "Worth it, wasn't it, young man?" he laughed, walking with them to the door and locking it behind them.

The account stayed open over the years. The payments continually became larger. Other accounts were opened. There were always bills. The farm prospered, but not sufficiently to supply all Mary's wants.

God blessed this home with two small children. With the coming of each one, there was much added expense. When the last one arrived, Mary insisted on having hired help five days a week. She positively could not manage alone. Hired help was expensive. An addition to the house was needed to provide adequate space for a room for the maid. Two years earlier two bedrooms had been added. Ray suggested moving back into the farmhouse. It was still standing unused. Mary would neither consent to this, nor to giving the maid the spare room.

Ray became so pressed with debts that he began selling off property and equipment. "Mary," he said one evening, about ten years after their wedding day, "we are going to have to start living differently. I must tell you we can no longer keep this up. I'm sorry to say we're going to lose the last two bedroom suites we bought. I can't make the payments." Ray was desperate. He pleaded for understanding.

Mary was irritated. "If you can't earn a decent living for us, I will have to go back to work in the office. I'm getting tired of just sitting at home anyway. I'd be happier in the office."

"Please, Mary, don't do that. I don't want to see you go back to work, and the children need their mother at home. Please, let's just stop living above our means." The long drawn line across his forehead and his rapidly whitening hair were beginning to give Ray the appearance of a much older man.

Mary would not hear to his arguments. "I'm going back to work," she insisted.

"But, Mary, unless we start living differently, we'll never make it on your salary and mine. We are being too extravagant. It is not necessary."

Seeing that he could convince her no other way, Ray resorted to the thing he hoped he would never need to tell her. "Mary," he said gravely, "we're just about to lose the farm and everything we have. We've got to do something quick. I'll have to just stop making payments on everything else and let it go, so we can get this mortgage paid up fast, or we will lose it all." Turning his pleading eyes to hers, he hoped that she could understand the situation and offer her help. He saw only the same rebellious determination to go on living as extravagantly as before.

Mary took a job in an office. Ray and the children saw little of her.

Her salary did not help at all in the problem. They lost the farm, their home, and most of the elaborate furnishings. Ray took a job with a farmer nearby. Soon they had to give up the nice home they rented for a small apartment.

Before her oldest child was out of school, Mary's health was broken. She gave up her job. She grieved over their poverty and complained about her husband's poor management. She pitied the children. How she had wanted to give them everything she used to long for! Now here she was—poor health, bad nerves, and nothing to offer her teen-age girls.

In her late thirties, Mary took seriously ill and passed away suddenly, leaving Ray to provide for a young family alone—leaving him without a home or money or any of the things he had in abundance when she married him. All those things had long ago been lost.

*   *   *   *   *   *   *   *   *   *   *   *

"Every wise woman buildeth her house: but the foolish plucketh it down with her hands."

*   *   *   *   *   *   *   *   *   *   *   *

Lois was kept very busy until she was out of high school. She spent most of her weekends at home with Father. Occasionally, she had gone to help Mary. She was glad when graduation was finally history so that she could spend more time at home. Now she could have a garden and can vegetables as Mother had always done. This saved Father very much.

When Lois was twenty-two, a young man, David Wise, was visiting in the community. He became attracted to Lois. He had a good Christian testimony and a pleasing personality. Lois consulted with her father before accepting the first date with him. Father seemed pleased and encouraged the friendship.

After a pleasant year of clean Christian courtship, Lois and David were married. An arrangement, which was satisfactory to all involved, was made to build an extra room for Father in the cozy little home they built close enough that Father could keep his job as long as he felt able. He had his meals with them and enjoyed the fellowship in their home. Father never felt like an intruder, and the young people enjoyed having him with them. Often his advice was sought in important matters. The day came that Father was no longer able to care for himself. David and Lois welcomed him into their home and cared for him as part of the family as long as he lived.

When Lois married David she was not unaware that he would have to borrow money to buy even a small farm. She was perfectly happy with the old furniture and secondhand equipment. The Lord prospered them until they were able, by careful saving and meager living, to pay off all their debts. During the first fifteen years of their marriage, their home was blessed with seven children, each one wanted and cared for and brought up in the nurture and admonition of the Lord.

Though David and Lois found raising their family a full-time job, there was always time and money for the work of the Lord. God had bountifully supplied all their needs. They realized that all they had was His, and used it accordingly. Nothing was wasted, nor was money spent for unnecessary items. Lois thanked God that she had learned to cook and sew when she was young. How she appreciated her godly parents and their rich heritage to her, though she never received a penny of earthly inheritance!

David could safely trust his wife with the checkbook or anything else he had. He knew she would not impose an unnecessary debt. He appreciated her sensible suggestions in business transactions. With each year of married life, David loved her more and saw new graces manifested in her life, which had always been filled with goodness and sweetness.

As each of the children grew up and left the home place to start new homes of their own, they left with a sense of appreciation and love for their parents, who had provided for them a place of spiritual refuge as well as physical care.

David and Lois had the privilege of seeing a large number of their grandchildren receive Christ and live faithful Christian lives. They were able to accumulate, through the years, a few earthly possessions to leave to their dear children; but of most importance, they were able to leave with them a true sense of values and a rich spiritual heritage.

*   *   *   *   *   *   *   *   *   *   *   *

"Every wise woman *buildeth her house:* but the foolish plucketh it down with her hands."

"Forgive Us Our Debts"

"One, two, three," John counted the slow, even strokes hoping in vain that the old clock would go on and strike a few more times. But no—the striking had stopped. How solemn each stroke sounded, as if to say, "Time is swiftly passing. Eternity is drawing near"!

It would very likely be another whole hour before another sound would interrupt his unwelcome thoughts. He had heard the clock strike one and impatiently waited for sleep to come—for hours it seemed, but then it struck only two. Too miserable to lie still any longer, he had walked the floor awhile, hoping to be able to relax and sleep. But now it was striking three and he had only dozed a short time.

His thoughts would not cease to trouble him. "Forgive me, Father," he had cried over and over, but still there was no peace. Never before had John sought forgiveness when he knew that he had grieved the Lord except that peace again flooded his soul and he knew he was forgiven. "Father, I know I have sinned," he cried again. "Give me victory over this sin, through Jesus my Savior, and forgive me."

Again the same little phrase stood out before him, ". . . as we forgive our debtors."

"Forgive us our debts, as we forgive our debtors." John did not wish to be forgiven as he had forgiven Aaron. He wanted to be forgiven according to the Lord's tender mercies.

"Forgive me."

"As ye forgive your debtors," seemed to be his only answer. And there was no peace in that answer—no assurance that all was well.

Finally, when the clock struck four o'clock, John could stand it no longer. Never to his knowledge had he refused to confess a sin of which the Spirit convicted him. But this was something else; how does one confess to his brother that he did not forgive him? What a hard sin to confess!

John again walked the floor. He could not tear his thoughts away from yesterday afternoon's incident. He had been milking when Aaron walked into the barn. Proud, arrogant Aaron, two years younger than John, had tried his patience to the limit in the past several weeks. His boasting and bragging were tiresome, and he seldom did his share of the work. John thought he could stand it no longer. Now here was Aaron, his head hanging, his shoulders drooped. He seemed to have lost his usual haughtiness. John hoped so. He hoped he had been brought down several notches, too.

And then the surprise came. Aaron walked straight over to John and looked him straight in the eye and said, "John, I've been mean and unfair. Will you forgive me? I know I haven't done my part, and I'm sorry about the boasting and bragging I've been doing. I know I have been guilty of exaggeration. But I have cleared matters with the Lord. Things will be different now. I am sorry I have so often made it hard for you."

John had been so completely baffled by the true note of humility that at first he had not said a word. Then Aaron had waited a moment, never turning his eyes from him. "Can you forgive me?" he repeated.

"I can forgive you," John replied with eyes downcast, "but it will take a long time to forget!"

Aaron stood motionless. When John looked up, he saw the

97

hurt look on Aaron's face. Aaron sadly turned away and began his chores.

The chores were finished, supper was over, and the family gathered for devotions. John suddenly became deeply convicted that his love for God had daily been growing colder. He had not been spending precious hours with the Lord as he had done a year ago. As the family knelt together for prayer, John did not hear Father pray. He had a matter to attend to between the Lord and himself alone. But somehow he could not feel that the Lord had forgiven him. There was no assurance.

Devotions were over and the family was in bed. John continued kneeling but could not find peace.

"Father, forgive me."

"As ye forgive your debtors."

Finally, he had gone to bed still troubled, to sleep only until one o'clock. The struggle had been going on now for three hours.

John dropped to his knees again, this time in true repentance. "Father," he cried, "be merciful to me, I pray, and forgive. Implant in my heart a Christlike forgiving spirit. I do not deserve the least of Thy mercies, but do not deny me, I pray. On the merits of Jesus' shed blood I humbly seek Thy favor and Thy help. I have done my brother an injustice. Lead me now to show Thy love to him. Father, I thank Thee for Thy pardon that forgives and remembers our sins against us no more. And I thank Thee for the Spirit's convicting power. In Jesus Name I pray. Amen."

With peace in his soul at last, John walked, with determination in his steps, across the hall to the room where Aaron and his brother Daniel slept.

"Aaron, Aaron," he whispered. Daniel slept soundly on as Aaron sat up. He rubbed his eyes.

"Time to get up already?" Aaron stretched and rubbed his eyes sleepily.

"No," John whispered, "not for an hour yet, but I have to talk to you now."

"All right," Aaron waited.

"Forgive me, Aaron. I was very unloving and unforgiving in my attitude toward you yesterday afternoon."

"Surely," Aaron replied. "And things will be different now, with the peace of God in both our hearts."

"Yes," John agreed. "Just think. He will remember them against us no more. What forgiveness! What wonderful love!"

As John crossed the hall again, his peace and joy knew no bounds. He felt a deeper love and gratitude toward God than he had known for months.

"God not only answered my prayer for forgiveness, but added an extra bonus," he thought as he crawled back into bed. "The spark of love that I felt was growing cold has again burst into a fervent flame. I must keep it alive by fellowship with Him."

"What forgiveness and love! What joy and peace!" John slept the restful sleep that one has when he is securely anchored without a doubt or a fear.

Once Too Often

Dorothy entered the living room, her eyes sparkling. "Mama, Henry asked me to ride to church with him this evening."

The younger girls were outside playing, and the babies were in bed for naps. Only Mama sat dozing in the living room. Papa often spent Sunday afternoons out with the young people in cottage meetings. Dorothy had stayed home today since Mama was not feeling well.

Dorothy was nineteen years old and had been looking forward to this first date with joyful anticipation. If any other young man in the church had asked her, she would have had to turn him down. Only Henry would get a "yes" from her.

The friendship grew for several months. Dorothy was happy—exuberantly happy! Why should she not be? Henry was a wonderful young man, a true Christian! Or Dorothy thought so for the first several months.

One Sunday evening changed the scene. It came as a shock. "Dorothy, let's not go to church this evening."

"Henry! You can't mean it," Dorothy exclaimed. "Don't say such a thing!"

Henry was grinning. "Sure I mean it. We've been regular church attendants. If we missed only one service, no one would miss us."

"Someone would," Dorothy contradicted.

"Who?" he wondered.

"God would," Dorothy reproved him. "Just why wouldn't you want to go tonight?"

"I'm tired. It would just be more pleasant to remain right here in your cozy living room with you alone."

Dorothy's mind whirled a moment. "What should I do?" The folks had already gone to church with the children. They would miss her, too, and wonder. "It would be pleasant to spend the whole evening here."

"We could study a chapter together and pray and have a profitable evening together, couldn't we?"

Dorothy did not answer.

"Don't you think that would be pleasing to the Lord?" he probed.

"Yes! any evening except Sunday. But for Sunday, God says, 'Not forsaking the assembling of ourselves together.' "

Henry laughed. "You are too serious minded."

Dorothy was hurt. "Too serious minded?"

"Henry!"

"Dorothy, don't look at me like that!"

"Come on, Henry, it's time to go."

"I mean it, Dorothy. Let's stay home. Will you . . . to please me?" He raised hopeful eyes.

"Why?" Dorothy asked again.

"Because I'd rather, just this once."

Dorothy hesitated, "Should I?" her thoughtful brow puckered. "If we could spend a profitable evening together in Bible study and prayer, what difference could it make? It would be cozy and comfortable here by the crackling fireplace."

"All right," she surprised him. "We will stay home this evening."

"Thanks, Dorothy."

Henry was plainly pleased with her, but Dorothy was troubled. "Have I done right to give in? Why would Henry want to miss church? He always seemed to enjoy going before. He is probably tired tonight and it won't likely happen again," she eased her conscience. The evening passed quickly. The proposed "chapter study" turned out to be a short part of their evening.

When Dorothy gave an account on Monday morning, her parents were very much displeased. "It won't happen often," she assured them.

"I hope it won't happen again!" her mother replied.

Dorothy was very sober all week. She worried about Henry's attitude more than she wanted to admit.

Following a pleasant Sunday afternoon walk two weeks later, Henry suggested, "Let's go for a ride." Dorothy glanced at the kitchen clock.

"We hardly have time. Till we get a bite to eat, it will be time to go to church."

"Are we going tonight?" he asked.

"Are we going? Of course we are!" she replied emphatically. "Of course we are going to church!"

"Let's go for a ride just this once," he begged.

"No," she answered, "not on Sunday evening."

"Why not?"

"Henry! You know why not. Because we should be in church."

"Dorothy, will you go for a ride with me this evening just to please me?" he waited for an answer.

"Should I?" she asked herself again. "I must have a good talk with Henry about his negligence, but this evening it's too late. It's almost church time." Dorothy started toasting cheese sandwiches.

"Will you?" he repeated. "Dorothy, it is such a pleasant evening, and we don't see each other except on Sundays. We need a little more time to talk some things over. Let's go for a ride."

"Maybe I should and then talk to him frankly about how I feel about missing church services."

"Yes," she answered at last. "We will go for a ride."

"Dorothy, you have given me a great pleasure." His happy voice was all the reward she could ask for her sacrifice.

The pleasant evening passed so quickly that Dorothy never got around to the subject she planned to discuss.

In spite of her parents' disapproval, Dorothy continued dating Henry and was seldom in church on Sunday evening. After a while he began coming Wednesday evenings, too, and prayer meeting was dropped, also. Her parents were alarmed and prayed and talked with Dorothy.

"I have done wrong," she admitted at last. "Yes, I will be willing to give Henry up. I see my friendship with him is coming between my Lord and me." Together they prayed while Dorothy confessed her waywardness and sought God's leading for her life. It was going to be hard, but with God's help she was willing to face the facts. She would write to Henry this evening. He would have her letter before Sunday. She would tell him they would not be seeing each other anymore in this way.

"Dear Henry," she began. "How shall I tell him? He won't accept it. He will want to talk to me. Oh, what shall I do? I am afraid if I talk to him, he will convince me. Lord," she prayed, "I will be true to Thee at any cost!

"Henry, our friendship must end. It is not drawing us closer to God, but further away from His perfect will for our lives.

"No, that does not sound right." Crushing the paper, she threw it into the wastebasket. Beginning again, Dorothy tried to carefully say each word right. She did not want to hurt Henry, but to let him know that she did not feel their continued friendship was God's will for them at this time.

"Dear Henry, I have enjoyed seeing you and spending our Sundays together, but . . ."

Dorothy stopped again, puckering her brow in deep thought. "But what?

"Father, help me," she prayed earnestly. "Direct my thoughts and pen."

Again the paper landed in the wastebasket. She began a third time: "Dear Henry, We have enjoyed spending our Sundays together. But I feel that we have not been giving God first place in our lives. We have been seeking only our own pleasure. I am going to ask you not to come and see me this Sunday. Let's pray about it and seek the Lord's will for our lives. We have been neglecting church attendance and spent very little of our time together enjoying spiritual things.

"I cannot feel that our friendship has been for our spiritual good, so it must end. Good-bye, Dorothy."

After signing the short letter, she read it over several times, sealed and stamped it, and sent it on its way.

What would Henry say? What would his reaction be to this? Henry never took "no" for an answer when he set his heart on anything. Dorothy spent much time in prayer and sweet fellowship with God in the next few days, often praying that Henry's heart would be changed, too, and that he would truly love and serve God.

Sunday came. Henry was not in the morning worship service.

"Surely he will not stop coming to church altogether. Henry would not do that! He must be sick," she decided.

That afternoon when the family all decided to drive over to Aunt Emma's, Dorothy said, "I believe I will stay home and rest today." She wanted to spend a quiet afternoon alone with the Lord.

A car drove in at three o'clock. Dorothy started. "This was just the time Henry always arrived." Perhaps that is why the whirr of the motor sounded quite familiar as the gravel crunched beneath the wheels on the driveway.

"Why would anyone come today?" Dorothy sighed. "I don't feel like entertaining company today." The banging of the car door and the footsteps were very familiar. Her pulse quickened as Dorothy jumped to her feet. She reached the window just in time to see Henry swing up onto the porch without coming around to the steps, just as he always did.

"He didn't get my letter! Oh, what shall I do?" When he knocked, Dorothy opened the door. Henry stepped inside, natural as ever. "No, he surely did not get my letter," she decided. "I will have to face him." She determined to do it bravely and with real conviction.

After a few brief sentences, Henry suggested, "Let's go for a ride, Dorothy."

"No," she answered firmly. "Did you get my letter?" Dorothy eyed him steadily. Perhaps after all he had and was just bluffing.

"Look, Dorothy, this is nonsense!" Henry shifted nervously. "You can't do this to me."

What could she say? Dorothy was floored. "Oh, I wish I had gone along to Aunt Emma's. If only I was not here alone." Dorothy thought frantically.

Henry was irritated. "Come on, Dorothy. The only fair thing for you to do is to come along this once and give me a chance to express myself. You are not being fair. Come on. Let's talk things over together."

"We can talk right here," she replied firmly. "I am not going for a ride today," she insisted.

"Dorothy, please, just this once more. I would like to talk to you alone. Soon your folks will be coming home and the children running in. You are not giving me a chance to express myself. You are not being fair."

"Henry, you know the children stay out of the front room when we are talking. If you have anything to say, you may say it. I have told you how I feel, and I still feel the same." Dorothy remained unmoved by his persistence.

Henry was also determined that he would not be so easily deferred from his purpose.

"Dorothy, your letter gave me something to think about," he began his new approach. "I have considered seriously your convictions and appreciate your stand very much. Would you please do me the favor to have a good talk with you this afternoon?" She just could not resist his earnest, pleading voice.

"Surely, there can be no harm in talking to him once more," she reasoned. "Perhaps things will be different." A spark of hope lit up her eyes. "Henry, I will be happy to talk things over with you today." Dorothy went to get her sweater. Coming back, she found Henry beaming on her, apparently well pleased.

Just as the two young people walked out across the porch, Papa and Mama returned.

"Oh, what will they think?" Dorothy worried, knowing how happy they had been with her decision. How they had thanked the Lord for Dorothy's renewed consecration and her willingness to give up her friendship with Henry when he proved unfaithful to God! "Will they understand?"

"Henry, I must talk to Mama a minute before we go," she said aloud. Quickly Dorothy walked over to the car. Henry waited patiently in the front yard.

"Mama, Henry got my letter and was really touched by it. He would like for me to talk things over with him just this once," Dorothy explained.

"Dorothy, you did that in your letter. His always 'just this once' is going to become once too often sometime if you keep on," Mama warned. "I wish you would not go."

"But, Mama, I think the Lord has spoken to him, too. I think he really wants to do better. It would not be fair to him if I didn't at least give him a chance to express himself. I am not going back on my decision, Mama. I mean to be true to God at any cost.

This does not mean we are dating again. I am only spending this one more afternoon with him. Then we will not be seeing each other anymore until we have both had time to pray about it and to prove ourselves. You wouldn't object to that would you?"

Mama's grieved expression showed plainly how she felt. Dorothy was convicted. She loved her parents and did not want to go against their advice—but there was Henry waiting. "Mama, please say that you would approve of it. Don't you understand how it is? I must talk to him only this once. I have not changed my mind at all about my decision."

"But you will change your mind about it if you spend the afternoon with Henry, I believe. I cannot approve of even one more visit at this time. Let him prove himself first."

"I have to be fair with him." Dorothy was frustrated. Why could Mama not see how it was? She was going to talk to Henry today, but, oh, how she wanted to do it with Mama's approval!

Without another word, Dorothy turned and hurried back to Henry. Their afternoon talk continued on through the evening. It was not that Dorothy wanted it this way. Oh, no, she was ashamed to face her parents Monday morning. Though nothing was said, she could feel their displeasure.

"Mama, I am sorry we missed church again last night," she began.

"I am sorry, too," was Mama's only reply.

"But we will not be doing it any more. I see Henry is not truly interested in living for the Lord. He is only interested in me. I told him not to come back." Dorothy's voice was truly penitent. "Mama, I am sorry I did not take your advice. It would have been better."

"Dorothy, I am glad you had the courage to stick to your decision and to tell him, though I feel, too, it would have been better not to have given in to him yesterday. He will very likely try other ways of winning you now if he is really determined, but don't give in," Mama advised. "If he does have a change of heart and proves himself faithful later on, there is plenty of time. Don't be hasty. A young man can put on a good front for a long time if he sees he is gaining his purpose."

Several weeks passed. Henry was in every service. He showed real interest in the prayer meeting. One night immediately after dismissal, Henry met her at the door. "Dorothy, may I take you home this evening?" he asked pleasantly.

Dorothy was so surprised and pleased that she almost said, "Yes," without thinking it over. It was hard to say, "No." Really, he had shown much evidence of a deeper spiritual life. Quickly Dorothy breathed a silent prayer for guidance.

"No, Henry," she replied hesitantly, "not tonight," and quickly walked out to the car.

"I noticed Henry talking to you last night," Mama mentioned on Thursday as she and Dorothy shelled beans together.

"Yes, he wanted to bring me home. Really, Mama, Henry has changed. I almost accepted."

"Dorothy, I would wait awhile longer and give him a chance to prove himself," Mama admonished the hopeful young girl. "He may only be trying to make an impression. We don't want to doubt the young man's sincerity. He may have really changed. I hope this is true. We will keep praying for Henry and just wait awhile."

"But, Mama, might he not become discouraged if he is really sincere and we act as if we doubt him?"

"No, Dorothy, I don't think it will work that way. If he is really sincere, he will appreciate your carefulness and patiently wait on the Lord."

Dorothy was quiet and sober all week. How she longed to spend a day with Henry again! Surely he had seen his spiritual need and had repented of his coldness. He seemed very different. "Why make him prove himself six months? Hadn't he faithfully proven himself a month already?" He could go on proving himself after they were dating, and she would help and encourage him.

Sunday came. "Dorothy," Henry shook her hand warmly in the entrance of the church, "I must see you today."

Dorothy was baffled. What could she say? He had simply stated that he must.

"I will see you at three o'clock." How excited he sounded! Before Dorothy could refuse, Henry went on. "Dorothy, let's talk things over again. Things are different now. I am living for the Lord from here on."

How could she refuse him now? It just would not be fair.

"May I come to your home?" he asked, convincing her that this was the right thing to do.

"Of course."

"Thank you, Dorothy." Henry turned and walked away.

Dorothy stood alone for some time. "Did I do right?" she wondered. "Mama will be displeased, but I will prove to her in time that I have not gone back on my decision to be true to God. Because I am seeing him this afternoon does not mean I will marry him, either. I just want to learn to know him better. I will talk to him this afternoon only to encourage him, and then we will wait a while." Dorothy was confident.

"No, Dorothy, I do not think this is wise," her mother counseled. "Just once will lead to more visits. You, too, must wait patiently till he has had time to prove himself. You know that you were not pleased with his conduct and attitude in many other areas besides his lack of interest in spiritual things. If he is really sincere, he will be true to God and wait for you.

"Sometime it will be once too often if you continue listening to Henry's 'just this once.' "

Dorothy could not see the necessity of such overcarefulness.

On Sunday afternoon Henry came. It would be easier to talk

things over as they drove than at home, so she accepted his invitation to go for a ride. Dorothy was pleased with his response to her convictions. She accepted his invitation for next Sunday also—then the next, and the next. It was the same. Soon the Sunday afternoon rides were longer and church services were often missed. In three months Henry and Dorothy were married.

Christ was not the head of their home, nor were His joy and peace found there. Dorothy often went to church alone or did not go at all. Her heart was broken. Her longings for a godly home were now far greater than her longings for Henry's friendship had been.

"Mama," Dorothy confessed with tears several years later, "I listened to Henry once too often!"

Publisher's note: It is very sad and unfortunate that Dorothy did not have a strong spiritual father to step into the picture to counsel her and to stand by her to see that she made her decision final. It was not fair to Dorothy to leave as large a part of the final decision up to her. They should not have allowed the car courtship. They should not have allowed her to continue dating Henry after his disloyalties to God and the church came into evidence. It would have been much easier for Dorothy to find the way if she had had this guidance and such restraints.

A Good Time to Ask

Ruth tiptoed lightly into Lucy's room. "Oh, at last she has fallen asleep." Ruth softly breathed a sigh. "Poor little Lucy, your breath still comes with great difficulty, even in your sleep," she worried.

Lucy had been sick for several days, but not as bad as she was this morning. "If only David were here!" Ruth thought. When he had left for work, Lucy was not up yet. They had not realized how sick she really was. Ruth knew that it would be nearly impossible to reach David by phone. He always left the office about 7:30 in the morning to go out on the job. Often there was no one at the office.

Lucy groaned and turned restlessly in her sleep. She whined weakly. Hot tears rushed to her mother's eyes. How could she bear to see her little daughter suffer like this all day? In the nine months since Lucy had come to brighten their home, she had always seemed to be a healthy child. But now she was very sick. Ruth noticed with pain how bright her eyes were as she stared almost unconsciously about the room. As she placed her hand gently on the hot little forehead, Lucy twitched and cried out.

"Oh, you poor little child; Mama didn't mean to frighten you." Ruth could not keep back the tears as Lucy continued to cry pitifully. How hot she felt! Ruth glanced anxiously at the clock. It was only ten-thirty. She felt she could not let Lucy suffer like this all day. There was no car at home. There was no

111

telephone. The concerned young mother could not go and leave the baby at home, nor could she take her out in the cold to the nearest neighbor.

Her thoughts turned to God, her only source of help. Oh, how sweet to be able to trust in God now!

Lucy quieted down again. Ruth stood watching her child. Her thoughts went back over the past few weeks. What a lot had taken place in those memorable weeks!

She began to think how different it would have been if this sickness would have come several weeks earlier. Ruth knew that at that time she would not have been able to look to her loving heavenly Father for help, nor could she have felt His presence near as she did this morning in her helplessness.

While the baby rested she mused, "What a difference Christ makes in our lives! How sweet to be able to trust in Him in time of trouble!"

David and Ruth, after spending the first several years of married life serving the devil, had recently given their lives to God. Confessing their sins and making restitution had not been an easy task. But what joy had been brought into their lives by taking this important step!

Ruth had received great peace and consolation from God's Word in the past few days. She knew her husband was also experiencing his new-found joy.

How different his conversation had been during the past few weeks, and what joy they had found in looking into the Bible together! Ruth found great consolation in the Scripture David read each morning before going to work. She could almost hear his deep, serious voice now. How different their days began now as compared to many days of the past years!

David also received great strength and consolation from the Word of God since he and Ruth had found the joy of regularly studying it together. This morning he had again left the house, feeling new purpose in life. "God has been so good to us, and has given us so many wonderful promises!" he exclaimed as he pondered the portion of Scripture they had enjoyed together this morning. How close he felt to God now!

David entered the office and received his instructions for the day. Soon he was on his way with a crew of men to Atkin's woods, where they would be cutting small timber for pulpwood.

All morning as he worked, David kept thinking of his little daughter. She had been asleep when he had left for work, but this was not unusual, because he had to leave early. David always especially enjoyed the mornings that Lucy awoke in time to give him a bright smile before he had to leave. Lucy had been a little fretful during the past night, so David had not been surprised that she slept late this morning. Try as he would to think only of her happy smiles and charming little ways, David's thoughts continually turned to other channels this morning. He worried and fretted and finally began to feel alarmed. "Was something wrong? Could Lucy be ill?" he began to wonder.

"Lucy has always been a healthy child," he tried to assure himself. But the uneasy feeling would not leave him. Lucy certainly had not been feeling quite well the last two or three days. But David could not understand the uneasy feeling that he had. She had not been seriously sick. Why should he worry so? Of course he would be very glad to have Lucy back to her normal self again.

Just then their morning text flashed through the mind of the worried father. "Ye have not, because ye ask not."

"Ye have not, because ye ask not." These words turned over and over in his mind. "Ye have not—" Then why not ask? No sooner had the idea presented itself to him than David, falling on his knees right there in Atkin's woods, asked for his desire. He prayed with full assurance that God would hear. "Why wait until later to ask?" he reasoned. "Now is as good a time as ever." Not knowing that his daughter was suffering great pain and a high fever at that very moment, David called in simple faith upon God for help. It was at exactly 11 o'clock that the concerned father felt his need and turned to the One he knew could give help.

"O Father," he prayed earnestly, "my little girl has been feeling ill and fretful. If it is Thy will, touch her little body with Thy healing power so she can again be her normal, cheerful self. And I thank Thee."

David arose from his knees and continued with his task of cutting timber, feeling a deep peace and calmness rather than anxiety and doubt. His day in the woods soon ended and David hurried home to his loved ones.

*   *   *   *   *   *   *   *   *   *   *   *

Ruth had been standing for some time, silently watching Lucy's pitiful movements, her short gasps for breath, and her delirious crying out.

The mother's heart was deeply touched. She felt she could not bear it any longer. Ever since ten-thirty, the baby seemed to rest only a few minutes, then would cry out again, thrashing about feverishly.

Suddenly she quieted and remained quiet longer than usual. She looked very pale and still. Ruth became alarmed. She touched Lucy's hand. It did not feel hot. She touched her head very gently. It, too, felt cool and this time Lucy neither cried out nor stirred. With relief Ruth bent nearer and caught the sound of Lucy's steady, even breathing. The young mother stood in wonder, watching the change that had come over her child. She could now leave Lucy's room. No noise or movement seemed to disturb Lucy now.

Ruth thanked God. Lucy surely was resting better.

At twelve o'clock Lucy rolled over. She smiled and cooed when she saw her mother. Reaching for the crib railing, she pulled herself up and began to bounce on the springy mattress. Giving little squeals of joy, she reached for her mother, who clasped her tightly in her arms, hardly able to believe her eyes.

All afternoon Lucy played and ate naturally. At the first sound of the garage door, she sat up and listened till it banged shut. Jumping up and down in her stroller, Lucy reached out two chubby little arms to her father as he entered the kitchen door.

Fondly taking the baby in his arms, David walked over to the stove where Ruth was preparing the evening meal.

"Has she been so cheerful all day?" he asked.

"O David!" Ruth exclaimed, "I can hardly wait to tell you about her."

As she went on to tell how very sick the baby had been and of the sudden change at eleven o'clock, David could not help interrupting her story to tell his own.

As David and Ruth wept for joy because of God's mercy and goodness to them, little Lucy played gleefully with her rubber doll. She seemed to be without the slightest sign of any recent illness.

The Atheist's Orange

The winds blew softly over the large ocean liner. Sister Miller walked slowly out onto the deck with her husband. Two more days of rocking and rolling over these ocean waves—oh, how good the shore would look! For days she had longed for the journey's end. The first several days had been the worst. Sister Miller had often been carsick, but that usually lasted only a few hours till the trip would end. Now, having been seasick for days, she was growing very weary of the journey.

This morning, since the weather was nicer and the water fairly calm, she decided to sit out on the deck awhile. The Millers had been seated only a few minutes when a tall, lanky young man walked toward them from the other end of the ship.

"Here comes John Owens, the young atheist I was telling you about," Brother Miller whispered to his wife. "He has talked to me every day for the past two weeks. I surely wish there would be something we could do to convince him of the foolishness of his way."

"Do you think he really believes that there is not a God?" Sister Miller asked.

"Good morning, friends," the youth greeted them warmly. He looked like a friendly chap.

"Good morning," Sister Miller smiled.

"Sit down with us awhile," Brother Miller offered, pushing a chair toward the young man. "Meet my wife."

116

The young man nodded. "Are you feeling better today?" he inquired. "Your husband tells me you are not very fond of traveling by boat."

"Yes," Sister Miller said with a smile, "I am feeling better this morning. I have not enjoyed the trip much though because of being seasick most of the time."

Mr. Owens and Brother Miller went on visiting for some time just like old friends. Sister Miller bowed her head in silent prayer. "Lord," she prayed earnestly, "help us somehow to be able to help this young man to know that Thou art God." Soon she began to feel seasick again. "If only I had an orange!" she thought wistfully. "I believe that would be something I could keep down and feel good on." As the wind blew harder and the waves rolled higher, she felt worse and worse. With her eyes closed, Sister Miller rested her head on the high back of her chair. She continued in prayer and fellowship with her Lord. "O Father," she prayed, "help me to feel better today. Father, I pray, somehow provide me an orange." A faint smile played across her face. "Why did I ask that?" she mused. "I will likely have to wait till we reach the shore for the answer to that prayer."

Mr. Owens kept casting amused glances in her direction.

"She is getting a good nap," Brother Miller said as he smiled.

"Yes," grinned Mr. Owens, mischievously reaching into the pocket of his jacket. Pulling out a nice big orange, he laid it gently in the lap of the sleeping woman. Withdrawing his hand he remarked, "Won't that surprise her?"

"Sure will," Brother Miller answered, "and she especially likes oranges, too. She often feels better on oranges when she has trouble with getting carsick. I've been wishing I could get some for her since we are traveling."

Just then the rocking of the ship rolled the cool orange against her hand. Sister Miller awoke with a start. A surprised

117

look crossed her face. She reached for the orange and held it up.

"God answered my prayer even sooner than I expected," she stated calmly, beginning to peel the juicy orange. "Just before I went to sleep I asked the Lord to send me an orange," she explained.

Tasting the sweet juicy slices, she pulled off several others, offering them to the men. "This is a very good orange," she said. "Will you enjoy it with me? I do believe I am feeling better already. I always feel good on oranges."

"No, thank you," Mr. Owens refused politely. "You eat it, Mrs. Miller." Till this time he had not uttered a word but wore the strangest look of surprise on his face.

"Where did the orange come from?" Sister Miller asked. When no one answered, she continued quickly, "Well, I know it came from the Lord. I asked Him for it and He sent it, but I was wondering by what means it got here on my lap."

"Mrs. Miller," the young man began in a subdued voice, "tell me, now, did you ask the Lord to send you an orange?"

"Indeed, I did," she replied simply. Looking into her honest blue eyes, he could not doubt her words.

Mr. Ownes shook his head and looked puzzled. "God answered your prayer!" he exclaimed. "God answered your prayer! I don't know why I laid that orange on your lap. I had no intention to. I was going to eat it myself. I can't understand—GOD—God! Yes, there is a God. No one could have that kind of faith without something behind it!" He sat quietly for a while, very thoughtful. The Millers united their hearts in silent prayer.

"I am convinced," he said at last. "There is a God! There is no such thing as not believing in God with people like you around. Will you tell me more about your wonderful God?"

With their hearts overjoyed, the Millers spent the remainder of the morning talking to the young man about the things dearest to their hearts.

Several days later when the ocean liner docked, John Owens stepped off onto the shore a free man—a child of God! He was eager to tell his loved ones at home the wonderful news.

"Bless Them That Curse You"

The sun was sinking low one autumn evening in 1675. Mahtako, son of Nauhaugus, chief of the Mashpee Indians, enjoyed the cool twilight on the woodland path leading toward the lake. Rounding a curve in the winding trail, he saw ahead a white man walking in the same direction. Immediately the young Indian recognized Simon Wenders, whose ill-kept clearing lay near the Mashpee village.

Mahtako quickly observed that Wenders walked with a decided limp, and that upon his shoulder he carried a small keg.

Mahtako attempted to slip unnoticed from the path, intending to circle the slow-moving white man. This motion was not made with hostile intent, for Mahtako, like most Mashpees, was a "praying Indian." The Mashpees had no dealings with the Wampanoags and other fierce tribes who at that time terrorized many small communities.

But Simon Wenders, like many white men, gave neither the peaceful nor the fighting tribes any reason to love him. Therefore, Mahtako took every opportunity to avoid this man and all other whites in his honest effort to keep out of trouble. Greatly had their innocent tribes suffered at the hands of cruel and heartless white men who were not only driving the Indians from their homes, but were unmercifully slaughtering many innocent and peace-loving people.

Wenders, turning at the moment of the Indian's quick

movement toward the woods, saw Mahtako and called him.

After a moment's hesitation, Mahtako unwillingly advanced.

"Ho, Brother Mahtako! It is well we have met. This silver shilling will be yours for rendering me a small favor."

Mahtako stood motionless, suspicion rising in his mind. Even in times of peace Wenders was not known to call an Indian a "brother," nor did he generally offer a shilling for such favors as he might wheedle or browbeat from a Mashpee.

"As you see," he continued, "I've sprained my ankle. And here is this keg of powder that I promised to deliver to the traders in the village beyond your tribe. It's getting late, and even at best I could scarcely reach the village before dark, much less so with this sprained ankle. Would you take the keg, Mahtako, and keep it with you in your tent tonight? Tomorrow—no need for haste—deliver it to the traders. Here, you have earned your silver shilling! I dare say it's easy earned."

Mahtako hesitated. Truly it was a good wage. But again suspicion arose, warning the cautious Indian to beware.

"The white men forbid the Mashpees to have powder in their wigwams," he said hesitantly. For in that time of little trust between the races, the English had taken unfair advantage of the Indians, making laws to prevent munitions of war from falling into the hands of even the neutral and friendly tribes, who were regarded with mistrust, as well as other tribes worthy of being feared.

"Oh, yes," nodded Wenders. "And a foolish law it is, for all men know the Mashpees to be true friends of the English. And it's only overnight. No one will ever know. And silver shillings are not often so easy to get."

Still Mahtako hesitated, fearful of the outcome. It was true that he did not feel bound by the unfair laws made by Englishmen, laws which he had no hand in making, and which, like all his tribe, he regarded as an injustice. But Wenders had misused him more than once, and the memory rankled.

Then in the mind of the praying Indian flashed the words of the aged apostle to the Indians, Richard Bourne.

Bourne, like the more-famous Eliot, had given his life to the ministry of the Gospel to the red men. Not only Bourne's words, but his saintly life had endeared him to the Mashpees. His doctrine, though strange to their ears, was received because of his own living testimony.

"Trying times be upon us," had said Richard Bourne. "White men have sinned against red, and red men against white, until now the battle rages. While the bloody heathen ravage there shall be little kindness, little but suspicion and perhaps misuse for many of your color in New England. You must bear yourselves meekly, as followers of Him who suffered for us all, remembering that your reward is not here, but hereafter. Show yourselves in all manner friends to the English, that none may have reason to suspect or complain of you in these perilous times. Bless them that persecute you; if ye be smitten on one cheek, turn the other also."

There had been murmurings among the Mashpees at this counsel, so foreign to every tradition and natural bent of the human nature. But Nauhaugus and his elders had counseled obedience.

No one denied the fact that the white men had cruelly overrun the Indians, denying them their rights, murdering their loved ones, stealing their children, and burning their homes. And all this was for no fault of the Indians. The white men simply wanted their land. The Indian's only crime was their persistence in claiming their rightful possessions.

What person would not finally take revenge and turn in full fury on his oppressor? This the Indians did, as all unregenerate human nature would do; that is, all but the Mashpee tribe, who had heard the sweet story of salvation, and who with one accord had received the Savior. Only their love for their Savior and obedience to God could keep them from joining the warfare.

Impatiently Wenders waited while Mahtako pondered the situation. Mahtako's thoughts were in a turmoil. Why should he do the white man a favor; much less, such a risky fellow? Yet, Christ's love goes the second mile.

"Mahtako will take the powder," said the young Indian at length. "But keep your shilling."

In a moment the young Indian had disappeared down the trail with the keg, leaving Wenders staring after him and then at the silver shilling in his hand, surprised at the sudden turn of events. Why had Mahtako so suddenly accepted the task, and that without pay? A little suspicion began to grow in the mind of the white man.

"Have I indeed played the fool?" he exploded. "But, no, even if the Mashpees are plotting, it's little they can do this night, and after that . . ." Hurriedly the surprised man sped down the path, showing little evidence of an ankle injury.

Mahtako, having a large number of fish traps set out, did not immediately turn home. "I will tend the traps," he said, "since there is no hurry to deliver the powder before morning. Then I will not need to come back out here tonight. Tomorrow morning I will deliver the powder. Maybe someday, if we prove ourselves friendly, things can be different for the red men," the praying Indian thought.

Late that night, with a string of fish in one hand and the keg in the other, he turned at last toward the Mashpee village, feeling a tingle of satisfaction because of the good deed he had done for an enemy.

After walking for some time through the dark shadows, Mahtako stopped suddenly.

The faint glow of a distant fire glimmered in the path ahead. No clearing or village lay there. Possibly a careless hunter had left a spark in the dry leaves. Every Indian knows the danger of forest fires. A small camp blaze could spread disastrously throughout this dry underbrush in minutes. Mahtako hurried toward the light.

Nearing the light, Mahtako hesitated. It was obvious that the glow came from a well-cared-for camp fire. Moving closer with caution, the faint sound of voices reached his ears—voices of white men. The Indian paused; then, full of curiosity, he crept nearer. What could they possibly be doing this time of night, in this dark place?

The voices came from a hollow, partly protected by large rocks. Knowing this forest well, the young Indian crept forward in the shadow of a large boulder. The voices grew louder. Angry sounds were heard. Mahtako stood breathless.

" 'Twill be the end of the red varlets in these parts," came the voice of the speaker. "And 'twill go hard if we don't get for ourselves the most of the Mashpee village land and their possessions," laughed the speaker harshly.

Then, with caution redoubled, Mahtako crept forward. "What now could have brought this on?" With a heavy heart and great concern for his loved ones, the praying Indian listened.

Straining his eyes through the darkness, the figures of half a dozen men could be seen, sitting round the camp fire.

Whiskey in abundance lay before them, to which these idlers helped themselves freely. Neither white men nor red had reason to love or respect them. All were armed. At this point, the effects of the whiskey had killed all sense of reason and caution. Their voices now raised beyond the point of prudence.

Mahtako trembled.

" 'Tis a cunning plan," the second speaker agreed. "Before morning dawns, Wenders and two other trusty men will set fire to Woods' barn, and leave there a coat that all the settlement knows to be an Indian garment. About the same time the rest of

124

us will begin firing shots into the building of Mattons. He, as well as the Woods, already fears and distrusts the Mashpees."

"What can all this mean?" Mahtako settled himself lower behind the boulder. "Whites destroying the property of other whites." Many misgivings and suspicions gripped the young Indian. "Surely these men have no fear of God before their eyes."

The thought of God filled his troubled heart with great calmness. Wenders was speaking again.

"After the shots are fired and the barn ablaze, we ourselves will run from the woodland as rescuers, with a toll of Mashpees in full retreat.

"Already beneath the door of the village sheriff lies a note, warning that in the dwellings of Chief Nauhaugus is a goodly store of powder!"

Another laughed loudly, pouring himself another drink from the jug before him. "And a goodly store of powder they shall find, thanks to Wenders," he finished boastingly.

"Yes, it's a clever plan," applauded another. "And after the pretended rescue, when the whole village, as hornets, rush excitedly from their homes, we'll lead them straight to the wigwam of Nauhaugus. There, after securing the powder, fate will be against the scoundrels. They'll be proven lawbreakers. After the battle, which will be sure to follow, we'll be the first to the field to claim the spoil."

"Will there indeed be a battle?" fearfully inquired a younger man.

Wenders again laughed, and with an oath declared, "With the men of the village in such a temper, and the Mashpees being Indians, though more sissy than most, there will indeed be a battle. But never fear," he added confidently, "with little but fish spears with which to fight, they can do but little more than give excuse for their own slaying. And as for the truth which may well be told after the battle, it's very little weight the word of any

Indian will hold."

Mahtako had heard enough. This fiendish plot he could well understand and, sure, it would work—just as the white man planned it. What could an Indian do? Where could an Indian plead? An Indian who loved his fellowmen—wished them no harm—tried to show them kind favors. Yet, what was his reward? These men, cruel and heartless, savage murderers of those who did them no harm, had all the advantage of the helpless Indians. How could such injustice be tolerated?

All through the settlement was distrust of all Indians, and Woods and Mattons, honest men both, had made no secret of their suspicion of the Mashpees—a thing which would render the pretended attack upon them the more credible. And the onslaught upon his own people, upon Mahtako's own father who ever befriended the whites, weapons or no weapons, sissy were the Mashpees! The wild blood seemed to boil in the brain of Mahtako! Weapons! These white men had put into his very hands the means of a just revenge! The fire below, themselves all crowded about it in the cool of the evening. A twist of the plug from the powder keg, a toss of the keg into the flames! He himself would be protected by the boulder. But the plotting white men should die a death more terrible than that which they had planned for the peaceful, praying Indians!

Slowly the keg rose above the head of Mahtako. But something seemed to stay his hand. It was the gentle face of Richard Bourne and the words of Richard Bourne, so often seen and heard in the rude pulpit of the little chapel he had built for the Indians with his own hands.

"Render not evil for evil. Bless them that curse you. Do good to them that despitefully use you."

Like the dark of the evening about him, long ages of barbarism lay behind Mahtako. But somehow through the words, and more through the life of the aged follower of a greater

Master, had come to the Indian boy a vision of a way of life better than the ancient law of revenge. Silently as he had come, Mahtako slipped away from the boulder. Not dreaming that a moment ago the death shadow had hovered above them, the white men plotted on.

Long past midnight, a frenzied knocking brought Richard Bourne quickly to the door. "Come," invited the aged pastor. "The latch-string is always out."

In a moment the faint glow of candlelight flickered across the ashen face of the Indian boy.

Richard Bourne looked kindly into the troubled eyes of the breathless boy, half spent with haste, then to the keg on his shoulder.

Mahtako gasped out his story, bit by bit, until the aged minister caught the intention of the wicked plot.

"Come," said the pastor. "Sit here and calm yourself."

"Do you believe me, Mr. Bourne?" Mahtako asked anxiously. "Here, see the keg! And I slew them not!"

Richard Bourne sighed deeply. "Yes, my son, I cannot help believing you," he assured the anxious youth. "Truly, I know the wickedness of these men of my race. Too much I have heard of their evil deeds," the aged minister grieved. "The day will come that God will scourge New England because we harbor such men as these."

"Almost I regret that I spared the lives of those murderers," Mahtako said fiercely. "Except for your words, Mr. Bourne, and for the love of my Savior, those men were all dead men now."

The aged minister sadly shook his head. "It is well for you and for your people that you held your hand, my boy. God grant thee grace never to take revenge. Their dead bodies would surely have witnessed against your race as an unprovoked attack. Then open warfare would most certainly have followed and the fault would lay with you."

127

Mahtako gasped. He had not thought of that.

"Can you save my people?" he demanded.

"Yes," said Richard Bourne. "Long before dawn trustworthy men will be stationed around the clearings of these men where the pretended attacks will take place.

"These men will be happy to witness against those false varlets you overheard and prevent the mischief they plan.

"Thank God for this testimony of yours, Mahtako, and I trust many other Mashpees will bear themselves as worthily as you! May God grant your tribe to live in peace and possess your lands in safety long after these villains are but a memory."

*   *   *   *   *   *   *   *   *   *   *   *

The work of Richard Bourne and his family among the Indians of Cape Cod is a matter of history. The Bournes are credited with holding their converts out of the hostile confederacy at a time when their aid might have been most disastrous to the struggling white settlements.

Also, the Mashpees still dwell on the Cape, while the more warlike tribes have long been "but a memory."

The Deacon's Leather Strap

For twelve years Paul Sanson had been deacon in the Locust Hollow Church. This small congregation of nearly fifty members loved the deacon and appreciated his conscientious efforts to fill his responsibilities faithfully. The congregation knew him to be a gentle, sympathetic man. He was firm, standing for the standards of the church; but his dealings were always in love.

Never did anyone guess that Brother Sanson had carried the leather strap with him constantly for twenty years! that is, never until one night during a series of revival meetings! Brother Sanson himself exposed the leather strap.

The sermon had been preached by Brother Kemp. God's Spirit was present, searching honest hearts. Many in the audience felt His convicting power as the Word was preached that night.

"We will sing one stanza of song." Brother Kemp nodded to the song leader.

Paul Sanson sat on the front bench. Without arising or announcing the number, he began singing prayerfully, "Softly and tenderly Jesus is calling."

The evangelist scanned the audience with a searching gaze.

Just as the last words of the first stanza were sung, the leather strap flashed across the deacon's mind. That leather strap he had carried for twenty years! Sometimes for a period of years it had not entered his mind. But now there it was again. What

129

would he do with it now—a deacon, sitting on the front bench leading the singing, pleading for submission from the people he served! How could he stand up and expose the leather strap now?

His conscience smote him so that he was unable to sing. Brother Sanson bowed his head. The congregation went on singing the refrain.

Brother Kemp stretched forth his arms in earnest entreaty, again pleading for surrender. "Why not confess your sin? Have peace with God. Christ offers you all this tonight if you will receive it—peace, joy, and power to overcome sin. Let's sing one more stanza." Brother Kemp bowed his head in silent prayer.

Brother Sanson, looking back at the song book, read the words, "Why should we tarry when Jesus is pleading . . . ?"

"Why should we?" he asked himself. The whole incident of the leather strap flashed through his mind in a moment of time.

Paul Sanson, a boy of twelve years, walking out of the barn just after the chores were finished, saw the leather strap lying there in the dirt. "That is just what I need to hold Rover," he had decided. Paul picked up the brown leather strap. "Yes, this is just what I need. It will hold him. No one will ever use this." Quickly he looked around; James was not anywhere in sight. "Oh, well, I'll just take it. It's surely something they threw away. It won't matter." With the leather strap in his hip pocket, Paul mounted his bike and hurried home. He had only been working for James for several weeks. He had been easy to get along with but was not the kind of man easy to talk to.

The long pause drew Brother Kemp's attention. Raising his head, he nodded to Brother Sanson. "Why hadn't he begun singing the next stanza of invitation?"

"Why should we tarry when Jesus is pleading?" Instead of singing, Brother Sanson arose to his feet. Facing the audience, he began. "First I want to confess that there is something hindering my peace with God. About twenty years ago I stole a leather

130

strap from the farmer I was working for. The Lord spoke to my heart about this sin; but I put it in the back of my mind, thinking it was too small a thing to matter. I want to make this right with James as soon as possible."

Brother Sanson took his seat and began the second stanza, "Why should we tarry when Jesus is pleading?" He sang with conviction. "Why should we linger and heed not His mercies, Mercies for you and for me?"

There was a deep peace and joy in his heart. There was nothing between him and his Savior. Now he could pray for those for whom his heart was burdened, with assurance that God would hear. The leather strap no longer hindered his life and prayers.

Blessings in the
Turnip Patch

"I'll never plant another turnip!" Elmer stated emphatically. He dropped wearily into the chair his wife offered him at the head of the table.

Lois smiled lovingly. "I hope you won't need to." She glanced apologetically at the meal before them. Bread and butter, and potatoes cooked with turnips. She had almost left the turnips out this time. But the potatoes would not last much longer. A few turnips added would stretch them a little further.

Following her glance at the steaming turnips, Elmer quickly added, "I like the turnips, Lois. It's just such hard work. I've been pulling and bunching turnips for more than three weeks now, and there are still thousands of them to pull. Every time I see those turnip fields the muscles in my back begin to ache."

"Yes, I know it is hard work." Lois remembered how she and Elmer had worked together in the turnip field last year. This year she could not help much because of the new baby. "I do wish you could find work or have a good market for something else that would be easier to harvest than turnips."

"I'll do something else next year. I'll never plant another turnip!" Elmer repeated his statement with emphasis on the "never."

That winter Elmer found a few small jobs to provide for his family. He had almost forgotten the turnips when spring came. Though work was still very hard to find, Elmer was fortunate enough to find a good job early in the spring, which he kept for several years. Of course, there were no turnip fields planted that spring, nor the following ones.

Elmer's wages were raised several times. He enjoyed his work. They were getting along well financially now. Then a call came to give up all and move to another small community to serve the Lord there.

Elmer and Lois considered this call seriously before committing themselves. There were now four small children to provide for.

"Yes, Elmer," Lois agreed, "I believe the Lord has called us and we should go. God has blessed us and has always provided for us. It may be hard, but I am willing."

Elmer was grateful for her willingness to leave behind the cozy home and friends to move into a new community, a smaller house, and poor prospects of a good livelihood.

The move was made. Elmer was again out of work. The fifth child came. Something would have to be done. Elmer and Lois had worked together, carefully planning a budget to keep out of debt. But there was a limit to how far a bag of potatoes could be stretched with seven around the table.

This problem, as was their practice, was laid out before the Lord.

"Father, we thank Thee that Thou hast always provided for our needs. We want to know Thy will and trust Thy care for us in all these things. We feel very much the need of a job and have not been able to find anything. Wilt Thou just lead us very definitely to the work Thou wouldst have us to do and we will thank Thee for it. We will gladly do anything—anything Thou wilt provide for us. Amen."

After praying about this need Elmer felt confident that God would open something for them that would enable him to provide for his family.

"Well, when are you going out to look for work again?" Lois asked, smiling. "Where will you look now?"

"I feel so confident that the Lord is going to provide something that I wonder whether I'll even need to go look for it," Elmer answered with new hope in his tone. "I really would hardly know where to look around here. I've been . . ."

Just then there was a knock on the front door, interrupting the conversation. Lois remained in the kitchen. She heard an unfamiliar voice.

"Mr. Good," he began, "I'm Mr. Jones from the Southeastern Produce Farms just across town. We need help badly and are scanning this neighborhood for workers. Would you be able to take a job a few weeks or longer?"

"Yes, I certainly would!" Elmer's answer came without a moment's hesitation. Why should he even take time to think it over? Had he not trusted God and expected just such an answer?

Lois was thrilled. "Surely God is pleased to hear when we just remember to come to Him with our needs."

The front door closed. Elmer went straight to the kitchen. "Lois," he called excitedly, "God surely had that answer on the way while we were yet speaking."

"When do you start?"

"Right away. Just as soon as I can drive over there. It's only six or eight miles. Why hadn't I thought of inquiring there before?"

With a heart full of praise, Elmer left the house with his lunch pail about a half hour later.

Nine o'clock that morning found Elmer Good bending over rows and rows of turnips. Stacks and stacks of bunches were already in the shed. Thousands more would be added before the season was over.

The praise on his lips was truly coming from a grateful heart as Elmer sank wearily into the chair at the head of the table that night.

"You look tired," Lois remarked lovingly, setting the food on the table. "Tell us about the new job."

"I'm pulling and bunching turnips," Elmer replied with a grin, "As soon as we can get caught up a little over on the farm, they want to start planting the late turnips."

"Turnips!" Lois gasped.

"Yes, turnips." Elmer's eyes sparkled when he remembered how he had been thanking the Lord all morning for answering his prayer. Never once had it occurred to him that this was the one job he did not want.

"It doesn't really matter what the job is, Lois. It's the job God gave me."

"But will your back stand it?" There was concern in his wife's voice.

"As long as it will, I'll do it. If it won't, then I believe God will provide something else. Let's thank Him now. Come, children," Elmer called as the bowl of steaming potato soup was placed on the table.

"There are lots of ways to make the potatoes reach further," Lois said with a twinkle in her eyes.

"Yes," her husband replied. "Tomorrow I'll bring home some turnips. Remember?"

"Father, we are grateful tonight for the good food Thou hast so graciously provided for us. We thank Thee for supplying all our needs and for the blessings we have enjoyed today. Amen."

Ten Years to Make a Deal

The little red hand on the temperature gauge kept swinging nearer to the hot side. Melody wondered what could be wrong.

"I'm going to have to trade this car off for a new one," she decided. "I cannot put up with an old undependable car when I have twelve miles to drive to work. Car trouble is not for girls."

Melody had a good paying job, a nice sum laid up in the bank, and hopes for a raise in the fall. Car payments should be no problem for her. How nice it would be to own a new car!

As she neared the station just outside of Centerville, Melody noticed the gauge warning of danger. "I had better have this checked," she decided, "before I go on home."

First the radiator was checked. "Plenty of water," the attendant called, reaching for the oil stick. "Say, young lady, did you know you have trouble ahead?"

"No, what now?" Melody wondered.

Holding the oil stick up near the window, he asked, "See those bubbles? That means there is water getting into the oil somehow. I don't know just where it is coming from, but I know water drops on the oil spell trouble."

Melody sighed, "Well, what shall I do? Is it safe to drive it home? Is it something you can fix for me?"

"Yes." The attendant scratched his head with a greasy hand. "But I could not fix it tonight. It may take a long time to find the trouble. This is an old car." He looked up. "Are you sure you want it fixed?''

"I have been thinking about trading it for a new one," she admitted. "But I am not sure I am ready yet."

"Well, young lady, I will advise you that this would be a good time. You let this get any worse and you won't get a thing for this old car. If you trade it now, you might get a good deal. This car looks good, better than it really is. But I have been doing your mechanic work long enough to know it is not worth what it would likely cost you to get it fixed."

Melody turned the switch thoughtfully. The old car sputtered several times, then started. It was only three miles to home. "I'll see," she said. "Maybe Uncle Joe will have something to suggest."

"You had better take my advice. I know what I am talking about. Kent's Auto Sales has some good deals on now." The attendant waved as Melody pulled onto the highway again.

"Tomorrow is my day off. Perhaps I should go in and see Mr. Kent. It might pay better than trying to keep this old thing running." Melody drove slowly on. "If I were home, Father and the boys would know just what to do. Maybe Uncle Joe could take off awhile in the morning to help me find another car." Melody did not trust her judgment in buying a used car, and three hundred and fifty miles from home was too far to get help there. "Uncle Joe is a good mechanic, too, and he will help me." Melody pulled into the driveway, glad to be off the highway.

On Saturday morning Uncle Joe was glad to accompany her to Kent's to advise her in the deal. "Yes," he had agreed, "you had better get another car and get at least a little something out of this one while you can."

At Kent's, Melody scanned the lot for a nice-looking car. The blue Ford looked good. Uncle Joe thought the green Chevy had a better sounding engine. The salesman walked from one car to another, pointing out all the special features and good points of each one. Never once did he suggest that there might be anything wrong with one of them.

"What can I get out of my car?" Melody wondered.

"What is wrong with it?" the salesman surprised Melody by asking.

"Well," she stammered. Melody had not expected this direct question.

"It is just an old car," Uncle Joe helped her out. "A girl, driving alone, needs a newer, more dependable car."

"You don't know of anything in particular wrong with it?" He directed this question to Melody.

Uncle Joe had told her before coming in to Kent's, "Now don't go in there and tell them all that is wrong with your car. They are not going to tell you what is wrong with theirs."

"Really, I don't know," Melody thought.

"No," she said aloud. "It is just that I want a new car."

"All right, I can give you two hundred and fifty in a trade on the green Chevy. That would leave nine hundred and fifty for you to pay."

The deal was soon transacted. Uncle Joe drove the green Chevy home.

"I believe you have a good car here, Melody," he said after driving awhile. "And you were lucky to get two-fifty for that old Plymouth. Some guy is going to have a lot of trouble soon with that water getting in the oil, but it's not our trouble."

With a twinge of conscience, Melody nodded, "Yes, it is someone else's trouble." Her mind was not at ease. Was that fair and honest?

"This motor sounds good," Uncle Joe went on, "and the body is sound—no rattles. I noticed the tires are in good condition, too—two brand new ones on the front and the spare is in good shape."

Melody was pleased with the new car, but the deal bothered

her. Had she been honest?

The green Chevy gave her good service for years. It proved to be all that Uncle Joe thought it was.

Melody continued her downward course—a little dishonesty here, carelessness there, with fewer twinges of conscience.

Nine years later found the same Melody able to do or say almost anything without considering whether it was right or wrong.

But one day a dear friend prayed and the Lord worked and Melody became very miserable. This dear friend continued to intercede faithfully until at last Melody could no longer resist such love and yielded her life to God in sincere penitence. Confession and restitution were made. Once more Melody found true joy and peace. There was nothing now to hinder sweet fellowship with God.

Another year passed. With peace in her soul, Melody attended the Friday evening meeting in preparation for the Communion service on Sunday.

"How wonderful it is to be at rest and peace with God!" Melody appreciated her salvation more each day. Brother Mark brought a real heart-searching message from the Word. The Spirit spoke to hearts that night as Brother Mark spoke. "It is so important that we humble ourselves and confess our faults," he said. "There is just no other way to find peace with God."

"Lord," Melody prayed, "show me if there is anything in my life that is not pleasing to Thee. I will do whatever You ask me to."

With true gratitude in her heart to God, Melody recalled the time her sins were all taken away by the blood of Jesus. Again she thanked the Lord for His grace and pardon.

The green Chevy, which had been traded for another car five years ago, suddenly came to her mind. The deal she made at Kent's that Saturday morning ten years ago came vividly to mind. Melody tried to push it from her mind and meditate on the good message.

"When the Lord asks you to confess a sin He means just that, and He does not forget it, and time does not erase it. It must be confessed. He will be faithful to bring these things to your mind if you are willing to humble yourself and repent. Then He can bless your life for His glory."

"That deal at Kent's—was I honest?" Melody's hand went to her forehead. She wiped the perspiration. "Could this uneasiness be God speaking to me about that? Surely not—I have had peace with God for a year. After all, it was Uncle Joe who made the deal. Anyway, I really was not dishonest. I didn't know for sure—I wasn't dishonest!"

"Were you honest?"

Melody did not know. Brother Mark went on. His voice showed deep concern and earnestness.

"Why didn't you tell the other fellow that the water pump wasn't working on that old car when you sold it?" he asked.

"What? Is he talking to me?" Melody looked up startled. Brother Mark went on, "And when you were taking that new job, why did you try to leave that false impression?" Melody heard no more for a few minutes.

"Lord, I will. I will confess my sin. Father, forgive me and give me grace. O Father, give me wisdom in making this right. May my life never bring reproach on Thy holy Name. Amen."

Melody raised her bowed head, trying to keep her thoughts on the message.

"Ten years," she thought, "ten years to make a deal. But I am going through with it now!"

With that settled, Melody again turned her thoughts to the Word being preached. She thoroughly enjoyed the remainder of the meeting with the peace of God in her heart.

The Power of Prayer

Sara awoke with a start. She rolled over, rubbing her eyes. "Dan will not return until late tomorrow evening," she recalled sleepily. Sara had been left alone only on very few occasions. When it was necessary for Dan to make hurried business trips, she had often accompanied him in the first few years of their marriage. Since Becky had come three years ago, it was necessary for her to remain at home more often.

Drifting back off to sleep, Sara was suddenly awakened again. She felt vaguely uneasy. Had she heard something? She could not be sure. Sara had a feeling there was someone in the house. She was wide awake now. Never before had the young mother been afraid of being alone with her little daughter. But now the night seemed dreadful and endless. Sara started to sit up then dropped back quickly. Yes! She had heard something! She hardly dared to breathe. Every movement or noise seemed a threat of impending danger. The footsteps which she heard crossing the creaking boards of the kitchen floor halted the instant her bed began to squeak. Now everything was still again, too still. This deathly silence struck fear to her heart even more than the noise had. Where was the intruder? What was he doing?

"Oh, what should I do?" Sara felt like screaming, but no one could possibly hear except the intruder. There was no telephone in the house. Sara tried to collect her thoughts and decide what must be done. By the dim light of the moon, Sara could see through her open door into Becky's room across the hall.

"Lord, help us," she breathed. "Should I go to Becky?" Just then the footsteps moved farther across the front rooms. The hall door opened. The suction from the open front windows drew Becky's door shut with a bang.

Sara's trembling hand flew to her mouth to muffle a frightened outcry. Every muscle tensed painfully. All was quiet again, frighteningly quiet.

"Dear Father," Sara prayed silently, "give me wisdom, and protect us. Help me to trust in Thee."

The footsteps came right on down the hall, past the rooms in which they were sleeping, and into the back bedroom. Sara could see a dark form moving past her door, but could make out no more. The hall was darker since Becky's door blew shut.

Her throat felt tight. Sara felt as if she were going to faint. She could not breathe. Drawers were being opened and shut in the next room.

"Mama, Mama!" Becky cried out. In a flash Sara was across the hall and at the little girl's side. "Who came in our house?" Becky asked, seemingly sensing that there was something wrong. Quickly Sara's hand gently covered Becky's mouth.

"I don't know, Dear," she whispered, gathering the frightened child in her arms.

"I must not let her know I am afraid," Sara decided, courage rising with responsibility. Tremulously she whispered, "God is with us."

"But what is wrong, Mama?" Becky persisted.

Sara did not answer immediately. She suddenly remembered that Dan had brought home a large sum of money last night. There was not time to deposit it in the bank before leaving. The money had been put in the back room.

"Mama," Becky whispered, "will God take care of us till Papa comes home?"

"Yes, Dear," her mama assured her, "but let's not talk now."

The rummaging in the back room continued. Sara felt like running—but where? The nearest house was more than a mile away. The very air seemed tense with danger. She dared not move.

"But, Mama, can't we pray?" Becky persisted again. "Can't we ask God to take care of us?"

"Sure, Becky, we will talk to God." Sara dropped to her knees, still clutching the child in her arms. Silently she poured forth her earnest petition for protection.

"Mama," the baby begged softly. "Please pray aloud so I can hear you." She snuggled closer in the protective arms.

Gathering all her courage with a silent plea for more, Sara began in a clear steady voice, "Father in heaven, we commit ourselves into Thy loving care. Protect us we pray. Be with us through this night and we thank You. And Father, bless every soul in this house tonight in Your own good way. Amen."

"Now we can sleep," the chubby three-year-old stated matter-of-factly. Sara laid her back on her bed and crawled in beside her.

"Are you going to sleep with me?" Becky clasped her mama's hand delightedly. Her steady, even breathing soon revealed that the innocent little one was fast asleep.

Not another sound was heard. For some time Sara lay quietly listening. The fear had left her. She felt calm and secure. The Father's presence was her comfort. Sara slept soundly till the morning sun streaming in the window awakened her to a calm, quiet day.

The intruder had left no traces behind him. In the kitchen all was in order. Sara made a careful check in the back bedroom. Several drawers were standing open including the one which held the large sum of money. But apparently nothing had been touched.

For two years the mystery of that night remained unsolved.

"Mr. Dan, Mr. Dan!" accompanied a loud banging on the front door one night just as five-year-old Becky was being tucked into bed.

Dan hurried across the hall to the front room.

"Good evening," he greeted the excited young man pleasantly. "Step inside."

"Mr. Dan, I know it's late, but please, could you come with me to the hospital?" he begged.

Sara followed her husband to the front room. Jim, one of Dan's employees, stood in the open doorway. "I just came from Winston General Hospital," he explained. "Hank was hurt in an accident. He is dying. Mr. Dan, he keeps calling for you. Dr. White said you should be sent for, so I have come."

"Hank dying?" Mr. Dan started across the porch, "Surely he has not been drinking this time." Dan remembered the many times he had nearly been forced to discharge this hard-working young man because of his one bad habit—drinking. But things were different now. Hank had been with Mr. Dan for nearly five years. Often he had wondered whether it was worth his effort putting up with this kind of help, but how richly he had felt repaid when several months ago Hank had made a complete change! He was a new man from that day on. Never had he touched another drop of intoxicating drinks. Hank showed evidence of the New Birth in every area of his life. Mr. Dan thanked God for this answer to their prayers.

Sara spent the long, quiet evening in intercession for her husband and his former employee. When Dan did not return for two hours, she went on to bed. Her good-hearted husband would gladly spend the entire night with the suffering man.

"Mr. Dan," the dying man groaned painfully. "I must tell you something."

"Yes, Hank. What has happened?" Mr. Dan bent over the

suffering form as a concerned father over a beloved son. He had been closer to Hank than to many of his employees. "Hank, is all well?" The older man clasped the weak, trembling hand on the bed. "Is there anything I can do for you?"

"Sir, let me talk now, I haven't much time." Hank's breath came in short painful gasps. "Yes, He saved my soul." A faint smile crossed the pain-drawn face. "I am ready to go after I tell you this."

Mr. Dan waited silently for Hank to proceed.

"Two years ago your wife's prayer kept me from theft and possibly from murder, for which I was prepared, if necessary, to get a large sum of money you left in your house one night with your unprotected wife." Hank paused. "She was protected, yes, she was! But I did not know it until I heard her pray."

Mr. Dan had been listening in shocked silence. So Hank was the intruder that night. And he would have committed murder.

"O God, thank You for the power of prayer!" the grateful man breathed silently, almost forgetting the man on the bed before him.

"Good night, Mr. Dan. I will see you over there. Thank God for the power of prayer." The words of the dying man faded into silence. Mr. Dan was left alone with his thoughts. His wife would be at home awaiting his arrival because she had faith in the God who answers prayer!

"Button, Button, Who Has the Button?"

Lois sat at her desk, thoughtfully tapping the eraser of her pencil on the letter she was trying to write. Her mind was too distracted to read. She gave up trying and threw her book on the table.

Nineteen-year-old Lois Culp, teacher of the junior class in Sunday school and an active Christian worker in her church, was confronted with one of the most perplexing problems that she had faced since she had become a Christian.

"O God!" she groaned. "If You'll just help me out of this mess, I'll be careful, ever so careful to see that nothing like this ever happens again."

It all began the day she and Rachel worked together an hour or so after the other girls had gone home. The shirt factory seemed quiet and deserted, unlike the usual hustle and bustle going on there. Lois was pleased with the opportunity to earn a little extra money by working overtime each evening for several weeks.

After they had gathered up the last scraps of material and placed them neatly in piles in the cutting room, both girls began gathering up buttons that had dropped on the floor or were carelessly left lying around by thoughtless workers. After placing several buttons on the counter, Lois noticed with surprise that Rachel was putting the ones she picked up into her pocket.

"Rachel," she said, "you're not planning to take those home,

146

"Yes," Rachel answered shortly. "They may as well go home with me as in the garbage can, hadn't they?"

"I suppose so," agreed Lois in a doubtful voice, "but are you sure that's where they'll go if you don't take them?"

"Well, certainly," Rachel retorted, disgusted at Lois' persistent questioning. "Who ever heard of a large firm like Hall & Grant saving every little thing lying around. I've seen lots more wasted around here than a few small buttons. I'm sure the others all just sweep them right out. What I can salvage from the garbage is to my benefit."

"Well, if that's the case, I may as well have a few, too," Lois decided, scooping them from the counter into her pocket. "Dad and the boys are always losing buttons."

Each evening, a few more buttons were added to her collection. By the end of the month, Lois was surprised at the number of buttons she had accumulated.

It was the last Wednesday in the month, which meant staff meeting. Each worker put away his work a few minutes early, and everyone gathered in the office, where the manager was nervously tapping a rhythm with his foot as they took their seats.

"Must have something extra on his mind today," Rachel whispered to Lois as she slipped into the seat behind her.

After preliminaries, several matters of business were taken up, some changes were made in various departments, and new assignments were given.

"Now," the manager said, slowly running his fingers through his hair, "There is one more thing—we've been coming out awfully short on buttons during the past several weeks. Whether it is due to carelessness or to counting errors, I'm not sure. I am confident that none of you would steal, even a button; let's be more careful with supplies."

Lois flinched. Her face burned as a hot wave of embarrassment and fear washed over her! She was sure her cheeks were crimson. She had an urge to glance at Rachel, but knew she dare not, lest she make herself more noticeable. Greatly relieved when the meeting was dismissed, she walked out hurriedly.

A few minutes later in the car, she burst out, "O Rachel! What are we going to do? I thought they were to be thrown out; therefore, I might as well have had them."

"Yes, that's it," Rachel answered. "We actually did not steal. Neither of us would have thought of doing such a thing. Really, I don't think we're obligated to do anything about it. Of course, we'll not take any more, but those that we have—well, we'll just forget them! We didn't actually steal them, you know."

"But, Rachel, don't you think we should return them? After all, they don't belong to us. My conscience will bother me as long as I keep them."

"Lois, I don't even have the least idea how many I carried home, do you?"

"No," she answered uncertainly, "but maybe we should talk to the manager and explain," Lois persisted.

"Never!" Rachel argued hotly. "That would be foolish! He has confidence in us, even more in you and me than in some of the other girls, I'm sure. He'd never trust us again, and it's not as though we had intentionally stolen them, you know."

"I'm still uneasy about the buttons," Lois ventured as she pulled up in front of Rachel's house.

"Forget it, Lois," Rachel urged, starting up the walk toward the house. She did not think of the buttons again that evening.

With Lois it was different; buttons were all that she could think of. Buttons were all that she could dream of. And in the morning, almost before she got her eyes open, her father was begging her to sew on a missing button quickly before he went to work.

Several weeks passed. Now on this particular evening, unable to concentrate on reading or writing, Lois was thinking of buttons again. Thoughtfully, she tapped her eraser on her desk.

"Why, oh, why did I do it for a few little buttons?" she asked herself. Then again, for the hundredth time, she recounted mentally the whole incident from the day the first button was taken until the day Rachel had convinced (?) her that it was not necessary to do anything about it since they would never have intentionally stolen them.

Finally, so miserable that she felt she could put it off no longer, Lois, feeling like a thief, fell to her knees and poured out her soul to God. Tears, wrung from inward pain, filled her eyes and bubbled over. "Father," she prayed in agony, "whatever You ask me to do, I will do. Only, Father, somehow keep me from bringing reproach to Thy Name."

She reasoned, "If I should return the buttons or confess, what will they think of my Christianity? And I, a Sunday school teacher . . ." Going over the whole business again and again, Lois hoped earnestly to find some other way to peace, without confession. Finally, after giving up in despair, she admitted that she had sinned in taking what did not belong to her.

"Now that I see it and know I've done wrong," she struggled, "what will I do, confess it, spoil my reputation, and have peace; or, conceal it, spare my reputation, and have no peace?"

The burden, weighing very heavily on her heart, seemed to crush out her very life. The longing for the peace she had once known was so great that Lois, before rising from her knees, promised God to get everything straightened out before another day passed. She went to bed and slept soundly.

The following morning she started for work a few minutes early, hoping to see the manager alone.

"Good morning, Lois," he greeted her, "I'm glad you arrived early. I've been wanting to talk with you."

"Oh, no!" Lois shrank. "Why didn't I confess it immediately. Now if he approaches me about it, he will think I confessed only because I was caught. Her thoughts troubled her greatly in the long moment he stood gazing at her.

Mr. Hall, thinking his own thoughts, watched with wonder at her apparent ill-composure.

"I've been watching you," he began slowly, "and have noticed that you are honest, do good work, and are careful with equipment and supplies. I think you have come to the place where you are eligible for promotion."

"But, Mr. Hall," she interrupted breathlessly, and proceeded to confess in detail the things he did not know about her, expecting, in response, a flare of anger in which she would be fired instead of promoted.

She paused, wondering what was going on in his mind, knowing (?) that she had lost an opportunity to be a true Christian witness, and also an opportunity for promotion.

"Lois," he said quietly, "now I know I've found an honest girl. Now I'm sure you're the girl I'm looking for!"

The others were entering the factory. Mr. Hall turned and walked away. Lois's head was in a whirl. She would need a few minutes of quietness to be able to actually realize all that had just taken place and how merciful the Lord is.

The Hardest Earned Dime

Cutting cress, lettuce, and spinach, or pulling and bunching small green spring onions or round red radishes was not an easy job. And standing behind that little stand out by the roadside was tiresome, too. But that was not the half—the garden had to be worked, hoed, cultivated, and the seeds planted, then weeded, and dusted for bugs. "Gardening is not an easy way to earn a living!" Anna decided after trying it several years. "But it is a way to earn a little extra, and something I can do at home with the children." Dan's wages just never quite reached and every dime she could earn helped a little.

By Thursday evening the cress and lettuce were getting so thinned out that Anna decided, "I can't cut any more till next week. It must have time to grow a little. That cress surely is selling well this year. I wish I had more." But when Anna thought of putting out more vegetables and all the work connected with it, she decided that her garden was big enough.

On the way in to the house, Anna noticed for the first time a nice patch of wild cress by the stream. "Why, it looks almost as nice as what I've worked so hard for!" she exclaimed. "I wonder if I couldn't just sell this." After examining it more closely, Anna had to admit that it was not quite as nice but it was worth a try. She set down the yellow plastic pan, and began snipping. She stopped with three nice large bunches of wild cress. "I will try this tomorrow morning. That was an easy thirty cents if these three sell."

On Friday morning Anna again set up the stand, displaying the nice fresh vegetables. "Wild cress—10¢ a bunch" she wrote in black letters on one white card.

"I wonder if the customers will buy it if they know it grew wild." Anna did not like the looks of that sign. She picked up a little card from the table: "Cress—10¢."

"Why not just go on using this card? The cress has been selling so well. They won't know the difference if I don't tell them." Anna stood back, looking at her nice display. "At least not by looking at it—they may taste a difference." Slowly she picked up the new sign again—"Wild Cress."

"No, I don't like the looks of that. And I'm sure the finicky Mrs. Wilson won't either. She always comes for fresh vegetables every Friday morning. There comes a red car now." Quickly she slipped the "Wild Cress" sign under the shelf.

The car slowed and pulled off the road. "Good morning, Mrs. Glick. Are your vegetables nice and fresh this morning?"

"Yes, indeed. They are fresh and tender." Anna stepped back so that Mrs. Wilson could inspect her produce.

After picking up a half dozen bunches of onions, she found one that suited her. Next she picked up a small plastic bag of spinach. "If I knew I could get some cress as sweet and tender as we got here several weeks ago, I would take another bunch of cress. Those are nice large bunches. They're still 10¢?"

"Yes, any bunch you want for 10¢," Anna answered, wondering, "Should I tell her? She won't buy it if I do. Is it honest to keep quiet?" "We need the money so badly and it is perfectly good cress. Why not sell it? That is an easy dime."

"Yes, I think I will take this one," Mrs. Wilson decided at last. "I hope it's just like what I got the other week. I don't usually care much for cress but that was good. You always have the best vegetables. I would so much rather buy here than at the store, and here I know I can count on an honest deal!"

"Why did she have to add that? Of course she can count on an honest deal! I have always been honest. There is nothing dishonest about selling my own wild cress."

"Certainly not—if you are not misrepresenting it!"

"But I haven't said a word where it came from. I have not misrepresented anything," Anna thought disgustedly. Why did this little 10¢ deal of cress have to cause such a disturbance in her mind?

"Is there anything else?" she said.

"This is all. How much will it be?" Mrs. Wilson repeated irritably.

"Oh, I am sorry. Oh—let's see. What do you have?

"Shall I charge her for the cress? Should I ask her if she would want wild cress?

"A 15¢ bunch of onions, the bag of spinach, and the 10¢ bunch of cress. That will be 50¢," Anna said hesitantly.

"Perhaps I had better ask her about the cress."

"Thank you," Mrs. Wilson said, handing her a half dollar. "I'll see you next week," and she was gone.

Anna watched after the car. "Surely that wasn't dishonest," she argued. "I simply sold her my own cress and she could look at it and decide for herself whether or not she wanted it. I neither forced it on her or misrepresented it."

"Why then didn't you leave up your little 'Wild Cress' sign?"

Anna pulled it out and looked at it. "Why didn't I? Because she wouldn't have bought it if I had!"

No more cress sold that day. "At least I have one easy-earned dime," thought Anna that evening.

"One hard-earned dime!" That worrisome voice that had been speaking all day, disagreed. "One hard-earned dime! You haven't finished earning it yet. You aren't finished with that bunch of cress. Remember, you are honest. You will tell her it is wild cress. She only lives two miles down the road. You go tell her this evening yet."

"But she asked for the cress—I only gave it to her."

Finally, seeing that she could not still her conscience or have peace, Anna admitted her wrong. She went to her bedroom and dropped on her knees to seek forgiveness. Arising from her knees, Anna glanced at the clock. It was only four-thirty. Dan would not be home for an hour and a half yet. The meat and potatoes were in the oven. "Why not go tell her now?"

Anna slipped into her coat, then, bundling up the babies, got into the car. How humiliating it was to walk up to Mrs. Wilson's fine brick steps with a dime in her hand to ask if she wants to keep the wild cress!

She rang the bell and waited—no answer. She rang again. After waiting a long while Anna went back to the car and found a small note pad.

"Mrs. Wilson," she wrote,

"I am sorry about the cress I sold you this morning. It was wild cress. What I sold you several weeks ago was different. If you do not wish to use the wild cress, I will be glad to return your dime next week when you stop by."

Anna Glick

Anna walked up the steps again and slipped her note in the screen-door handle. "What will Mrs. Wilson think when she gets home and finds this note?" she wondered. "If only I had left my little 'Wild Cress' sign up! That would have been so much easier than having to give an explanation like this now."

Anna drove home slowly. The meat and potatoes were soft by five-thirty. "I'll fix a salad of cress to go with it," she decided. When she went to get one of the bunches of crisp green cress, Anna noticed her little sign still lying beneath the shelf. Quickly she placed the "Wild Cress—10¢" on the last bunch of cress.

"Whether this will sell or not, I don't know. But if it does, at least it will be an easy-earned dime. And if it doesn't, it won't cost me a trip to town or the humiliation of another confession."

A Man's Soul

"For what shall it profit a man, if he shall gain the whole world, and lose his own soul? Or what shall a man give in exchange for his soul?"

These words (Mark 8:36, 37) kept turning over and over in Jacob's mind. It was early in the spring of 1920. The weather was beautiful for getting out the crops. There was much work to be done in the next few weeks. Jacob was a busy farmer. His three hundred acres were his pride and joy.

The next farm, owned by Paul Miller, was also a prosperous one and well kept. The white board fence between the Miller and Bender farms always had the appearance of fresh paint. The cattle were well fed and the pastures green and lush on both farms.

While Jacob Bender milked his twenty cows, he could not help thinking of their value and of the value of his farm. Why, some of these cows gave one-third more milk than the average cow. In fact, no one in Grassy Banks had cows to compare with these—at least, no one but Paul Miller. And these large fields of corn he had just finished planting would bring in some cash this fall, unless something very unusual happened.

"But what is all this really worth?" Jacob wondered. "What real value are bountiful harvests?" Jacob had felt rather uneasy for some time. He had to spend so much time on his large farm that there was seldom time for anything else. "The value of one soul is worth far more than the whole world," he pondered. Yes,

Jacob had taken care of his own soul's need, knowing that there was nothing worth exchanging for one's soul. But there was Paul Miller's soul. Paul was a fine neighbor, but not a Christian. He had no time for church, no time for God. No, Paul had no time for Christianity. He, too, was a busy farmer.

After living next door to Paul for about two years and often working together on their farms, Jacob considered Paul a very close friend. He enjoyed very much working with this good-natured neighbor.

This morning while Jacob milked his prize cows, he kept thinking about the worth of a man's soul. And always Paul Miller's soul seemed to be calling for help.

"But I can't approach him as a sinner," Jacob reasoned. "I might insult my best neighbor. Paul might even become angry if I asked him whether he is a Christian," Jacob worried, remembering the time he had gotten Paul to go to a Bible school program. That was last summer. Paul reluctantly consented, only because his little daughter had a part on the program. How well Jacob remembered how after the service the minister, shaking hands with Paul, had asked, "Are you a Christian?" Paul seemed very much embarrassed and answered, "I'm certainly not a heathen." Later he had told Jacob he did not think people had any right to ask such personal questions. Paul had never gone to church again and Jacob was afraid to ask him. They got along so well that Jacob did not wish to hinder the relationship.

"But how about his soul in the Judgment Day?" Jacob worried. "How will he feel toward me then?" Jacob pondered these thoughts seriously. "After all, I will also have to give account to God." Jacob tried to work out a plan to relieve himself of his responsibility toward his neighbor. "I will witness by a quiet Christian life," he decided, "rather than by words. Then he cannot take offense."

But the Spirit continued to speak to Jacob, urging him to

speak to his neighbor about his soul's need.

Jacob realized that probably he could more freely talk to Paul than any of their neighbors because of their closeness. "But suppose he turns against me then, and I wouldn't even be able to be a good witness to him in working together," Jacob excused himself.

All that summer, Jacob could not rest or push from his mind the urgency of Paul's need of salvation. In every way possible, he showed good Christian attitudes and made a definite effort to be a witness for Christ, except by word of mouth. Jacob could not bring himself to go to Paul and tell him about his concern for his soul, though he spent many sleepless nights worrying about the lost condition of his friend and about his own responsibility in the matter.

The rains had fallen. The crops had grown and it was again harvesttime. For the next several weeks Paul and Jacob would be working together from sunrise to sunset. This would be a golden opportunity to speak to Paul about his soul. This prospect filled Jacob's mind constantly in the days prior to harvesttime. How he longed to see his neighbor enjoy the blessings of a true Christian life! More and more, as they worked together, he could sense Paul's lack of peace and his longing for something to satisfy. Yet Jacob never had the courage to bring up this important subject.

During the days of harvest when they spent much time together, God spoke clearly to the Christian neighbor, urging him to warn the non-Christian.

Finally Jacob decided he would go. He would go to Paul and tell him how he loved him and appreciated him as a good neighbor and how he longed for his soul. Yes, Jacob made this same decision over and over and over, but he never found time to do it. There were always many things to keep a farmer busy.

Years passed. Jacob and Paul continued on as before. They were neighbors on good terms. There had never been anything to

A Man's Soul

mar their relationship.

Suddenly Paul was taken very ill. The doctors said he could not live. Jacob spent hours on the Miller farm when his own needed attention. He was still determined to witness for his Lord by Christlike actions. The night Paul had been taken to the hospital, Jacob could not sleep. "If only I had spoken to him about his soul," he cried, knowing that Paul was not ready to meet God. Jacob was in agony for several days till Paul regained consciousness. With great relief Jacob decided again to speak to his neighbor concerning his soul's need as soon as he was strong enough to carry a conversation. As time went on, Paul's recovery was miraculous. By harvesttime he was able to be out on the farm again. With some hired help, he continued to be a prosperous farmer.

Again Jacob put off the thing he knew he should do. For ten more years the Millers and Benders lived side by side. Jacob seldom thought of Paul's need.

In the spring of 1942 Jacob again felt pressed very heavily with his responsibility to his neighbor. "I just must speak to him soon," Jacob decided, remembering the serious illness he had suffered several years earlier. "I cannot put it off any longer." Recently Jacob had noticed changes taking place in Paul. He seemed to be becoming increasingly hard and indifferent. There had been a time when Jacob felt confident that Paul was about to yield his life to God and seemed almost on the verge of surrender. Now he seemed to be fast growing cold, even bitter. Now to speak to Paul would take much more courage than when they were younger men. Jacob's old habit of procrastination still had its hold on him. The Spirit again spoke plainly, more urgently than He had for years. "I will, I will go," Jacob decided with determination. "But not today."

The next morning Jacob with his family left for a short vacation. When they returned three days later, they were shocked to

159

find their neighbor's house empty and locked. The Millers had left a note with the neighbors for Jacob Bender. Because of certain circumstances they had sold out and moved to another state hundreds of miles away. They left their address and expressed their appreciation for the good neighbors they had had in Grassy Banks.

That was the last time the Benders heard from the Millers. More years passed. Jacob was no longer able to care for the farm. Two of his sons took it on partnership. Jacob helped what he could. His health would no longer allow him to put in a good day's work. Jacob spent quite a lot of time reading. One day, as he read Psalm 49, he came across this verse, "For the redemption of their soul is precious."

" 'The redemption of their soul is precious'! Paul Miller! How is it with his soul?" Jacob had neither heard from nor written to Paul Miller since they moved twelve years ago. Why should he think of him now in connection with this? Jacob felt condemned. Again, with great urgency, he was pressed with the need of speaking to his old friend about his soul's need. Jacob felt such a burden that he could no longer push it aside. He had put it off too long already. All these years Paul might have been enjoying a blessed Christian experience if he had filled his responsibility as a Christian neighbor. For years he had nearly forgotten, but now again it was as if God Himself had spoken in an audible voice, pleading with him to help this lost soul find Christ.

Humbly Jacob knelt by his chair asking God to forgive his negligence. He went to his desk and got out a tablet and a pen and began to write—first a friendly greeting, then the community news. Jacob stopped. "Now where from here?" He sat for an hour or more. He would finish it later. Yes, he was determined to write to Paul and to inquire whether he had ever taken care of his soul's need.

The letter lay on the desk for several days. Jacob tried again.

160

He picked up the old address book. Yes, there was Paul Miller's address. Would he not be surprised to hear from Jacob, his old friend from Grassy Banks! Jacob pulled an envelope from the drawer and addressed it. That was all he got done that day. The unfinished letter lay for two more weeks without being touched. Finally Jacob went back to the desk. "I just must get this letter off," he decided with finality. Jacob picked up his pen. Just then his wife came in with the *Budget*. Jacob scanned a few articles, then, turning to the letter from the community where the Millers had moved, he read: "Last evening at eight o'clock Paul Miller took his gun and walked outside. His wife heard a shot and went to see what he was shooting at. Paul lay on the back steps with a bullet through his heart!"

The words glared at Jacob. He was shocked. He looked at the unfinished letter, the addressed envelope, and the *Budget* in his trembling hand. Had anyone ever invited Paul to Christ, the solution to all our problems? Jacob sat in a daze. The Lord was revealing to him how his reputation in the community was an idol to him. It had its part in keeping him from witnessing. Was there any way he could ever be clear of his guilt? "Oh, for one more chance!" he groaned in agony.

"One more chance would do you no good," a voice seemed to say. "All your life you've had ample chances. Even this letter could have reached him in time. Possibly it could have even prevented this tragedy."

Never before had Jacob realized the importance of promptly obeying the promptings of the Spirit as he did now. "It is appointed unto men once to die, but after this the judgment"!

Shoestrings and Leather Glue

Wearily James trudged in the lane toward the house. He could not sleep again. He had not been able to sleep last night, or the night before. Now it was eleven o'clock. He had been walking since eight-thirty—walking through the orchard, around the barn, down past the stream, through the pasture field.

Heaving a deep sigh, he walked over the creaking porch boards as quietly as possible. Oh, to be able to sleep!

"I'll surely sleep tonight. I'm tired. I'm really exhausted. Perhaps a man over forty years old doesn't need quite that much exercise. But if I sleep now it will have been worth it."

James undressed and started to get into bed, then hesitated. Falling to his knees, he again tried to pray. Here was where the trouble had begun $2\frac{1}{2}$ hours ago. He closed his eyes. "Holy Father . . ." No more words would come. Before his eyes lay the same pile of shoestrings, only perhaps bigger; and the mounds of leather glue were now mounting, growing larger each time he dared to cast a glance. Shoestrings and leather glue! Shoestrings and leather glue!

Would he never be able to pray again? Could he never form words of praise, or make petitions known to the Father above?

"Why? Why?" he asked himself again and again. Shoestrings and leather glue! Shoestrings—each one so small in itself, yet what a pile they could make! What a large room of the brain it took to occupy these thoughts! No room was left for anything else. And the glue—sticky, smeary glue. How firm its grip was on his mind—glue that could not be pulled loose, could not be torn loose, could not be soaked loose—oh, that awful glue!

Finally James arose from his knees. He was exhausted. He climbed into bed. Had he prayed? Had he not better just start going to bed without praying? What was the use?

Shoestrings and leather glue!

Leather glue and shoestrings!

Finally James fell into a restless sleep.

*   *   *   *   *   *   *   *   *   *   *   *

About twenty years ago James had worked for a poor cobbler. As a boy, James had been good help. The cobbler, being the only one in the small but growing town, had had lots of business. The trade finally grew to become a small shoe factory. The best shoes to be had far and near came from the Cobbler's Shoe Store. James continued working for a number of years. The cobbler took great pride in using the best leather glue for his shoes, especially boys' school shoes. There was seldom a complaint of the shoes not holding. Yes, the shoes sold out of the Cobbler's Shoe Store were good shoes.

As business grew and more help was hired, there was much more waste of materials that several years ago would have been carefully saved and put to other use.

James well remembered harder times when these scrap materials would have been a precious savings. Even at this time, with two small children, the little amounts of the extra-quality leather glue which was being wasted would come in very handy at home. James began carrying a small jar in his lunch pail into which he carefully scraped a little glue each day. Also many shoestrings, which were carelessly left lying around, James picked up and carried home. He continued this practice for several years, until he left the small town for a better job in the country on a little farm. There James spent a few more years earning and saving what he could. His life with his family continued on much as before until one day, when in his early thirties, James met some Christian people, who by the help of the Holy Spirit led him to a saving knowledge of Jesus Christ.

After this experience, many things were different for James and his family. He had found a truly satisfying experience. He had made restitution and confession for every sin of which he was convicted.

James then enjoyed peace with God and felt His presence near and precious to him at all times. As a humble Christian man he often prayed that God's will for his life would be revealed to him. Very carefully he followed the leading of the Spirit according to the understanding he had.

For many years this peace and joy was not marred. There were times when the Spirit spoke to James about something of which he needed to be more careful, or of an incident which should be corrected. These things James prayerfully took care of as they arose, thereby maintaining that sweet peace and assurance.

Now, ten years after his conversion, the shoestrings and leather glue suddenly came to his mind and allowed him no peace.

"Lord, I've had peace all these years," he prayed. "I've never thought of those things as stolen goods. Why should they bother me now? You know, God, I truly want to keep a clean conscience; but if this is important why didn't You bring it to my memory when I was converted? It would have been easier then. I was making everything right then. Surely You don't mean I should go and confess that I stole those items? Not now—twenty years later. The shop may not even be open anymore."

"But you could find out whether it is still open," an inner

voice urged.

"But surely God wouldn't have given me peace all these years if I had sin in my life," James argued. "Surely all those things were cleansed by the blood when I was converted."

"Thou shalt not steal," burned into his troubled mind. "If I have taken any thing from any man by false accusation, I restore him fourfold." Why should these words come to his mind? He had not stolen anything—only picked up unused materials.

"Were they yours? Or were they another man's?" The inner voice seemed to continue the argument.

James was baffled. Never before in all his Christian experience had he run into anything this hard to submit his will to. He could not understand why this incident should lie forgotten all these years and now suddenly become so urgent. But one thing James did understand. God was asking him to go back to the small town of his childhood, look up the cobbler, and repay him for all the materials carried out of his shop.

During the years on the farm, things had often been hard. Even now there was only a very small savings on the closet shelf, and there were many things it should be used for. The family was larger now, and the farm had not prospered well. But James determined, as always before, to mind God, even if it took his last cent. Peace was more precious than money.

So one warm summer day found James, now in his late forties, boarding the train for his hometown, which he had not seen for nearly twenty years. The train fare was higher than he had expected. James wondered how much the cobbler would want for the shoestrings and leather glue. Nevertheless, the debt must be paid.

As the train neared his childhood home, James became very uneasy. How everything had changed! Could this be the right place? Could these new roads be through the same town? The buildings simply overwhelmed the country farmer. Clad in farm clothes, shabby but clean, he began to feel very much out of place as the train chugged into the new station. As James remembered the old station, there was only a sidewalk with a roof built over several benches. Now this modern station made James feel as though he were perhaps in Washington or New York City, by some odd mistake.

James inquired about the name of the town to know for certain. Finding that he was at the desired location, he tremblingly stepped off the crowded train. His heart sank as he looked up one street and down another.

Finally getting his bearings by a few old buildings that were still standing, he decided that the Cobbler's Shoe Store must be to the right.

Bravely he started in the direction of the water, each step becoming a greater burden. How could he face the old cobbler? Suppose there were lots of workers standing around? What would be the right way to start and the right things to say? James prayed for grace and wisdom.

Nearer and nearer he came. Tighter and tighter something clutched at his throat. James felt he would not be able to speak. Suddenly he looked up. Right there before him was the very spot where the Cobbler's Shoe Store used to stand. Now there was only a magazine store. Could this be right? Was there possibly some mistake?

"Could I help you?" a young man asked, stepping into the doorway and facing the stooped older man on the sidewalk.

"A-yes, yes," stammered James. "Could you tell me where the cobbler's shop is located?"

"The cobbler's shop," the young man repeated. "No, sir, I don't know of any cobbler in this city."

"Father," he called back to a dignified-looking man in the store, "do you know anything about a cobbler's shop?"

The man thought a minute. "You mean the large factory over

on Fifth Street?" he asked, walking to the door.

"Good day," James greeted the gentleman. "I was looking for an old cobbler who used to have a little shop here on this street."

"Yes, yes," the gentleman laughed. "That's the one. You must have been away from this city a long while."

"About twenty years," the farmer replied.

"The cobbler is now called the president," the man informed him. "He has his factory in the largest brick building on Fifth Street. The large factory is still called the Cobbler's Shoe Store."

"Thank you," James nodded and walked on toward Fifth Street. The buildings were larger and more modern in this section. James felt smaller and less able to face the great president as he turned the corner and saw the large structure before him bearing the name: Cobbler's Shoe Store.

For a moment James paused, almost ready to flee. Could he enter that building? Was it really necessary? The poor farmer trembled. "I've never stolen anything from here," he again began to justify himself. Quickly, James brushed these thoughts from his mind. He had heard God's call and was sure he was following His leading. He would not turn back now. Breathing a silent prayer as he went, James walked through the large glass doors.

"Holy Father," the broken man pleaded, "just be with me and put words into my mouth that will honor and glorify Thy Name. I thank You that I know You are with me in this place and will direct the steps of all Your children. Prepare the hearts of those with whom I will speak. May good come from this contact."

James found himself standing in a large hall, surrounded by doors. "May I help you?" a girl asked politely, from behind the large information desk.

"Yes," James answered. "I would like to speak to the president."

"The president?" she questioned. "May I see your card?"

167

"I have none," James replied. "But I must see him if it is possible."

"Is he expecting you?" she asked doubtfully.

"No, but it is very important. I must see him," James urged. How he wished he could get this thing over! If only he could have walked into the old cobbler's shop as it used to be! He waited while the girl leafed through several papers, hoping he would not be turned out. Would such an important, busy man even want to take time to talk to a poor farmer? Surely the value of the shoestrings and glue would be so small that the president would not even want to bother with them. But still James was determined to clear his conscience.

"He is on the sixth floor," the girl spoke. "He is a very busy man. Give your name to the girl at the desk up there. She will see whether he has time to see you this morning."

"Thank you," James answered, turning toward the elevator.

The ride to the sixth floor seemed long. James felt weak; the air seemed stuffy. He hoped he would not need to wait much longer.

"Could I speak to the president?" he asked the girl behind the desk.

"Your card, please," the girl held out her hand.

"I do not have one," James answered. "But I must see him, please."

"Your name?" she asked in a very businesslike manner.

"James Brown."

The girl rang a bell. Soon a gentleman appeared. "Take this man to the president's office. James Brown is the name. He wishes to speak to the president."

"Yes, ma'am," he answered, motioning James to follow him. They walked some distance down the hall. "Wait here in the hall just a moment. I will go into the office and speak to his secretary. She will tell me when he can see you. James Brown was the

168

name, wasn't it?"

"Yes," James swallowed hard. How would he be able to speak to such a busy man? Again James prayed for grace and calmness.

The young man was back. "Mr. Brown, I spoke to the president's secretary, Miss Smith, and she said the president is unusually busy this morning and that he does not recall your name or of having any business transaction with you. He can hardly take time to see you now. Would you like to leave a message with his secretary?"

"No, sir, I must see the president himself," James answered firmly.

"Would you like to tell me what the urgent reason is for your call? I will see what I can do for you."

"Yes," James answered humbly. "I worked for the cobbler years ago," he paused, running his hand over his damp forehead.

"Yes," the gentleman waited.

"While I worked for him, I stole some of his materials," James spoke with great difficulty. "I want to confess this to him and pay him for the materials." The poor farmer could hardly speak for the emotion he felt. His voice was cracked and broken as he stood trembling under the steady gaze of the younger man.

"I see," the man answered. "I will see that the president gets your message."

Again James was left alone in the hall until a few minutes later when the secretary came to the door and invited him into her office.

"You may go through that door over there," she said, indicating the door to the president's office. "Be seated until he comes in. I will tell him you are waiting in his office."

"Thank you," James offered weakly. This long waiting ordeal was making it harder for him. James was deeply impressed with the importance of this great man he must speak to, taking time he could hardly spare.

"How are you, Mr. Brown?" The president spoke coldly as he entered the door by which James had entered a few minutes earlier.

"I am well," James replied.

Silently the great man took the chair opposite James. He looked at him with eyes as cold as steel. "You wish to see me about some company property which you have stolen, I understand." The hard expression on his face did not change. "I am in a great hurry. If you will quickly tell me what items were stolen, I will have my secretary look up the prices and a bill will be made out which you may pay in there at the desk."

"I am very sorry," James began, "but I will not be able to tell you the exact amount of the materials stolen. However, I certainly do want to repay you. When I worked for you twenty years ago—"

"Please, Mr. Brown, I am very rushed this morning. Will you explain quickly?" the president retorted sharply.

James gasped and caught his breath. He had not expected anything like this. "I—I used to pick up shoestrings and leather glue," James looked pleadingly into the face of the other man. "I am not sure exactly how many I took. But I want to—"

"Please, please," the president interrupted impatiently. "Is that all? Was there nothing else?" As James sat shaking his head, the busy president arose from his chair. "Do you mean that is all you bothered me for? You have already wasted more time than a few shoestrings and leather glue could be worth. "Look, man, I'm busy," he shouted angrily.

"I want to pay you and tell you I'm sorry that I stole those materials when I worked for you," James spoke quietly. "Then I will go."

The president was furious. "You may go now," he shouted. "I cannot waste time talking about things that happened twenty years ago. Why do you bother me and waste my time?"

"I didn't want to come," James answered, breaking down and weeping like a child. "I didn't want to. But I had to. O sir, you don't know how I dreaded to face you and confess my sin. But I had to do it. I love my Savior who set me free from sin. When He speaks to me, I must respond and obey to maintain the wonderful peace He has given me. Sir, can you not see that I had to come?" As the tears flowed steadily down the farmer's face, the president looked on in wonder. Never before had he witnessed such a scene as this.

Humbly James pleaded with the great important man to try to understand how God had spoken to him, and that he could not resist the power and love of God.

The president dropped into his chair. Burying his face in his hands, he, too, wept. "James," he spoke at last, "James, you have something that few of us have. The peace you have is of far more value than this factory and all its shoes." Pulling a clean white handkerchief from his pocket the president wiped his eyes. "James," his voice trembled, "I admire your courage."

"I could not have done this alone," James replied softly. "The One who demanded that I come came with me. He will never forsake me. Oh, won't you bow to Him also? You will find all the needs and longings of your soul satisfied."

The president continued wiping his eyes. Low sobs frequently escaped his lips as the faithful Christian man very simply explained the plan of salvation to him. He spoke of God's love and mercy and of the wonderful peace and joy to be found in turning from our own way and yielding to Him.

"James," the president answered brokenly, "I've heard all this before, but it's been so long ago. My mother used to take me to Sunday school and pray for me. She taught me all about God's love and mercy but I spurned it all and turned to my own way. I haven't heard Gospel preaching for years; and it's been a long, long time since I've seen it lived out as I've seen it here today."

The president's voice was softened and the look on his face more tender as he continued. "James, you are forgiven. The shoestrings and leather glue will never be mentioned."

"No," James answered determinedly, "I will not be satisfied until I have paid for them. As I said, I cannot tell the exact amount, but I want to estimate and pay as near as I can for the goods I carried out of your shop."

"Did you carry any away in large amounts?" the president asked kindly.

"No, only one or two shoestrings at a time, and just a little glue, usually only a spoonful. But it did not belong to me and I must pay for it."

"Yes," the president answered. Together the two men figured as nearly as possible the value of the things stolen. The bill was paid and James felt a great burden removed.

The busy president seemed no longer in such a great hurry but was willing to listen to the poor farmer speak of his soul's need and the only remedy.

Finally James had to go. He was only disappointed that at this time the president was not willing to submit his will to God. James left the factory with a light heart and a prayer on his lips that the seed sown would yet take root and the other man would find the peace he longed for.

Two weeks after this incident, James was shocked when he read in the newspaper that the president of the Cobbler's Shoe Store had died very suddenly of a heart attack. James had neither seen nor heard from him since the day he had made his confession. Had the president responded to the call of God? James would probably never know on earth. He did know that the busy man had had one last opportunity. How thankful he was that he had not put off the thing he knew God wanted him to do!

"Whatsoever Ye Ask"

Sara walked up and down the hot, dusty rows of beans, shaking her head sadly. "We won't get enough beans this year to pay for the seed if we don't have rain soon." Some were completely withered. "No hope for them." She walked over to the tomatoes. "All the hard work I put into this garden—wasted. Completely wasted!" She sighed. "I hardly had the time to have a garden to start with and the seed was so expensive." The few tomatoes that had survived the drought, like the beans, could not possibly survive much longer without rain. "Even if we would have a good rain now, the crop would be poor. But at least a little would help."

The heat was depressing and the sight of the pitiful garden did not help at all. The air was unusually stifling this afternoon. Walking back toward the house where the children were napping, Sara thought bitterly, "I tried so hard. Why? Why such a dry year?" Looking up just before entering the back door, Sara noticed a dark cloud coming up over the house. "What a black cloud!" she exclaimed. It was moving right across the house.

Casting a dark shadow over the garden, the blustery cloud moved on. Almost without thinking, Sara looked up and cried impatiently, "Lord, whatever is in that cloud, let it come down!"

Having uttered her hasty prayer, she stepped inside, still feeling a bit resentful that her garden had not been watered sooner.

"What is all that racket? The children must have awakened."

The weary young mother started toward Donnie's bedroom. "He shouldn't be up yet—and such a fuss! He will have Debbie awake." The clattering noise grew louder and more persistent. It seemed to be coming from every direction by the time she reached the little boy's bedroom door.

Sleepily Donnie rolled over. Debbie cried out, "Mama!" The noise had already woke her from her short nap.

Bewildered, Sara stood in the hallway looking around for the source of all the noise. Rushing to the window, she soon discovered the cause of the awful commotion.

"Hail," Sara cried, "and such hail I have never seen!" It was dashing against the house, bouncing and rolling across the walks. It seemed the windows would soon give way under the pressure of it.

"Mama!" Debbie cried again, and Donnie sat up wide-eyed. "What is it?" he asked, staring out the window.

"It is hail, Donnie," Sara replied quietly.

"Why is it raining hail?" the four-year-old asked. "Why is it hitting our house?"

Sara looked away. "Why is it raining hail? Why is it?" she asked herself soberly. "Perhaps because I asked for it. I didn't know what was in that cloud, but, of course, I expected rain."

After a half hour, quietness reigned. Sara walked to the back door. There lay the large hailstones, almost covering the porch. The yard and—yes, the garden. Where were the beans and tomatoes now? Well, if they were still there, they must be buried under the hail. They were not much before, but now—they surely would have been better off without "whatever was in that cloud." Sara stepped outside again. Walking between the rows of beans, she stopped time and again to raise a torn, beaten, mangled plant, only to see it drop limply to the ground again. The few stems that had not been completely cut off were so torn and twisted that they would never stand up again.

The air felt cooler and less depressing. More clouds drifted lazily across the blue sky. Sara looked at them closely. The air felt damp. "Those clouds look like rain. Oh, my garden needs rain!" The bitterness had gone, and Sara now felt her helplessness and dependence on the Lord. Three little words kept coming to her mind. "Whatsoever ye ask . . ." "I should ask for rain for my garden." Suddenly she stopped. "My garden—I don't have a garden! No amount of rain would help now."

Then the truth dawned on her, but too late. "Perhaps I should have asked for rain sooner. The next time I will ask for whatever He sees is best for me, rather than demanding the thing that looks good. He sends the clouds and knows what they hold. I'll leave the decision to Him when to send and when to withhold." Sara sadly walked to the house. "No beans to can this year. No tomato sandwiches for lunch throughout the summer months."

The phone was ringing. Quickly Sara stepped inside.

"Hello.

"Yes, I was outside, but that is all right. I was ready to come in.

"No, I wasn't working in the garden.

"Raining?" Sara looked outside, "Why, yes, it is raining here, too, now. Wasn't that awfully big hail?

"You mean you didn't have any hail over there! Why, we are not half a mile apart. Yes, it surely did hail here."

Sara hung up the receiver. "Yes, the Lord promised, 'Whatsoever ye ask . . . ' I am surely going to be more careful in my asking after this."

The Crop That
Couldn't Grow

"Good morning, neighbor," Amos called out as he pulled on the reins of the team he was driving. "I see you're not setting out any tobacco this year again."

"Yes," John replied, straightening up. Until now he had not noticed the owner of the farm across the hill coming by in the horse-drawn cart. John had been intently weeding his new bed of strawberries. If a living could be earned raising strawberries, he was determined to earn his that way. He would do all in his power to make the crop a prosperous one. Only the Lord could make it grow.

"There's no one in these parts raising strawberries," Amos stated. "Tobacco is the only money crop around here."

There was a short pause.

"You have always done good on your tobacco, haven't you, John?" the big man on the cart questioned.

"Until last year," John answered, a broad smile of satisfaction crossing his face.

"I noticed last summer as I drove by several times that you hadn't set any out," said Amos. "I figured you'd already retired. Now this—strawberries are hard work. Well, so is tobacco, but then you've got a substantial payoff; and besides, this country isn't suited to strawberries."

John remained quiet, waiting for Amos to finish.

"These look all right," Amos continued as he climbed down

off the cart to examine the nice crop of berries more closely. "But as I say, they're not suited to this country. Likely they'll grow one year and fail the next. Now tobacco—I've seldom seen a crop to fail in all this area. Say, John, why did you change to strawberry growing?"

"Well, Amos," John began slowly, glad for this opportunity. "As you say, I've always raised tobacco, and for big profits; that is, until last year."

"Yes. Then last year you never set it out. I was wondering why," Amos asked pointedly.

"But I did plant tobacco seed last year," John contradicted his neighbor, "and at a great expense."

Amos's mouth dropped open. He did not say a word.

"I bought the best seed. I had my ground prepared and in the best possible shape."

"Last year was the best tobacco-growing year we've had in ten years," Amos almost shouted. "Everyone of our neighbors will agree. No one around here has ever sold so much per acre, nor any so nice. Why, most of us took in almost double what we'd earned the year before, and we didn't do bad that year."

"Right," John agreed. "That's why I won't set any out this year, because it had every chance to prove itself last year."

"John, I don't understand. You didn't lose your crop last year, did you?"

"A total loss! My crop last year was the most total crop failure I've ever seen. And I know why," he finished triumphant-ly.

"I certainly don't understand." Amos looked puzzled. "I thought you hadn't set any out. I never saw a plant around here."

"That's right. There never was a plant on my farm last year. But, I did buy the seed, prepared the land, and—well, that's where the crop failure comes in. Then I prayed."

"You what?"

"I prayed!"

"You prayed?"

"Yes, indeed, I prayed. And God sure answered in a mighty powerful way. That crop of tobacco just couldn't grow, under the best of conditions. I asked the Lord to show me if tobacco raising was wrong. Now, Amos, you know neither you nor I would use the stuff. But we went right on raising it. I began to get convicted that it was wrong."

"But, John, they'll get it somewhere. If we don't get the profits, someone else will! It's not as though that would stop them all from using it."

"Well, I reasoned that way a long time. But last year I decided to give the Lord a chance. You know, all we can do is get it in the ground and the Lord makes it grow. That part of it isn't in our power."

"Yes, yes," Amos mumbled, shaking his head doubtfully.

"Well, I prayed. I told the Lord that this thing had been bothering me. I didn't know whether it was pleasing to Him or not—our raising tobacco."

Amos mumbled something under his breath.

Quickly John went on. "I said, 'Lord, if You don't want me raising tobacco, just don't let this crop grow, and I'll never plant tobacco again.' Well, as you've said, the season was perfect. The rains were just right. I had everything I needed and gave the seeds the best of care. But I'm telling you the truth, Amos, not one seed ever sent one plant above the ground. I waited and waited. Everyone else's crops were thriving. Of course, they hadn't asked God to use this means of showing them His will. I had, and He showed me. Amos, I'll never, as long as I live, plant another tobacco seed."

Amos grunted, shook his head, and started back toward the waiting cart. "See you, neighbor," he called without looking around.

Amos was talking to himself as he climbed into his cart. "John's a good farmer—always has had the nicest looking tobacco fields in these hills. That crop just couldn't grow? Nothing else could have kept it from growing but God Himself!"

In the Shadow of His Hand

It was prayer meeting evening. Grace was glad. What a lift this midweek meeting gave her! They had two worship services on Sunday, then a whole long week. Yes, the midweek meeting was surely needed, and Grace was there unless there was a real reason for not being there. No, this doesn't mean being too tired, having company, or any such small interference. Those things could not induce Grace to miss midweek prayer meeting. Never!

Humming an old hymn, Grace dressed Donny, her two-and-a-half-year-old son. He always went with her to church. "Now we're ready," she announced. "Come with Mama. We're going to prayer meeting."

The car was old and sometimes caused trouble, but it did usually get where it started out for. It sputtered and choked, but finally got going. Grace eased in on the gas to keep it moving smoothly. A few houses down the road she stopped to pick up several neighbors. They all knew that they could depend on Grace when they needed transportation to church services. The church house was across the hill. The old Chevrolet groaned and pulled, and finally reached the top. Grace changed to second gear, knowing that the downgrade was very steep. She had a little too much speed. Lightly Grace hit the brake. Nothing happened. She pushed harder—the car was gaining speed. Grace began to feel alarmed. She reached for Donny and pulled him down on the seat beside her. The old car was speeding on. Grace held the brake on the floorboard now, but it did no good. The car had gained such momentum now that it was almost out of control. Pumping the brakes did no good. A car was approaching from the opposite direction. Grace knew that she had no control of the speeding vehicle. She helplessly called on God.

"O God!" she cried in this moment of distress. "It's all up to You. If we get out of here safely, it's only because Your hand has control. I can do nothing." Not a word was uttered in the car as it crossed the path of the oncoming car just an instant before it passed. The old Chevy circled into a filling station, just missing the pumps, at an awful speed. Grace held the wheel, knowing it was God's hand doing the steering. She was under the shadow of His hand. Before swerving back out into the highway, the old car passed a telephone pole so close that Grace thought, "This will stop us!" When it missed, she took fresh courage. The second she was on the highway, a car passed, and another was coming from the other direction. The old Chevy slipped between them. Grace kept her hand on the wheel, and her trust in God, silently committing all to Him. After coasting a short distance down the road, she was able to gain control and bring the car to a stop.

Though she was shaking, Grace triumphantly praised the Lord. "It was only God who brought us to safety," she said. "Surely He has some purpose for our being here or we would not have escaped in this way. Praise the Lord! We are under the shadow of His hand."

"The Angel of the Lord"

Observations of a number of people

A busy mother walked to the window to check on her three-year-old son, who had been playing in the front yard. What she saw frightened her too badly for action. She had neither voice nor strength. She could only call on God for help. There was no way she could reach the baby in time.

Johnny was running full speed, chasing a big yellow butterfly. The chase was taking him directly over the path of a large, coiled rattlesnake. He was not ten feet from it when his mother reached the window.

Just at that moment two small, brightly colored butterflies fluttered almost directly into Johnny's face. Johnny's little arms flew up. He caught one and turned to follow the other one, which was flying in the opposite direction.

Mother ran to the door and caught up the baby in her arms as he passed the house. Father ran out to kill the snake.

"Oh, I was sure he would run right over the snake," Mother cried. "How glad I am that the butterflies happened over just then!"

"Why, that was no 'happen,' " Father answered gravely. "For I say unto you, That in heaven their angels do always behold the face of my Father which is in heaven" (Matthew 18:10).

*　　*　　*　　*　　*　　*　　*　　*　　*　　*　　*　　*

Ada walked home from the little white church. Her heart was filled with song. Never had she been this happy. Today Ada had given her heart to the Lord. For a long time she had felt condemned, knowing that she was a sinner; but not until today did she receive Christ as her own personal Lord and Savior. Now all her fears were quieted; the heavy burden was lifted. Ada knew that her sins were taken away by the blood.

How every one of the members of the little white church rejoiced that morning when they learned of Ada's decision! Ada wondered at the joy it could bring to the whole congregation for one child to do what is right. But, most of all, Ada marveled when Sister Brunk said, " 'Likewise, I say unto you, there is joy in the presence of the angels of God over one sinner that repenteth' " (Luke 15:10).

*   *   *   *   *   *   *   *   *   *   *   *

Brother Brunk, the aged bishop, sat with bowed head. The burden was heavy. Through all his ministry he had sought to lead his people in right paths. Only by God's help had he been able to keep a spiritually minded group of people living a life of separation from the world. Always he had taught loyalty to God and His Word, His ordained ministers, and the church. That was when the church stood firmly for nonconformity to the world. But, alas, something was happening, not only in the church in general, but even in Brother Brunk's congregation. Worldliness was slowly creeping in.

Brother Brunk was sure that it was the Lord who had spoken to him, calling him to a life of separation, not only from the world, but from all those who loved worldliness, even in the church. No longer did he have the authority to use the discipline needed to keep the church pure. Brother Brunk knew that it was God who had called him to minister to the people, and to God he would someday need to give account. God very definitely led the aged bishop to break all ties with any organization that was not living according to the Scriptures.

Many thoughts troubled this saint of God as he pondered the right thing to do. "Will the people be willing to separate themselves from worldliness to follow God?" he wondered. "Will they see the necessity of breaking with an organization of people who are turning their backs on God and His plain Word? How can I do this alone?" he wondered, contemplating the cost of such a move. "I will be true to my ordination vows at any cost," he decided. And suddenly the sweet assurance that God was very near to lead and to give strength and courage flooded his troubled soul with joy. The words of God to His people of old came to his mind: "Therefore now go, lead the people unto the place of which I have spoken unto thee: behold, mine Angel shall go before thee . . ." (Exodus 32:34).

*　　*　　*　　*　　*　　*　　*　　*　　*　　*　　*　　*

Dan went to work. There were about a half dozen men in his crew. Today they would be working on the roof of a large two-story building. Dan tried the scaffold. It seemed safe. He always liked to be sure. Soon he was on the roof with several other men. A few men stayed below to help from there.

In the middle of the forenoon everything seemed to be going well. The roof was nearly covered with tar paper. After the last piece had been cut, Dan stepped off onto the scaffold again, holding his open knife. Just below him John was stooping over, gathering up scraps and tools. Somehow, before the knife was closed, Dan lost his grip on the handle. The knife flew through the air; it flipped, turning the point of the blade down and was headed directly for the back of John's neck. At the same instant John stood up. The knife missed his nose only by inches and sank into a board at his feet. John looked up.

" 'The angel of the Lord encampeth round about them that fear him,' " Dan repeated.

" 'And delivereth them,' " John finished, looking at the sharp blade buried several inches in the hard wood.

*   *   *   *   *   *   *   *   *   *   *   *

Lois cheerfully went about her duties, cleaning the kitchen, feeding the baby, and dusting the front room. She hurried a little more than usual. Her garden had done quite well. There were several more bushels of beans to pick and can.

Roy had already gone to work, leaving her and the baby alone, when Lois noticed an old man walking down the road. She looked again. It was seldom that anyone passed their house. Who could it be? He had a long white beard, shabby clothes, and carried a large pack on his back. He looked very tired. Who could it be? Lois was sure it was not any of their neighbors. Why should a traveler be walking this long, lonesome road?

Lois continued her dusting, casting anxious glances out the front window. Sure enough, he was turning into their lane. Lois could think of nothing but stories of tramps she had often heard. But no tramp had ever traveled these parts that she knew.

Lois quickly decided to lock the front door and take the baby and go into the bedroom till he left. She had no time for entertaining tramps or hucksters this morning. But, no, she could not make herself do it. His face looked kind and tired as he drew near. He knocked. Lois answered the door.

His honest brown eyes impressed her. His appearance was that of a good, kind father. "Could I get a meal here?" were his only words.

Lois remembered that she was alone and that she was busy and that this was only a passing stranger. But there seemed to be something irresistible about him. "I will prepare your breakfast. Sit here on the porch and rest till it is ready." She was always careful not to invite men into the house when Roy was not home lest she give the enemy an occasion for evil reports and thus bring reproach on her Lord. She brought him a glass of cold water, for which he was very grateful.

Quickly Lois went to the kitchen and fried the last two slices of ham and two eggs. She set out a pitcher of orange juice and bread and butter.

"Here," she said as she brought him a tray attractively prepared. "Your breakfast is ready."

"Thank you," he answered kindly. He bowed his head for several minutes before partaking of the good food. Lois busied herself about the house until he had finished.

"Thank you," he said again when he handed the tray back to her. He picked up his pack and started down the road.

Lois wondered all day about her strange visitor while she worked with the beans. "Roy," she said when he returned that evening, "I had a most unusual visitor this morning."

After she told the whole story and mentioned that none of the other neighbors had seen the man anywhere in the community, and how strangely she had felt that this man deserved a good meal, he answered, " 'Be not forgetful to entertain strangers: for thereby some have entertained angels unawares' " (Hebrews 13:2).

*   *   *   *   *   *   *   *   *   *   *   *

Vernon felt defeated, completely defeated. He felt unwanted. He was not needed. The church had no use for him. Vernon was sure that the Lord had wanted him to preach. And he wanted to preach; more than anything else, he wanted to preach. Why could the church not see that God was calling him? Why would they not ordain a man whom God had called?

Yes, Vernon had been in the lot twice. Both times he had felt very sure that God had called him. This time he would be the one. But no, each time the lot fell on someone else. Vernon became impatient. God had called him to preach. If the church would not do something about it, he would have to take the initiative and do something himself.

Vernon began conducting meetings. He began going from one member to the other, trying to get support. But he could not feel that the Lord was blessing his ministry. Finally, in desperation, Vernon committed his way unto the Lord. In humility, he asked God to show him what His will was and whether he should go on with the work. One Scripture flashed into his mind: "And the angel of the Lord said unto him, . . . behold, I went out to withstand thee, because thy way is perverse before me." Vernon felt now that he had taken the wrong way and was ready to seek help. He went to the bishop of his congregation.

"Brother, I believe I have failed. I was sure the Lord had called me to preach, but the church did not use me. Now the Lord has showed me that what I've been doing is not pleasing to Him," Vernon confessed.

"Vernon," the bishop answered, "you do still feel that the Lord has a place for you to fill in the ministry though, don't you?"

"Yes," Vernon answered humbly. "I can't get rid of that feeling. The Lord has definitely called me."

"Don't try to get rid of it," the bishop answered. "But let me ask you one more question. Did the Lord set a date when this call should come?"

"No," Vernon answered thoughtfully. "No, I hadn't thought of that."

"Just wait patiently," the bishop advised.

Vernon very humbly took his place in the church as a faithful member. He served in whatever area he was called upon to serve. Several years later God called him through the church, and he was ordained to the ministry.

Lost, Everyone to the Rescue

"Ronnie, let's go pick some more huckleberries this morning," Mama called.

"Oh, good. Will we go up to the woods?" Ronnie's eyes danced with delight.

"Yes, Ronnie." Mama beamed on the happy four-year-old boy. "Go and get your little sand bucket so I can wash it. You may put your berries in it."

Ronnie ran out and was soon back with the bucket. While Mama washed it, Ronnie went to the back door and whistled for Queenie. The little brown cocker spaniel bounded up onto the porch, jumping and wiggling. Yapping delightedly, she greeted her young master when he stepped outside. Mama followed with a large pail and the little sand bucket.

Mama and Ronnie started up the hill toward the woods. Sometimes Queenie was in the lead, sometimes following close behind. It was a happy party that reached the huckleberry patch about a half hour later.

After picking the big blue, juicy berries for a while, Ronnie set down his bucket beside Mama and ran to play with Queenie.

The boy's laughter and the puppy's barks kept the mother informed as to where they were playing.

"Ronnie, be careful when you run about. There are lots of big holes where the trees have been pushed over. This morning the holes are full of water because of all the rain we've had."

"Yes, Mama, I will be careful." Ronnie ran on, following Queenie. The beautiful, fragrant flowers were fresh after the recent rain. The woods seemed to be a happy place this beautiful morning.

The large bucket was almost full of the delicious berries when Mama suddenly noticed that everything was very quiet. The only sounds were the songs of the birds.

"Ronnie, R-o-n-n-i-e!" Mama called. Quickly she ran up several paths, calling and listening. When the child did not answer for several minutes, the worried mother became greatly alarmed. She rushed toward the edge of the woods. In the clearing, there was no sign of the boy and his dog.

Dropping to her knees by a fallen tree, she cried to God for help. "Keep my little son safe till I find him," she prayed earnestly. Then, rising to her feet, she again sought out other paths. There was no trace of footprints on any of these trails. Several times along the way she paused and breathed a hurried prayer for guidance. Convinced at last that she should call for assistance, Ronnie's mother reluctantly left the woods and hurried down across the clearing.

With many backward glances, she rushed to the nearest farmhouse.

"Please," she called to the man beside the barn. "My little boy is lost up in the woods. Would you gather a group who would help to search for him?"

While the farmer rounded up a group of men, the worried mother hurried back up to the woods, still calling, listening, and praying. Almost an hour had passed now. She began to look more carefully around the large water holes. With rising fear, she thought of the snakes and other dangers one could encounter in the woods.

The country school was dismissed. All the older children with about a dozen men were soon racing up the hill. The entire woods could be combed by noon with a group this size.

"Keep in sight of each other," the men instructed the children. "And watch out for the holes. Be careful of stepping into the dense brush because of snakes. Everyone, head straight through the woods toward the other side. Call Ronnie's name occasionally as you go."

With this advice the party started through the woods to the rescue.

"R-o-n-n-i-e! R-o-n-n-i-e," his mother called often as she walked along near the group of schoolgirls.

"Do you think he could have been kidnapped?" one of the girls spoke in low tones as they neared the opposite side.

Now a new fear clutched at her heart. "Surely no one would kidnap Ronnie." But he certainly did not seem to be in the woods.

Just then a glad cry rang out from behind the rescue party. "Ronnie is safe." Quickly everyone turned and ran toward the sound of the welcome words.

His mother was first to clasp Ronnie in her arms. "Ronnie, Ronnie," she cried, tears streaming down across her cheeks. "Where have you been?"

"Mama, don't cry," the innocent child pleaded. "I just followed Queenie. She went down to Mr. White's farm and crawled under the house. When Mrs. White saw me crawling under the house, she made me come back. Please stop crying, Mama. I could have found my way back alone. But Mrs. White wanted to come with me."

All the neighbors were touched by the scene. How glad they were that they had joined in the search, though the innocent child felt very confident! He did not know that he had been lost, nor that there was a large group of anxious searchers in the woods.

Drying her tears and setting Ronnie on the fallen log beside her, his mother again dropped to her knees, this time with thanksgiving and praise to the watchful heavenly Father.

This happened thirty years ago. Ronnie was lost for several hours among the holes and pitfalls and many other dangers of the woods. A large group of concerned people came quickly to his rescue.

Today Ronald is lost again! He is no longer an innocent child. Nevertheless he is the same Ronnie. He is lost amid much greater dangers—the snares of the devil and the pitfalls of sin. His concerned mother pleads, "Everyone to the rescue. Pray!"

Confess Your Faults

Norman kicked at the gravel as he walked shiftlessly along the road. "What's the use anyway? I've tried and *tried* and *TRIED!*"

He stooped down and picked up a smooth, flat stone. For a long time he watched as ripple after ripple, ever widening into larger circles, proceeded from the little splash the stone had made in the water before him. He threw another stone and another. The circles continued to move, always outward toward the banks. How far they reached, but only to die out in the stillness of the stream in a short while! Norman stood motionless. Would his life be like this—always reaching out and out but finally dying out without ever having reached anything?

"What's the use?" he asked again in an audible voice. His tone was so hopeless that had anyone heard the fourteen-year-old speaking he would surely have gotten the impression that the youth almost despaired of life itself. And really, he did.

Norman was raised in a good Christian home. He loved his family. There had been no tragedy or hardship to cause such despair. No. Norman's life had been rather level and easygoing; that is, until about a year ago.

At the age of twelve Norman had realized his lost condition before God. He spoke to the pastor, Brother Daniels, about his need. The young boy was pointed to Jesus, the only remedy for sin. Norman surrendered his will and received Jesus as his own personal Lord and Savior. He was very happy for a time. How bright the world had looked then. His newfound source of victory over sin brought much joy.

As the days and weeks passed, the tempter came repeatedly, placing before the young child of God the enticing allurements of the world.

Many times as Norman faced these temptations with the Word and confidence in God, his faith was strengthened by victory through Christ.

But now at last the tempter had won a victory. Norman had told a lie he just could not confess.

Norman walked back toward the gravel road and picked up several more small stones. He threw them into the still water and waited to watch the circles ripple outward.

"Why don't you just confess and find peace with God again?" the gentle Spirit pleaded.

"But it has happened so often. Soon no one will trust me at all," Norman worried. "I don't want to be like this. Why, oh, why don't I think before I talk! I have had to repent of no other sin as often as that of lying. I just can't—"

"All liars shall have their part in the lake which burneth with fire and brimstone."

Norman turned and started down the road with these words burning into his troubled mind.

"I certainly don't want to be a liar. I did not intend to tell a lie. I just answered before I thought." Norman was truly sorry that this had happened again. It seemed he was helpless to overcome this one sin.

"If we confess our sins—"

"But I've confessed so often," Norman thought, sighing heavily. "What would Brother Daniels think if I came back and told him I lied to him this morning on the way to school?" His thoughts carried him back to the troublesome incident.

"Good morning," Brother Daniels had said, pulling to a stop beside Norman. "Want a ride? I'm going past the schoolhouse."

"Sure," Norman replied. He climbed into the old black Ford, glad for this unexpected lift. He was a little late this morning and a ride would help.

"How is school?" the pastor asked.

"Going pretty good, I think," Norman replied.

"Do you like the new teacher?"

"Yes, we all like him, but he is strict."

"Yes," Brother Daniels said with a smile. "Makes you all behave, does he?"

"Sure," Norman answered. "But he is so stern about getting all our lessons done and done right, too."

"I see. So you are really learning something?"

"I guess so. I got 100 on every spelling lesson this year." Norman had been so proud of his unbroken record—until yesterday.

The car stopped. Norman hesitated. "Why did I say that?" For a moment Norman sat, contemplating telling about the broken record.

"Here we are," Brother Daniels spoke, turning to the waiting boy.

Norman lifted the latch and started to get up. He did not raise his eyes. "I must have just forgotten for an instant that I missed that one word yesterday. I did not intend to tell a lie."

Norman did not speak. He closed the door and watched Brother Daniels drive away. The bell was ringing. Norman walked across the school yard. "If I had said that yesterday it would have been true," he argued with his troubled conscience.

"But today it is not true. You misspelled one word. You no longer have an unbroken record of 100."

Norman took his seat. All day he worried and tried to find some way out. "I just can't go and tell Brother Daniels I lied."

Over and over in the past year Norman had faced other such

experiences. How he wished he could overcome this one fault that caused him much trouble!

As Norman walked on down the gravel road, he finally reached a decision. Though the struggle was a hard one, he was determined that this thing should not rob him of his peace with God.

"I will go and tell Brother Daniels just how it is. Maybe he can help me somehow to find victory over this thing." Having made up his mind, Norman hurried his steps toward the pastor's home.

"Brother Daniels, may I speak to you alone?" Norman asked when the door was opened.

"Surely." The pastor stepped out onto the porch. "Let's walk down along the river," he suggested. "There we can have a good talk." Together they walked along in silence for a while.

Finally Norman began. "Brother Daniels, I lied to you this morning about my spelling grades." He went on to explain how he had made the statement about having an unbroken record of 100 until yesterday when he missed one word. "I really did not intend to tell you a lie. But after I had said it, I did not have the courage to change it then." Norman went on to confess that this thing of speaking untruthfully had been a constant problem to him.

Brother Daniels remained silent for a while. "Norman," he said, "to overcome this fault that you find yourself so often guilty of, you must understand the seriousness of it. 'Lying lips are abomination to the Lord.' "

"Yes, I know," Norman cried, "but how can I stop saying things before I think? I don't want to tell a lie, or plan to tell a lie. But before I think, I have said something that is not true."

"Norman, do you really want to have victory over this?" Brother Daniels asked earnestly.

"Yes, I do," the boy replied sincerely.

"Enough so that you would be willing to confess this fault?"

"Why, of course, Brother Daniels. I have over and over had to go to a number of different people and make confessions for untruths I have told."

"Norman, first of all I believe you need to make this problem a definite matter of prayer. Seek God's help, knowing that in your own strength you cannot face the enemy of the soul. Then I believe it would help you to confess to our congregation what you have just confessed to me." Brother Daniels watched Norman's expression change at this last suggestion.

"O Brother Daniels, I can't do that. Do I really need to do that? After all, I've confessed each lie to the person it was told to. Must I also confess publicly?" Norman was really perplexed. How he wanted to do what was right, but why should this be necessary?

"Norman, you do not have to do what I suggested," the pastor replied. "Sometimes, yes, real often, this is a sure way to defeat Satan in our lives. He has had the victory. You cannot overcome this one fault. Would you not be willing to put forth this much effort to defeat his purpose in your life?"

Norman heaved a deep sigh. He was not ready to answer. Why should he have to do this?

"Confess your faults one to another, and pray one for another," Brother Daniels quoted.

As Norman walked on home alone, his heart was lighter; the guilt was gone. Yet there was a struggle. "Why should Brother Daniels suggest such a thing? Why should I confess publicly? What will people think?"

Suddenly Norman began to realize that all his thoughts were concerned with what people will think. "What will God think?" he asked himself seriously. "In His Word He has said, 'Confess your faults.'"

"O Father," Norman prayed that night before going to bed,

"I really do want to have victory over all sin. Do help me to watch my words more carefully. And give me courage and an opportunity, and I will confess this fault to the church."

Norman went to bed assured of God's help and blessing in his life.

The opportunity came the next evening at prayer meeting. Norman heard the Spirit's voice and promptly obeyed. Following his confession, there were others who confessed their besetting sins.

This experience was a real milestone in Norman's young life. With renewed courage and a stronger determination to watch his words, Norman found that a memory of this night often helped him to overcome the habit of untruthfulness he had formed in youth.

Yes, the tempter still came; but, having submitted his will to God, Norman found that there was strength to overcome. There was victory through Jesus!

Time to Unravel Them All

It was a pleasantly warm evening. The usual group attending the little mountain mission had been growing until the building was at last filled to capacity. Now, this last Sunday evening had brought out a record crowd. Never had the small sanctuary boasted this large a congregation. The audience joined in singing; the house filled with the melody of well-loved hymns.

Esther, sitting near the front, could scarcely keep her mind on the message as Brother Sheldon endeavored to bring to all a clear picture of the price paid for our salvation. Try as she would to follow the message, her mind wandered constantly to the blond, curly-haired girl, surrounded by her friends, who she knew would be watching her from the back of the church.

Theda never sat alone, nor lacked companions. Her popularity not only reached the entire valley, but also penetrated neighboring communities. Wherever youth gathered, Theda could be found in the center, her rippling laughter and gay witticisms could be heard above all. She constantly had the attention of most of the young men, much to the displeasure of some of her closest friends; but, to remain in the group, one must be a friend of Theda Lambert.

Theda also had a hard time keeping up with the evangelist. How could one so young, so beautiful, so anxious to tell her friends about the party planned for next Saturday night keep her mind on the message of a country preacher with a bothersome southern drawl? Now she was having a good time and was so engulfed in it that the needs of her soul were easily pushed into the future. Yes, Theda was a Christian—at least a church member. What else mattered?

To Esther it was a more serious matter. "O God," she prayed, "Help me to understand Thy will for my life. Lead me to a closer walk with Thee. Lord, I pray, cleanse my heart of envy and jealousy."

Again, Brother Sheldon's voice was pleading with each soul to accept the love of One who paid a very great price for our redemption, to have assurance of His daily presence and a glorious future with God, rather than to enjoy the pleasures of sin for a season.

After the benediction, Esther, longing for the companionship of which she knew so little, joined the group of youth on the lawn. Immediately she realized that she was an unwelcome intruder. Quietly, with bitter feelings, she slipped away.

"Why, oh, why can't I be a part of the group?" she lamented. "Why am I always alone while the others walk smartly to the luxurious autos of handsome young men? Does it pay?" These thoughts troubled Esther as she slowly made her way to the family car.

Esther knew she could be one of the group. She, too, could be invited to the parties by making only a few small changes—or were they small? She could break down all the convictions she had through the instruction of her parents and pastor. She could be young and gay, closing her mind to spiritual matters, putting them into the future just as the others were doing. Of course, they all planned to act like Christians as soon as they settled down to family life.

Theda, in her charming way, went on telling the group around her of the grand party she was planning for the coming Saturday night. She scarcely noticed Esther's quick departure.

Esther's name was mentioned by a few in the group. But then came the inevitable decision: Esther would never enjoy this party. Little did they realize how Esther's heart ached for their friendship, nor that at the present moment she was pouring out her troubles to a sympathetic listener, who, sensing her disappointment at not being accepted in the group, had followed her to the car and tried in the best way she could to comfort her.

Esther did appreciate very much the interest and concern shown her by her friend, Alice. Alice was neither her age nor a very close acquaintance. Still, it was better than being alone.

"But, Alice," she said after some time, "I can't see that it pays. What do I have? The others are all having fun." The usually sunny Esther looked like a storm cloud about to burst. After much encouragement to remain faithful to God, Alice left a slightly comforted Esther to consider the gain or loss alone. She had assured her that she would be happier in the end, though Theda now appeared happier. The past—Theda moving in and stealing her friends, one by one; the present—Brother Sheldon's message, God's love; the future—here Esther stopped; she would remain faithful! She committed the future into the hands of God.

For Theda, Saturday night passed glamorously, delightfully. More Saturday nights were spent in hilarity and fun. Fewer Sunday mornings found Theda in church. Ocassionally on a Sunday morning she could be found in church on the back seat, whispering, giggling, and looking very smart in her new gray suit, with cheeks unusually red and lips crimson. Bob, proud of the race he had won, would be at her side.

Wishing to impress the other girls, Theda told them of her engagement to Bob, the most handsome, most popular young man in the group.

"I know," she said, "he has a few bad habits and rarely attends church services, but after we are married it will be different. We plan to have a happy Christian home."

"But, Theda," exclaimed one of the young girls, horrified, "Bob drinks, doesn't he?"

"Yes," Theda had to admit, "just a little." She defended, "But he never gets drunk."

Alice, passing by at that moment, was shocked to hear Theda speaking that lightly of a very serious matter. A drinking husband—a Christian home—a happy family? To Alice it was poor reasoning, utter blindness! "At the first opportunity," she resolved, "I must speak to Theda of the danger in which she is involving herself."

Very soon the opportunity arrived. Theda became enraged and asked Alice kindly to mind her own affairs.

"But, Theda," Alice pleaded, "some day the threads you are weaving now will be the design of your life."

Sharply on the defensive, Theda retorted angrily, "What difference is it to you how many threads I twist and tangle and knot; when I'm old I'll have plenty of time to sit down and untangle them all." With a light, "I'll have my fun while I'm young," she walked away, completely ignoring her friend.

Alice and Esther, with many other Christian friends, constantly remembered Theda in prayer, burdened about her indifference to the Word of God.

Time went on—Theda was happy, very happy. She was going to be married. She and Bob had chosen the house they would buy. Their car was paid for. They could easily make the payments on their house with the income Bob was earning; then, too, she would continue with her job until they could buy some of the extras they wanted.

At last, the great day came, clear and beautiful! The young bride was living in the clouds. The mountains were aglow with gold and crimson. At eight o'clock that evening Theda and Bob were pronounced husband and wife.

* * * * * * * * * * * *

Two months passed. Bob and Theda had not been seen in church, but there was no time for that—now there was a hard struggle to meet payments.

Bob began coming home later each week. Theda scolded. She never knew when to have supper. No longer was it a pleasure to cook for Bob. He did not seem to be enjoying the meals anymore. Theda became careless about cooking supper. There were times when Bob was forced to prepare something for himself, which was very provoking after a hard day's work.

Theda argued, "After all, haven't I worked all day, too?"

Bob began eating before coming home, occasionally coming in very late. These nights Theda retired alone. She realized that Bob was beginning to drink more. Before long, he was coming home dead drunk.

Never before in her life had Theda been treated cruelly. Now, as a result of Bob's fits of temper, she was often left with bruises. After one such experience, Theda remembered Alice's advice to be careful. She remembered Esther who would never have a "good time," and who was seldom asked for a date. Even now, Esther was cheerfully serving the Lord without a life companion. How Theda wished she were free once more!

"O God," she travailed in anguish as she fell on her knees, "must I pay a lifetime for my foolish blindness?"

Very early on a midwinter morning, Alice was alarmed when she received a call to come immediately to 704 25th Street. She knew at once that it was Theda speaking. But what had caused the distressed call?

Alice left as soon as possible. As she neared the house she listened. Great racking sobs could be heard within. She knocked, trembling. Slowly she pushed open the door and entered. The odor that greeted her was equal to that of a tavern. Bob lay sprawled on the floor, a pitiful sight.

On the drive back to the valley, Theda told the whole story of her lonely and fearful nights in the recent past. "What can I do now," she begged of Alice, "after finding myself in these dreadful circumstances as a result of my life of sin and pleasure, my lack of consecration and faith?"

Alice, heavy-hearted, could find no answer.

Theda, fearful that Bob would carry out his threat to take her life, successfully concealed where she was staying for a few days. Her parents had welcomed her into their home. But now her mother was fearful for the safety of the entire family if Bob should find out that Theda was there.

Her short-lived security and ease came abruptly to an end on Friday night when Bob made his appearance. He demanded that Theda return home at once.

A week passed. All her friends, wondering how Theda was getting along, were praying much both for her and for Bob.

Late one afternoon, Alice received another call. "Alice," begged Theda, "please send a message to my father to come for me immediately." Theda was found in critical condition, in need of medical and spiritual help.

She was with her parents only a few days when Bob came again, begging her to come home. Once again he promised to live a better life.

In a few weeks, the news spread over the valley that Bob and Theda had a third member in their family.

Little Bobbie, who was to have a Christian home, was now suffering at the hands of a cruel, drunken father. Theda's heart was broken.

*   *   *   *   *   *   *   *   *   *   *   *

Two years had come and gone since the revival held by

Brother Sheldon. Again, the mountain mission was filled to overflowing. Esther, bright and happy, was in her place in the front of the church where she was singing the old-fashioned, soul-inspiring hymns. Her heart was at peace with God.

After dismissal, Alice, seeing Esther's radiant smile, asked her if she remembered her struggle of two years before.

"Yes," replied Esther humbly.

"Did it pay to serve Jesus?"

With tears in her eyes, Esther answered, "Never again will I even compare the pleasures of sin with the sweet fellowship that is mine in Christ Jesus."

Publisher's note:

We are grateful that Esther received the help that she needed regarding her social relationships. However, we regret that there were apparently many spiritual needs that the church seemingly sadly neglected.

The Winds Obey My Will

The leaves had already fallen. The trees stood bleak and bare against the blue October sky. The rains had been few in the past month. Even the grass was dry and brown. The strong south wind began to blow in hot gusts against the backs of the neat rows of houses along Oakland Road.

Most of the men had gone to work by the time the sun came out brightly enough to drive the women in from their work in the gardens and yards. The houses were close enough together to encourage neighborly chatting, but this morning when the hot wind began to blow, most of the women on Oakland Road preferred the indoors. A few of the women also had gone to work, leaving their children in the care of one of the teen-age neighbor girls.

Debby did not want to go out and play this morning, but begged Lucy for a story after her mother went to work. Lucy laid aside her dusting rag and went to entertain the child. After all, that was what she had been hired for. It was very warm inside. Lucy took Debby out on the back porch.

The next house was quiet. The heat seemed to have stilled the whole neighborhood.

In a house farther down Oakland Road Grandmother Miller sat drowsily in front of her quilt. She would stitch awhile; then her head would begin to nod. "What an unusually warm day!" she exclaimed to her daughter.

"Yes, Mother," Anna answered as she went outside to feed

the chickens. But very soon she rushed back inside. "Mother, I thought I smelled smoke as I crossed the back porch. There is nothing burning in here, is there?" Anna checked all the burners on the kitchen stove before going outside again. Assured that all was safe, she went about her chores, leaving her aged mother alone in the house. Grandfather was working out in the shop.

Just as Anna came around the corner of the chicken house, she again had a strong sensation of something burning. Looking up, she saw her father in the doorway of the shop, sniffing the air. "Do I smell smoke?" he asked anxiously.

"I keep thinking I smell smoke also," Anna replied. "You haven't burned anything this morning, have you?"

"No, I certainly haven't. Not in this kind of weather!" he exclaimed. "And I surely hope all the neighbors will be careful with fires. If this large woods behind us caught fire on a day like this, I'm afraid not a house on Oakland Road could be saved. With that strong wind coming right across that woods and all our houses so close—no, I'm afraid we wouldn't have a chance."

Lucy had told the restless little Debby only a few stories when she stopped and asked, "Debby, do you smell smoke? It seems there is smoke in the air!" Lucy began to look around. Now the back door opened at the next house.

"You're not burning trash over there, are you, Lucy?" her neighbor called.

"No," Lucy called back, "but I certainly thought I smelled smoke. . . . " One by one the neighbors began to appear in their doorways. Alarm began to spread all up and down Oakland Road as everyone began to realize that there was no doubt—the woods were on fire! There were no telephones. The nearest fire station was miles away. There was not a man at home on Oakland Road with the exception of Grandpa Miller, who was about eighty years old. What could be done? Little groups began to form in the backyards and along the roadside. The smoke began to circle high above the trees, coming down in great dark puffs on the little white houses.

A car was coming down Oakland Road. Someone stopped it and quickly showed their neighbor from the next road the trouble they were in. Quickly the man went for help. In a short time cars and men from miles around began pouring in Oakland Road. Before they arrived, the women had begun pumping water and had rows of buckets waiting, which the men eagerly grabbed and then rushed into the woods. They all worked frantically for an hour. It seemed no progress was made. The fire came dashing toward them with fierce gales of wind constantly forcing the men to back up. Closer and closer it came. The fire was getting hotter. The whole woods seemed a raging inferno. The women could no longer pump water fast enough. They were losing. Soon they would have to flee for their lives. The courageous fire fighting went on, the laborers knowing that soon they would be forced to give up.

It was getting so hot up by the pumps in the backyards that the women were starting to leave their posts and flee with the children. At last the fire trucks came! The exhausted men dropped back to let the fresh firemen take over. With better equipment and a good supply of water, everyone hoped the dreadful ordeal would soon be over. But it could soon be seen that the fire was leaping straight toward Oakland Road. The walls of the vacated houses were too hot to touch. Surely they would soon go up in flames. Children screamed as the frightened women rushed away from the hottest section with them. The flames were now leaping twice as high as the trees. The sky was black with smoke. The wind continued to blow with intent purpose, straight toward the neat little white houses on Oakland Road.

The Miller home was at the west end of Oakland Road farther from the fire. A large group gathered there to watch with the aged Millers.

"Sisters," Grandmother said calmly, "let's kneel for prayer. God still rules the wind." Every woman and child humbly knelt at Grandmother's suggestion; some with confidence and trust, submitting to God's will, and others trembling in fear and dread of what was taking place outside.

*   *   *   *   *   *   *   *   *   *   *   *

The firemen soon saw that they were fighting a losing battle and were about to retreat, with scorched faces, singed hair, and lungs burning with the awful smoke, when suddenly a blast of wind from the north turned the wildly leaping flames directly back over the burned trees and brush still blazing in the awful heat. The firemen watched astounded. Never before had they seen anything happen this suddenly. They dropped their fire fighting equipment. The Oakland homes were out of danger. The flames swept back across the ashes, gradually dying out.

Not a home on Oakland Road was damaged. God had changed the wind just in time.

Grandmother's prayer was answered and the people of Oakland Road knew that the winds still know the voice of Him who ruled them centuries ago.

"God Is Our Refuge"

"Oh, where are kings and empires now
    Of old that went and came?
But, Lord, Thy Church is praying yet,
    A thousand years the same.

We mark her goodly battlements,
    And her foundations strong;
We hear within the solemn voice
    Of her unending song.

For not like kingdoms of the world
    Thy holy Church, O God!
Though earthquake shocks are threat'ning her,
    And tempests are abroad."

The small congregation of Cedar Grove sang the words with heartfelt meaning. Reverently they had gathered to worship the Lord that morning. The earthquake shocks of World War I were, in reality, threatening their little flock. Looking to God, they remained firm and strong. Their joy was full: God was their refuge and strength. They had found in Him a very present help in trouble.

"Unshaken as eternal hills,
    Immovable she stands,
A mountain that shall fill the earth,
    A house not made by hands."

Orie, the song leader, walked to his seat. The congregation sat silently waiting till he was seated. Brother Martin, the superintendent, arose. "We greet you in Jesus' Name," he began, "the Name of the One who is closer to us all than a brother." After Brother Martin read a short passage of Scripture, the congregation knelt for prayer. Brother Martin's deep voice brought their earnest petitions to God. "We pray especially that Thou be near our young men who are suffering for Christ's sake. Just give them courage to remain firm and true to Thee, O God. May not one of our number give up or become discouraged by these cruel mockings or imprisonments. Strengthen us. For Jesus' sake. Amen."

The Sunday school classes took their places, and were followed by an inspirational message from the Word of God. After services were dismissed, there was very little of the light or frivolous talk that is very often heard in God's house. Soberly the sisters greeted one another, extending sympathy to those whose husbands were not able to be present. Only about half of the men in the congregation were in church this morning. The others were being held in jail for the stand they had taken as conscientious objectors. These were the days before any provision was made for exemption from war for religious beliefs.

The brethren, too, greeted each other warmly with the kiss of charity, encouraging one another to hold fast, remaining firm and true to the end.

The minister, Brother Hershberger, was not present. To the crowd gathered around her, his young wife told about the evening he was taken. An angry mob had gathered outside their house, shouting insulting and cruel remarks. He and his wife had stayed inside. Soon everything grew quiet. There was a knock at the door. John and Mary were on their knees beside the bed at the time. He arose. "Mary," he spoke softly, "I'll have to go."

"O John, must you answer the door?" she begged, tears

coming to her eyes. "Maybe they would think we aren't at home," she added hopefully.

"No, Mary. I must go to the door. The car is in the driveway. They would know we are here—and I believe I should answer a knock on our door anyway."

Mary arose from her knees and started to follow her husband. "No, no," he said, "you stay here." John walked through the bedroom door. The pounding on the door was louder and the voices more impatient.

Mary dropped on her knees. "O God, spare my husband," she cried. Many of their friends had already been in prison for six months. They had suffered greatly and were put through severe tests in an endeavor to cause them to give up their faith.

Many of the brethren had endured physical torture. A few had even been put to death, "not accepting deliverance; that they might obtain a better resurrection." Mary's thoughts were in a turmoil as she heard the front door open, her husband's calm voice, and the harsh voices of the angry men outside. Soon the door closed. She listened for his step. The house was quiet. Where was he? Had he gone outside?

"O my Father," she cried, "spare my husband, if it be Thy will."

All remained quiet for some time. Mary arose, trembling. What had happened? She walked out into the living room. No one was there. No one was outside. Two cars were leaving. Mary turned and ran to the back door. She opened the door and called, "John, John!" She went outside and walked around the house and entered the open front door. Inside, she again dropped on her knees. John was gone.

A number of the brethren and sisters were wiping tears from their eyes when Mary finished. Offering their prayer support, the little group comforted Mary concerning her husband. God had always delivered His own—if not from death, then by a more glorious deliverance through death. Mary committed all into His hands.

"God's will be done," the aged bishop, Brother Mast, exhorted them. "Let us all be true witnesses for Him in these trying times so that our lives might honor and glorify His Name."

"I saw a group going up toward your house last evening," one brother remarked. "Did they come in and speak to you?"

"Indeed they did," the bishop replied. "They came up to the door and shouted for me to come outside. When I opened the door several men grabbed me and stripped me of my clothes. Others were waiting with buckets of tar which they dashed on me from the top of my head to my feet. I could hardly breathe." Men and women listened, wondering where all this would lead to. Things seemed to be getting worse. Their neighbors began to hate all conscientious objectors.

Brother Mast went on. "After this, bags of feathers were thrown on me which clung to the sticky tar. Then, laughing boisterously, the men left. I never would have been able to get rid of the tar if my wife had not gotten a nice tub of warm water ready and helped me to clean it off. I believe I would have died. The stuff almost suffocated me." The aged bishop, calm and serene, encouraged the others to remain true, whatever the cost. "If we fail to be true to God, we all know that we will lose our souls. If we are firm and true, we cannot lose more than our lives, and that would only mean reaching our eternal reward sooner. Take courage, brethren. 'God is our refuge and strength'!"

During the weeks that followed, several families moved to Canada. Others were looking at farms in other states where the persecution was not so great. Orie, with his widowed mother and two sisters, remained in Cedar Grove. Not often was Orie heard to speak, but his testimony in the community was one which could not be spoken against. He was often used as song leader of the Cedar Grove Mennonite Church. At the beginning of the war,

Orie had been too young to be drafted. Now the war lasted so long that Orie was sure to be called. His mother worried. Orie had always shown a fine Christian spirit, but he was so young. One day the call came. It was sewing circle day. As the sisters gathered with heavy hearts, the sewing was laid aside and the meeting was changed to a prayer meeting. Many more men were being drafted, and many were still in prison. Today Orie's mother was not present. She had sent word that Orie had been called for induction in the army. Special prayer was offered for the faithful young man.

Orie said "good-bye" to his mother and started out, not knowing what the day would bring forth. He knew that God was his refuge, and was content. " 'I will not fear what man shall do unto me,' " he quoted calmly before kissing his mother good-bye that morning.

Soon word reached the Cedar Grove people that Orie, too, was behind prison bars for his faith that was it was wrong to fight and kill. Seeing the things the others had endured did not hinder him. Orie would not turn back on God. For weeks he had nothing to eat but dry bread and water. There was no bed in his cell—only hard, cold cement. His health began to fail. Still Orie remained true to God. His trials were cruel. The days and nights were long, but by the grace of God, Orie remained cheerful. Many of the prisoners and guards often stopped to listen as hymns of praise came from the small cell where Orie spent several months.

Homes in the Mennonite community were splashed with yellow paint. Horses were stolen and their farm implements damaged. The neighbors would know whether these queer notions were convictions or merely an easy way out of the war. Their boys had to go—many never returned! Why should some people be exempt from helping to protect the country in which they lived? Many who had been good neighbors turned enemies of the Cedar Grove people. At last the war ended. The prisoners were released. Cedar Grove again began to grow.

God had never forsaken those who had been faithful to Him. He "is our refuge and strength, a very present help in trouble."

Great Things

At ten-thirty on Sunday morning, Esther climbed the stairs to her small classroom in the corner of the balcony. The girls were all there, ten of them. She casually noticed that Doris and Rosie were not sitting together. Doris had taken the back bench. This was unusual but Esther attached little significance to it.

"Let's bow our heads while Doris leads us in prayer," she opened the Sunday school hour.

After a brief hesitation, Doris led in a short prayer.

"We have a very interesting and practical lesson today," Esther began. "Someone tell us, without opening your quarterly, what the lesson is about."

"It's something about the Christian experience," one of the teen-age girls answered. "I don't remember the title."

" 'My Duty to My Brother,' " another girl added.

"Yes," their teacher continued. "I think, without doing injustice, we could title it 'My Duty to My Sister' in our class."

"Rosie, will you read the first verse, starting with Matthew 18:15 on through the verses in Matthew 5. You may each read a verse around the class. Then we will pause before reading the verses in Luke, for your thoughts and questions."

These Scriptures were read. Then all was quiet. Esther tried in vain to get a discussion started. She received almost no response from the girls.

Her two best talkers remained silent. Several others answered

216

some questions in a few words. Rosie and Doris said nothing, but sat without lifting their eyes.

Esther discussed this portion of Scripture and went on to the next, trying to bring in many practical applications.

While Esther went on through the lesson this morning, she sensed a strange tenseness among the girls. She silently prayed for wisdom in the words she spoke.

Esther dismissed the class a little early. It had been unusually hard to teach today.

After the morning message Esther chatted awhile with the girls before going home.

When Esther arrived at home, thinking on the morning lesson and how unusually quiet the girls had been, she suddenly remembered that neither Doris nor Rosie had spoken to her after the service. These two girls, usually the friendliest and most talkative in her class, had slipped out unnoticed.

*   *   *   *   *   *   *   *   *   *   *   *

After dismissal, Rosie hurried out to the car. She was very unhappy. This morning's lesson had made her even more miserable than when she had studied it alone Saturday evening. Then it had seemed easier to apply it to another, today it seemed every verse applied to herself.

"I'm not at fault," she reasoned. "So it's not up to me to make the first move to be reconciled." But her conscience was not that easily quieted. "Doris and I have always been good friends as long as I can remember. I've never wronged her, more than a few childish quarrels we used to have. I've always thought Doris was a friend I could trust—till she told that lie about me last week. I can't imagine why she would say such a thing. Well, before we're ever friends again, she'll have to confess that she wronged me!"

217

"Rosie, if ye forgive your brother . . . ," her conscience warned.

"I'll gladly forgive her, if she asks for forgiveness," Rosie argued.

"You could make it easier for her to confess if you still showed a loving attitude toward her. You must love her in spite of her faults."

"Well, I don't hate her! I'm not the guilty one; it's Doris!" Rosie defended herself. "She is acting hateful—as if I had wronged her. She doesn't show any sign of being sorry."

"But it is your attitude that you need to be careful of," the Spirit continued to reprove the offended girl.

Rosie was wiping tears when her parents came to the car.

Mother looked anxiously into her troubled face, but asked no questions.

"Doris won't even speak to me!" Rosie exclaimed accusingly.

"Did you speak to her?" Mother asked quietly. "You came outside so fast, I wonder if anyone had a chance to speak to you."

*   *   *   *   *   *   *   *   *   *   *   *

Doris paused only a minute after the benediction, then hurriedly slipped out the side door and started walking home. Tears streaked her face as she walked slowly down the dusty lane, alone.

"Oh," she almost groaned. "I never thought it would come to this."

Glancing back toward the church, Doris hoped to see Rosie following her—but no, she must walk alone. "I can't blame her. It is all my fault," Doris accused herself. "Oh, if only I had thought before I spoke! Poor, dear, sweet Rosie. How can I ever make it right. I never intended to lie about her."

"But you did! Now you must confess it."

"But I really didn't mean to do her any harm. I never expected it to turn out the way it did. Who would have thought all the girls would hear it so soon, and believe it? I know it is awful! But I don't know what to do. She wouldn't understand if I tried to explain." Doris was weeping bitterly now.

"Confess your sin. Confess that you lied," the Spirit urged.

"I could, if only she wouldn't have given me such a cold shoulder. But really, she makes it quite impossible. Oh, I wish she would have walked home with me today!"

"You really didn't want her to or you would have asked her."

"Well, I don't usually ask her. She always walks when it is nice weather."

"But you could have spoken to her today and invited her to walk with you. She probably feels you wouldn't want her after what you said about her."

"I couldn't! She left too soon!" Doris argued with her guilty conscience.

All afternoon she worried and grieved over her sin, but was not willing to face her responsibility and confess it.

"If only Rosie would act like her old self, I could confess it and we would be friends again. But she makes it impossible to talk to her about it."

*   *   *   *   *   *   *   *   *   *   *   *

On Sunday afternoon, Esther often visited her Sunday school girls. Today, before starting out, she prayed earnestly for two girls who she felt were surely facing some difficulty. She knew nothing of what the difficulty was, nor would she have guessed the bitter feelings between the girls she thought were close friends. She had not exactly planned to visit either Doris or Rosie today, but now she felt led to go in that direction.

Doris was not especially surprised to see her Sunday school

teacher walking up the lane, nor was she as pleased as usual to see her.

"I guess she has heard. Oh, what a lot of trouble I've gotten into just because of a few little words! I'd give anything to take them back now."

Doris was rather nervous as she went out to meet Esther.

"Let's go for a walk," Esther suggested after several unsuccessful attempts to start a conversation.

Doris surely was not acting normal.

"This is a lovely day for walking," Doris stated without much enthusiasm.

"Yes," Esther agreed, "I almost envied you and Rosie walking down this lovely lane together at noon today while I had to go the other direction. I supposed the anticipation of this pleasant stroll together was your reason for leaving so soon," replied the unsuspecting teacher. "I was sorry I didn't get to talk to you girls."

"Yes, it was a pleasant walk." Doris exclaimed quickly, relieved that Esther had not said what she feared she was going to.

Immediately after she had spoken, Doris realized she had told another lie. "I mean—," she gasped. "I mean it's a nice place to walk. But Rosie didn't walk today, you see," Doris stammered.

"Oh, I thought she left with you, as usual. I hadn't noticed."

"You hadn't noticed what?" Doris asked nervously.

When Esther looked steadily into her eyes, she turned her head.

"That you didn't walk together," Esther answered.

"Oh?" Doris stopped, looking into Esther's face.

Her conscience was speaking so plainly that she felt sure her teacher must know.

"Esther, I'm so sorry. I'm so sorry! I'd give anything now to take it back. I really didn't mean to do her any harm." Doris was weeping.

Gently Esther pulled her down beside her on a log by the road. She was bewildered. "I don't understand, Doris."

"O Esther. Rosie always has been my best friend, especially since we became Christians two years ago. When I lied about her last week, I never dreamed it would have the effect it did. I'd give anything now to take back what I said," Doris sobbed. "She hates me. I know it is my fault. But—oh, if only we could be friends again!"

"Doris, I know nothing about this," Esther said slowly, touched by the girl's evident grief. "You don't need to tell me what you said about Rosie; but if you have wronged her, I am sure you know what you need to do about it."

Esther paused.

Doris, again bursting out in sobs, cried, "I know, Esther, and I wanted to ask her to forgive me this morning. But she wouldn't give me a chance."

After talking and praying with the burdened girl for some time, Esther left. Doris knew what she would have to do, and only she could do it.

The sun was still high in the west as Esther walked out the lane, alone. When she came to the fork, she decided to walk on up and see Rosie awhile.

How her heart ached for the two girls! How their young lives had been marred by this unpleasant experience! "Only the Lord Jesus can bring about a reconciliation between them," she mused, and breathed a prayer that He would continue to work with them.

Rosie was sitting in the hammock out under the maples in the backyard. She did not see Esther coming until she spoke.

"This looks like a lovely place to spend a quiet afternoon," she greeted her.

"Yes," Rosie jumped. "You surprised me. I hadn't seen you coming up the lane."

"May I join you?" Esther asked, walking toward the hammock.

"Sure may, and welcome." Rosie slipped over to make room. She laid her Bible and quarterly up at the end.

After chatting pleasantly for a while, Esther rose to leave. "Will you walk a little way?" she invited.

Rosie looked perplexedly, "Oh, no," she answered confusedly. "I didn't, because—well, because it's up to her to take the first . . ."

"I asked, 'Will you walk along part way,' " Esther clarified her invitation, feeling sure the girl had misunderstood.

"Oh, sure," Rosie answered, very much embarrassed at her blunder. "I thought . . . ," she was getting in deeper all the time. "I thought you asked why I hadn't walked with Doris this morning." Rosie was blushing deeply now. "Really, Esther, I am not at fault."

When Esther made no comment, Rosie went on, "I wasn't going to say anything; but since I've said this much, I'd better explain. I don't know if you have heard the lie Doris told about me or not. If not, you must be the only one who hasn't."

Esther was shaking her head. "No, I haven't heard anything about you that I think you would not want to hear, so I'd rather not hear it. And maybe it's not as bad as you think."

"But, Esther, don't you think she should confess that before I'm obligated to act as though our friendship is the same?"

"It surely is too bad that you missed that lovely walk together," Esther said, evading her question.

"But she rushed off without speaking to me," Rosie defended herself, "as if I had wronged her. She is at fault!"

"Couldn't you have made a special effort to speak to her and walk with her to prove you still love her?"

"But, Esther, she hurried off; she didn't want me to walk with her."

"Are you sure?" Esther cautioned. "Maybe she was longing to walk with you."

Rosie gasped, startled. "Esther, she has been treating me hatefully . . . won't even look at me."

"Maybe she is ashamed."

"She doesn't act like it. She could come over and talk to me if she wants to be friends. She doesn't!"

"Are you sure? Possibly she's longing to renew your friendship and doesn't have the courage to face you because she knows she has wronged you and hurt you deeply."

"But, Esther, I haven't wronged her. Must I go to her? It seems to me it is her responsibility to ask my forgiveness."

"Yes, Rosie, she needs to confess her sin; but maybe you could make it much easier for her to do that if you showed her you still love her in spite of what she did."

Rosie sobbed. That was just what she knew she ought to do.

"Esther," she said, trembling, a faint smile playing at her lips, "I believe I haven't seen my responsibility or my fault for trying to see hers."

For the second time that afternoon, Esther stopped by the roadside to pray with one of her dear girls.

"Rosie," she said as they parted at the fork in the road. "I'll be praying for you."

"Thank you, Esther, and thanks for helping me to see my problem."

Rosie started up the dusty lane from which Esther had come an hour ago.

Doris thought she saw somone approaching from way up the lane. She was not quite sure who it was. She hoped and prayed.

*   *   *   *   *   *   *   *   *   *   *   *

At twenty minutes past seven, Esther glanced out the window

of the church to see the folk gathering in. It was a very pleasant evening. She looked up the dusty lane and saw a beautiful sight: Doris and Rosie had just rounded the curve, coming toward the church, with their arms lovingly entwined around each other.

" 'The Lord hath done great things for us; whereof we are glad,' " she breathed silently.

Prayer Changes Things

Linda had been working all evening on the new blue dress. This was the first one she had made by herself.

Mother sat sad and silent in her rocker. She offered to help with the handwork when Linda had become very frustrated an hour ago, but Linda only answered, "No, I cut and sewed it all alone and I want to do the handwork alone, also."

Mother then walked over near the window where Linda sat stitching and grumbling. "This is the hardest stuff to sew," she complained.

"Linda, I wish you would have chosen something more practical. I am afraid this material will not wear well. I'm sure this was more expensive than lots of other materials which would have worn much longer. You know we cannot afford things we don't need. This is much harder to sew, too, than some of the more practical materials would be."

"O Mother, I know all that," Linda replied. "But I want one good, nice-looking dress. The other girls all have more expensive-looking clothes than I have. I want to look as nice and attractive as the other girls. You don't seem to care how I appear," she finished accusingly.

"Yes, Linda," Mother sounded hurt, "I care very much how you appear. 'But let it be the hidden man of the heart, in that which is not corruptible, even the ornament of a meek and quiet spirit, which is in the sight of God of great price.' " Mother softly quoted these searching words from 1 Peter. "We don't need expensive clothing to appear our best in God's sight. And what else matters as much as what God thinks? Who else is it on whom you are so concerned about making a good impression?"

"But, Mother, I know that matters most! But, why must I appear more poorly dressed than anyone else at church?"

"You don't necessarily need to," her mother assured the young girl. "But neither do you need to have such expensive clothes to make a better impression. In God's sight a meek and quiet spirit is of great price; and when you are clothed with these, then at least in God's sight you are well pleasing. Without the meek and quiet spirit, neither God nor God's children can appreciate you as much, though you wear the most expensive clothing. 'In like manner also, that women adorn themselves in modest apparel with shamefacedness and sobriety; not with broided hair, or gold, or pearls, or costly array; But (which becometh women professing godliness) with good works.' This is why I think we should be more concerned about pleasing God than men. God has plainly told us what is pleasing to Him. And one of the things that is displeasing to Him is wearing expensive clothing. So when we choose our materials we need to be very careful to choose the ones that are practical and worth their price rather than those that look the nicest and may soon wear out."

"But, Mother, this was such a pretty blue. It is just the shade I look good in." Then Linda held up a tiny strand of delicate white lace about two feet long. "I bought this to put around the neckline and sleeves," she stated simply, without looking up.

"Linda, you have never worn a dress with lace on it. I do not want you to sew that lace on your dress." Mother spoke these words firmly, looking straight at Linda.

Now Linda looked up. "Why not, Mother? All the other girls are wearing lace since the Wood family came here, and all their girls wear lace. Well, most of the other girls, at least."

"Linda, it makes no difference how many other girls are wearing lace. I do not want you to start wearing it, because our church standard says we should not wear lace; and above that, the Bible teaches us that we should not wear worldly and unnecessary adorning and that we shall not spend our money for that which has no value. Besides this, about the girls wearing lace—just exactly how many girls have begun wearing lace? The Glenn girls are the only ones I have noticed besides the Woods."

"Millie Good had lace on her last new dress," Linda defended herself. "And Joyce and Donna said they are going to put it on their new summer dresses, and I think the rest all will, too."

"Linda, I am sorry this is happening in our church. I do not want you to add to the worldliness and drift in our church. I am sorry you spent your money for that piece of lace. But that is spent now and I am going to ask you to throw the lace in the trash can. Do not sew it on your dress." With these words Mother had gone over to her rocker in the corner. With her Bible in her hands she had remained silent for over an hour in deep meditation.

Linda felt rebellious and determined to dress just like the others were dressing. She picked up the lace. "I'm not going to throw it away!" she thought stubbornly. "That cost me thirty-five cents of hard-earned money. This blue needs a little dainty white trim to make it look its nicest." Linda cast an impatient glance at Mother's sad face. She was rocking and reading, seemingly confident that Linda would obey without further words.

"What if I just don't listen?" Linda said to herself. "What if I just go ahead and sew it on? What will she do about it?" Linda remembered what an argument Millie had with her mother when she put lace on that light green dress—"but she won out!" Linda smiled with satisfaction—"and I will, too." With determination Linda laid the lace carefully around the neckline. How neat it looked! This was prettier lace than Millie had on her green one.

It ought to be. It cost a lot more.

Linda began stitching. Her thread tangled. The lace slipped and was almost hidden at places. Her stitches were showing badly around the already neatly finished neckline. How she wished she could ask Mother to help! But that would never do—not this time! Linda glanced at Mother again. Her eyes were closed. Her lips were moving slightly. Something struck Linda—it almost took her breath away. She sat motionless for a moment. "Mother is praying. She is praying for me, I'm sure. Suppose she is asking God to save her daughter from the worldliness in the church. Suppose she is praying for a submissive, obedient heart in her daughter. Suppose—

"How will God answer her prayer? How can He if I rebel and stubbornly insist on my own way?" Linda's heart condemned her. She felt miserable. She looked at the lace again, then at Mother's face, so calmly confident. How beautiful her face looked, how serenely joyful and full of confidence in her prayer-answering God! The pretty, dainty lace had lost its attraction by the next time she looked at it. "Why do I want it anyway? What purpose does lace serve?"

"Whatsoever ye do, do all to the glory of God" now came to Linda's mind.

"Will this lace glorify God?" Linda asked herself. She knew it could not. Linda bowed her head in humble submission now as she began to see her stubbornness and rebellion. "O Father," she prayed, "I've been so rebellious. I have wanted to please the flesh more than to please Thee."

With determined fingers Linda began picking out the thread that was recently stitched in. "The lace will have to go!" she said aloud. "I cannot wear it to the glory of God."

Mother looked up with a pleased smile. "Shall we thank the Lord together for answering prayer?"

"Mother, I knew you were praying for me," Linda smiled.

"You asked God to speak to me when it looked like I wasn't going to listen to you, didn't you?"

"Prayer changes things!" Mother answered confidently.

Carol's Second Chance

" 'My country! 'tis of thee, Sweet land of liberty,' " sang Carol joyously as she dusted and polished the mirrorlike furniture in the girls' apartment. Carol, with several other girls, now called these beautifully furnished upstairs rooms her home.

Downstairs were the old ladies who were spending their latter years in the Country Haven, a small home for the aged.

With a light heart and spring in her step, Carol was quickly finishing her daily duties.

" 'My native country thee, Land of the noble, free,' " the happy girl continued her singing.

Life had been good to Carol. Her health was good. She was earning easy money and enjoying her work. Really, she was proud of her country.

With the last mahogany table polished, Carol, still singing, went on down the hall to put away her dustcloths and wax. It was still early in the afternoon, but several of the other girls were already off duty. There were only a few ladies in the home at the present time, so the work was lighter than usual.

The remainder of the afternoon would be spent in relaxing together, while the old ladies rested downstairs. Brother Daniels, the superintendent of the home, would walk across the yard to his home and spend the afternoon with his wife and two small daughters.

Passing Dorothy's room, Carol pushed open the door.

"Finished now," she called, then stopped, looked again—"Well, I know Dorothy was here a minute ago. I wonder why she went back downstairs. She probably went over to the front parlor to wait for me," Carol decided, and went on down the hall to put away her things.

"Dorothy," she called, sticking her head in the parlor door a few minutes later. "Well, where can she be?"

Walking on down to Esther's room, Carol hoped some of the girls would feel like hiking this afternoon.

After knocking, she pushed open the door, surprised at not having gotten an answer.

"How strange! Esther was lying here across the bed a few minutes ago when I was cleaning this end of the hall. I wonder what those girls are up to now." Carol listened—everything seemed strangely quiet. Walking to the head of the stairs, she wondered, "Surely the girls haven't all gone out—surely—" Slowly she went down to the first landing. Somehow the whole building seemed awfully quiet.

At the bottom of the steps she stopped again. Carol was not singing now; a sudden fear struck her heart. Quickly, she went to the end of the hall where the offices were. Seldom were they completely deserted. No one was in sight.

Slowly, thoughtfully she walked to the other end of the hall, a certain fear gnawing at her heart. At least the old ladies would be there, she would not be completely alone.

Baffled, she went from one room to another. Every room was empty! "It just can't be!" she cried, as the sudden horrible thought that struck her now penetrated to the very core of her being.

"Behold, I come as a thief. Blessed is he that watcheth" (Revelation 16:15). "In a moment, in the twinkling of an eye" (1 Corinthians 15:52). "We . . . shall be caught up together with them in the clouds, to meet the Lord in the air"

(1 Thessalonians 4:17). "Watch ye therefore, . . . Lest coming suddenly he find you sleeping" (Mark 13:35, 36). Was it possible that the Lord had come and caught her unprepared?

These thoughts rushed through her mind in jumbled confusion. "What can be the meaning of all this? Surely they are all here, somewhere! Or, could it possibly be the Lord had come. Is this the way it would be—everyone suddenly gone?—Oh, it just can't be. It can't possibly be true. But, where . . . ?" Turning, she ran up the stairs, hoping to see the girls, yet fearing lest her fears were true. Again she stopped on the landing, looked out of the large window; no one in sight, not even the superintendent's little girls. How strange! How very strange!

At the top she paused. A terrible weakness overcame her. "What if it is true. No! There must be someone here."

"Girls," she cried. "Oh! What can I do? Surely I must be dreaming." But everything seemed very real.

A thousand tormenting thoughts kept pushing, crowding in confusion through her brain. Now, how clearly she could see her rebellion against God; her lack of trust and confidence; her unwillingness to submit to His will! Many things seemed plain and clear now, things that she just could not see before (or was not willing to).

Rushing back to Esther's room, her mind in a whirl, she paused only long enough to notice her housecoat draped across the front edge of the bed as if it had been suddenly dropped there. But, still, no sound was heard; no one was in the room. Carol went on to the end of the hall, looked out of the small window, trembling, wondering, "Can it be true?" Oh, how strange the sky looked; so clear and blue, so strangely blue, with big white billowy clouds floating slowly by! Weakness, complete and overwhelming, overcame her, a longing and desire for one more privilege to beg for mercy. Then, remembering the love and mercy of God, she dropped to her knees, crying out in anguish of soul,

"O my God, for one more chance. Father, provide some way for me. If You will yet extend to me, mercy—Father, I'll be faithful to follow Your leading. I'll give You my life—my all."

Carol arose from her knees. A deathly stillness prevailed.

"Lost, forever lost!" she shivered, remembering that once the Lord had come it would be too late to call for mercy. "Forever . . . too late!"

Again she dashed down the stairs, past the first landing, on to the bottom where she grabbed the banister for support.

Her own heartbeats seemed to thunder in her ears. "Too late, too late!" Trembling, blindly stumbling, she again made her way to the office, weak and faint. Stepping through the archway of the first office, she noticed that the door to the back office was closed. She crept closer, pressing her ear to the door, passionately hoping to hear a sound.

"Oh, someone is in there!" There were soft voices from within. Carol's first impulse was to fling open the door and rush in. She checked this desire. Turning quickly, she tiptoed out of the office. A great relief flooded her soul, leaving her dazed. She fled upstairs. Looking out of her window, she noticed several old ladies sitting out on the lawn chairs, the superintendent's little girls running across the lawn to meet their papa. The sky had taken on a more natural color. Fleecy white clouds floated softly past.

In her own room, Carol fell on her knees. Bursting into uncontrollable sobs, she cried out to God. "My Father, have mercy on my soul, O my God; and I will keep my vow." Carol went on naming her sins one by one. She confessed all. Ready now to submit to God's will, she again promised, "I will submit to Your will and plan for my life." This time it was with assurance that God was hearing her plea. Rising from her knees a short while later, Carol flung herself across her bed, weeping, thinking of what might have been; thinking of God's tender love and of the utter foolishness of rejecting it.

Brother Ira's Problem

"Good morning, Brother Ira." The young minister greeted the elderly man at his door. "Come right in."

Ira Good walked into the kitchen where Sister Baer was just finishing her breakfast dishes. "Good morning, Brother Ira," she greeted warmly as she dried her hands on the kitchen towel. Sister Baer walked on in through the living room, leaving her husband alone with their guest. Brother Ira looked troubled. Perhaps he wanted to talk to the minister alone. Sister Baer went on down the hall where the children were getting ready for church. She would dress and then help the younger girls with their hair. She could hear the men talking now but was unable to understand the conversation. However, she could sense from Brother Ira's tone of voice that something was troubling him. What could it be? Brother Ira was one of those pillars in the church, strong and solid, who we seldom even think of as having spiritual problems.

"Have a chair," Brother Baer invited. "We'll just sit here and visit awhile. I believe the children have most of the rooms occupied while getting ready for church." It was more than an hour till church time, enough time for a good visit.

"Thank you, Brother Baer." Ira took the chair he offered. With his elbows propped on the table, Ira rested his chin on his hands. He heaved a deep sigh.

Brother Baer waited. He was sure that this faithful, much-appreciated member had some problem to cope with that he wanted to talk to someone about. He felt very inadequate to try to help this seasoned saint with his problems. Still he realized that all help comes from God and that God had chosen him as a vessel through whom He could work.

"Brother Baer," the troubled man began at last. "I am deeply burdened with a problem that is developing which I can't seem to overcome."

"Yes." The minister was sympathetic.

Brother Ira went on. "First, I feel I should apologize to you for the way I've been sleeping in church." Brother Ira looked very much ashamed. "I don't want to do it. I have tried every way I know to stay awake in church; but it seems that when I get in and sit down, I just fall asleep." His voice plainly spoke of the contrition he felt. After humbly confessing this weakness and asking the minister's forgiveness, Ira continued. "Besides the hindrance it may be to you in your preaching, I'm sure it is an even greater insult to God, to sleep in His house when His Word is being preached." Brother Ira shook his head sadly. "I've tried to overcome this thing but have not been successful, so I've come to you for help." He paused.

Brother Baer had listened attentively. What was the right thing to say? What help could he offer a man who slept in church? For a moment the minister was puzzled. He breathed a silent prayer before speaking. This problem was real to Brother Ira. He could not brush it off lightly. The minister had certainly noticed recently how many people slept in church. Brother Ira was not the worst of them. His head had nodded several times, to be sure, but this dear brother had never been caught slumped down in his chair as if he intended to sleep. And he was older. Sometimes there were conditions of the body for which a person was hardly to be blamed for drowsiness.

Brother Baer spoke thoughtfully. "Brother Ira," he asked,

"do you ever fall asleep when you sit down to eat?"

"No," he answered, "I don't know that I ever have."

"You've still got a pretty good appetite for a man your age, haven't you?" the minister asked. "You know, Brother, I wonder, if you should lose your appetite, whether you might not start falling asleep at the table. Of course, while you're enjoying your food, you're not likely to," he spoke kindly.

Brother Ira had listened and caught the idea. "O Brother Baer," he pleaded earnestly, "pray for me that I will not lose my appetite for spiritual food. Perhaps that is where the trouble lies; I've lost interest or failed to really desire the spiritual food. Can it be?" Brother Ira was truly broken. He realized his need and had a great desire to have that need filled.

"We will certainly be glad to pray for you," Brother Baer agreed. "You know that there are ways to cultivate a good appetite. If you never went to the table or smelled the good food, you would not have as great a desire for it as you have when it is before you. You taste it and it's very good. Then you want more. Haven't you often found that at times you are not very hungry until you have tasted a choice dish? This will immediately whet your appetite."

"Yes, I've found that this is true," Ira agreed.

" 'O taste and see that the Lord is good,' " the minister quoted. "Possibly a little more time spent with God and His Word at home would whet the appetite sufficiently to keep us awake when we are at His table, feeding on His Word," Brother Baer suggested. "Also, I realize that we ministers do not always take time to seek a message from the Lord and study His Word to prepare ourselves for His use as we ought to. This may be one reason our people are sleepy in church sometimes."

"Thank you, Brother," Ira said, rising to his feet. "I believe I see where I can cultivate a better appetite." Brother Ira went home.

The minister knelt by his chair. "O God," he prayed "give me a message this morning that is fresh from Thee and will awaken our church and whet the appetite of the people for Thy Word."

"All the Hay Is Lost"

Jason and Nelson were brothers. They had two large farms. Neither could be said to be a better farmer than the other. The farms, located in the rolling country of Pennsylvania, were a picture indeed, envied by many local farmers. The brothers were thrifty and energetic.

There was only one major difference in the two men. As a boy, Jason had received Christ as his personal Lord and Savior and had lived a faithful Christian life ever since. His radiant testimony was known for miles around.

Nelson, in many ways, had the same pleasing personality and easygoing ways as his brother had, though he had never yielded his life to God.

Often the brothers worked together. They made many plans together and discussed new and better ways of farming. Usually they were in agreement on any major issue. Only in religious matters they did not see things alike.

All week they had been baling hay; half the week for Nelson, the other half for Jason. There was about one more day's work. After a good long day, then all the hay would be in. It was late Saturday evening. And it looked like rain! The hay would get wet. Only one more day would have saved it. But tomorrow was Sunday. The weather had been threatening. Maybe it could be saved tomorrow, but Monday would surely be too late. "Shall we get the rest of it in tomorrow?" Nelson asked.

"Tomorrow?" Jason remarked with some surprise. "Do you know that today is Saturday?"

"Yes, indeed," Nelson remarked tersely. "And I know tomorrow is Sunday."

"Well, that should answer your question, Brother. Tomorrow is Sunday! Tomorrow is the day the Lord Himself set apart for rest and worship."

"Yes, and the Lord Himself gave us this crop to harvest," Nelson replied. "I believe He expects us to be good enough stewards to take care of it and get it put away."

"The Lord knew this crop was here when He sent the rain," Jason replied.

"All right," Nelson added. "The only way to save the hay is to put it up tomorrow, if it's not raining then already."

"Tomorrow is Sunday and I will not work, even if I lose all the rest of the hay," Jason replied firmly.

"Well, you will lose it all if you don't get it tomorrow," Nelson argued. "I just can't see it that way. You can rest if you want to. I'm going out to get my share. Yours can lie there and spoil if you don't come out and help."

"All right," Jason agreed.

On Sunday morning the sky looked threatening. It looked as if it were set for heavy rains. Nelson was out baling hay almost before day light. He worked as hard as he could go all day. It began to sprinkle just a little in the morning. He worked faster, determined to save the hay. The showers were heavier in the afternoon. Nelson kept at it, and by evening had all his hay in the barn.

Sunday morning was a pleasant time for Jason and his family. They got up and had worship together. They went to church and received spiritual food and strength. In the afternoon Jason relaxed and enjoyed the fellowship with his family and a few friends who stopped in. It had been a damp, dreary day; but

Jason's home was filled with the sunshine of love and contentment. He had not a worry about the hay. The Lord had always provided for their needs, and Jason was confident He would continue to do so. By evening the sky suddenly began to clear. The night was warm and windy.

Monday morning dawned bright and clear. The sun shone very hot before Jason could get through his morning chores and get to the field. About seven o'clock, he went in for breakfast and morning devotions. Then Jason went out to the field. The hay was in perfect condition for baling. The sun was hot and oppressive all day. By evening Jason had all his hay in and in good condition. As he came by Nelson's barn in the evening, Jason smelled a warning signal. Then he saw the heat waves rising and the steam oozing out of the cracks and around the windows. Jason stopped the tractor. He ran toward the barn. "Nelson!" he called frantically. "The hay is heating."

He rushed inside. There was the seething, steaming mass! Nelson was working frantically to get the hot, molding hay outside before it caught fire. Jason pitched in and helped. For several hours they worked without a word. Maybe they could save some of the hay. It had been too damp when it was put up. If only he had known that the rain would be over and the sun would shine on Monday! How much better off the hay would have been in the field!

When they finished, dark clouds were rolling up and thunder rumbled in the distance.

"Maybe we'd better go over and check yours," Nelson suggested.

"I think mine is all right," Jason replied without a hint of boasting.

Both men were exhausted and decided to retire. As they walked by the moldy hay, Nelson shook his head sadly. His only comment was, "All the hay is lost."

240

"By Their Fruits"

About twenty young men gathered outside the large barn at the new experiment farm. These men were conscientious objectors.

James joined the group to take his instructions. He felt strange and uneasy. He knew all about farming and dairying, sure. But this was different. James was raised on a dairy farm. It was a carefree life with lots of outdoor freedom. He loved the farm. But here everything had to be so exact and done differently than at home. James doubted that he would enjoy this as much. But he was determined to do a good job. This was a wonderful privilege that the government had granted the young men who could not conscientiously participate in war. James felt keenly his responsilibity to show his appreciation by a life of careful obedience and respect for those in authority.

Most of the young men had been here several months already. For some of them the two-year term of service was almost over. In a few days James had sized up the entire group, forming impressions of nearly every one of his work partners for the coming months.

Dave and John, who had been nicknamed "The preachers," seemed to be the most conscientious and serious minded in the group. Paul, John, and George were fine fellows, too, and honest workers, always willing to do more than their share.

Now Carl and Don were quite different, always shirking their duties, shifting responsibility, playing pranks, and many times spoiling the testimony of the whole group at Balmy Acres Farm.

As a Christian youth, James was deeply concerned for the testimony of their group. The community folks about them naturally watched these young men carefully, critically. If they were too good to go out on the battlefront with their own boys, then their lives at home should also be different.

" 'By their fruits ye shall know them.' Yes, this community is surely watching the fruits of our lives and we need to be careful," James had decided before coming to Balmy Acres. "If we are truly born again, then they will not be disappointed in us. But 'a corrupt tree cannot bring forth good fruit.' If our fruit is not good, we have no business being here."

After James had worked several weeks with these young men, Paul and John began making preparations to return to their home communities. Their terms of service were over. They would be missed because they were conscientious workers. Others would soon take their places.

"Don and I are going to Greenville Friday afternoon," Carl offered, "Would you boys like to ride along out there to catch your train home?"

"Sure would," Paul replied. "That would be a lot better than taking a bus over to Greenville Friday afternoon. Thanks."

James had been wanting to get to the little filling station on Route 11 to talk with Thomas Hamon again. He had several good talks with him since they first met on the train about a month ago. Tom seemed sincerely interested in spiritual things. If he was an honest seeker, James wanted to give him every opportunity to know the truth. Tom had always seemed open to the truth. So when Carl offered, "Ride along to Greenville with us, James," he readily agreed.

"I'd like to ride along partway."

Here was his chance. James had Friday afternoon off this

week, too. "Partway?" Carl asked.

"Yes, I'd like to ride along out to Hamon's Station on Route 11. That's only about five miles, isn't it? I could walk back."

"Sure," Carl agreed. "You are welcome to ride that far. What do you want at Hamon's?"

"Just want to talk to Tom awhile," James replied. "He's the young man I met on the train coming out here."

"Yes," Carl nodded. "But you'd better ride along to Greenville this time. You don't often get to a big town around here. You can talk to Tom any time or we could stop in there on our way back."

"No, thanks, I'll just stop off there on your way in to town."

"All right, but you'll miss a lot of fun," Carl replied. "Tom's a nice guy. I always buy my gas there. We're big friends, too. I think he really likes most of us fellows. He always takes time out to stop and chat awhile with any of us, or even for a game or two of pool occasionally. Once he even fired up that old Chevy of his and tried to race this new Ford. Of course, I beat," Carl chuckled. "I think he knew I would. He is good-natured. Always tries to please his customers."

"Carl, you don't mean you would go out on the highways racing and violating laws when we are here as a part of a group of conscientious people, do you?" James asked, shocked at the careless attitude expressed by his friend.

"Oh, I don't have a habit of it," Carl squirmed. "But you know how it is; a nice fellow like Tom expects you to have a little fun with him. If we want to be friendly with our neighbors, we'll have to do a few things they enjoy."

James shook his head sadly. He said no more at the time. But he was deep in thought as they neared Hamon's Station Friday afternoon. Did Tom really expect such actions from the young men whose very purpose for being here was in obedience to the Word of God? Surely he would know that this was not consistent.

When the fine new Ford pulled in at Hamon's Station at two o'clock, Tom was out at the front pumps, waiting on a customer while another waited on the other side of the pumps.

Carl swung around to the side pumps, frightening the attendant who was waiting on a truck there.

"Careful! young man," he growled. "Slow up a little."

Carl laughed. "Hi, Tom," he called across the lot. "Big business this afternoon? How about filling me up quick. I have to get these boys over to Greenville to the train." Carl pulled out his watch, apparently uneasy.

"Sure," Tom answered good-naturally. "Be with you in a minute." As quickly as possible he finished his business with the customers out front and hurried over to Carl's car.

James glanced at his watch. "Three hours to go fifty miles. Carl knows good and well there is no hurry. Why does he act so rushed?"

"Hi, James," Tom called, walking past the door just as James crawled out. "I haven't seen much of you for several days. Guess you don't get around like Carl does, not having a car."

"No, I don't often leave the farm," James replied.

"All through," Tom called, slapping the shiny fender. "Run along, young man. Don't miss that train."

When Carl revved up the motor, Tom acted as though he would race him. "All right, pour it to her," he called, and Carl took off spinning wheels and throwing gravel. What a noise those spinning wheels made, squealing onto the hard-top! Several people turned around, scowling.

"Crazy guy!" Tom muttered sourly, half under his breath. "He won't be satisfied till he smashes that Ford. Thinks he's smart! He'll learn when he cracks it up. Law-abiding citizens! I doubt if many of them are!" Business kept pulling in; cars were waiting in a line at the front pumps. Tom hurried away, leaving James standing alone, bewildered, wondering how he would ever talk to Tom now concerning his soul. He had thought Tom had confidence in him, but now he did not seem to have confidence in any of the conscientious objectors.

"By their fruits ye shall know them." Sure, Tom was only judging the fruits he had seen. He had no reason to believe that they had anything he did not have.

Tom was busy for a half hour. When the lot emptied, he walked on inside.

James was hurt. Tom knew he had stood around all this time, waiting to talk to him. He had walked right past him without a word. Taking a coke from the icebox, he had pulled up an old crate and sat down with the men inside. It was evident that he had no intentions of talking to James. Slowly James turned with a heavy heart and walked the five miles back to Balmy Acres.

"I can't talk to Tom today," he decided. "He seemed so open before, and now this. Will he ever be interested again?"

"Today Is the Day of Salvation"

Joseph had just gone to work. Ellen went back to her dish-washing. Hot tears streamed across her face and dropped unheeded into the dishwater. "If only he could see his need of a Savior!" Ellen cried out, broken-hearted. "If only Joseph were a Christian, too!" How Ellen longed for Christian companionship! "If only I had known Joseph better before we were married!" They had been married for eight years. Bitter years of disappointment they had been! Five children had joined them during these years, adding to the responsibilities and cares of the home.

Only two years had passed since Ellen, realizing her lost condition, had cried to God for mercy. After giving her heart to the Lord and fully yielding her life to Him, she had prayed earnestly for her husband and the children. But it seemed he only grew harder each day. Many hours she had spent weeping and praying, determined to be true to her Lord. The cost had often been great! Joseph had said that she would not hold out a year and he meant to prove it by trying her to the limit of her endurance. By God's grace she had always proven to be a loving, faithful wife and true to God, unyielding under the pressure of sin and hatred that surrounded her life.

This morning, struggling with heartaches and fears, her faith almost failed. "Would he never yield?" She was sure he had often been fighting conviction, but he would not give up—not Joseph! He was a man who did not want anyone's help! And he did not want anyone to tell him what to do—no, not even God Himself!

Ellen was burdened for the children. How could she teach them to love their father when he was cruel and unfair, or to love her Lord when their father mocked and scorned all she tried to teach them? Ellen almost felt like giving up. It was not that God had not been faithful—oh, no! He had always been faithful and given grace for every trial when she looked to Him. But this morning the burden seemed very heavy. Joseph had not done or said anything to cause this unusual burden this morning, but it was just there.

"Come unto me, all ye that labour . . . , and I will give you rest." What a sweet message of love from the Father came to her just now!

"Yes," she responded gladly, "I will come to Thee." The heavy burden had often been lifted by spending time alone with God. So, looking to Him, Ellen dropped her morning tasks—they could wait—and walked into the bedroom. There she dropped on her knees. "Father," she cried, "I am so weary this morning. I do thank Thee for Thy love and the assurance of Thy presence with us. Keep me true to Thee at any cost, and speak to Joseph this morning. Just bring him to his knees before Thee, Lord, so that he, too, might yield his life to Thee and enjoy peace and rest. Mightily convict him today! May he be convinced of Thy love and pardon and be willing to come to Thee."

After laboring thus long on her knees in intercession for those she loved, Ellen arose and resumed her duties about the house. The children were playing contentedly in the yard this morning, glad for the nice weather.

The busy young mother now went about her work with a calm assurance that God in His own time would answer her prayer in His own good way. A feeling that all was well now possessed her, for all things had been committed to the Father. She could rest in His love and go on with a song in her heart. Dishes were washed and put away, and a nice custard was in the oven, baking for supper—Joseph's favorite lemon custard. Soon she would need to fix some lunch for the children.

*   *   *   *   *   *   *   *   *   *   *   *

After leaving the house, Joseph jumped into his white Ford, just as he would any other morning. Out on the open highway, he stepped harder on the gas pedal and sped across town. He was a little late, nothing unusual though. He often left late enough to have to rush to make it on time. But somehow this morning Joseph felt uneasy. Was there someone watching him? He was breaking the speed limit, but no more than usual. "Why this uneasy feeling?" Quickly glancing in the rear-view mirror, he assured himself that no officer was around. But he could not shake off that awful feeling. Someone must surely be following! He looked again—no apparent reason for alarm. Joseph tried to shake it off, but without success.

"Well, is there some evil foreboding?" Something surely was wrong! Joseph could not get away from it. "Is there some danger ahead?" Joseph laughed a hard coarse laugh. "What is wrong with me? Am I getting chicken?" He stepped on the gas and rolled on another mile or so.

"You are not ready to meet God! Not ready to die! Not ready for eternity!" kept ringing over and over in his ears.

"No, I am not," he admitted. "I never have been and don't plan to get ready for a few years yet. Oh, yes, sometime I will—but not now. I am still young!"

Joseph was thoroughly disgusted with himself. Why should he be hearing such a sermon this morning in the quietness of his car? He had not gone to church for years. Nor had he read his Bible. What could have brought this on?

"Prepare to meet thy God!" The sign on the corner stared him in the face. But it had been there for years. He had often seen it, but never before had it screamed at him as it did today. By the time Joseph reached the mill, he was trembling so that he could hardly walk from the car to the open doors near the office. He walked in and straight over to Mr. Wells' desk.

"Good morning," Mr. Wells looked up. "You don't look well, Joe. Something wrong?"

"May I have the day off?" Joseph asked in a husky voice.

"Yes, sir, you have some time coming. This would be a good day for you to take it."

Joseph turned without another word and got back into his car. He was not at all sure what he was going to do, but he knew he had to do something!

Driving back across town, Joseph began doing some serious thinking. "I have got to get right with the Lord," he concluded at last, pulling to a stop at the edge of the woods.

"Won't the men sneer when they hear this? Yes, there will be much to face, but I am determined. It can be done. Yes, Christ can make a life completely new. Ellen has proved it. If He can save me after the life of wickedness I have lived, I will surely live for Him the rest of my days!" Somehow Joseph felt sure that the Lord would save him and was calling him now, and he meant to respond to the call.

"How can I confess all these things?" he cried out in despair as one sin after another stared him in the face with frightening proportions. "And what will I do about—" Here Joseph stopped, almost afraid to face the reality of the decision he had made. "How can I face all this?" Joseph almost despaired to carry out his intention to get right with the Lord as the Lord in mercy continued to speak to him, showing him the cost. "No, I will not give up now. I will not turn back," he cried determinedly, walking on back the narrow path deeper into the woods. When he was hidden from view of the road, the large, rough-looking man fell to his knees in true brokenness.

"O God," he cried out in anguish, "I have sinned."

It was a long, hard struggle to give up his will to accept the lordship of another. But when he reached this point of submission, sweet peace flooded his troubled soul.

His first desire was to tell Ellen of the victory he had found through Christ. "But, how much I must confess to her!"

Joseph started toward home. He had no doubts about how Ellen would receive him and his confession. He could depend on her proven loyalty and faithfulness in spite of all his unworthiness.

* * * * * * * * * * * *

"My, how the morning did fly!" Ellen exclaimed. "Can it possibly be eleven o'clock already?" When she walked back to check with the kitchen clock, Ellen noticed a car outside the window. "Why, it's Joseph's car. Whatever could be wrong? He has never come home at this hour—except the day he was fired." Ellen looked worried. She walked to the back door just in time to hold it open for her husband to enter. He did not appear to be hurt, nor did he seem angry as he had been that other day. Without a word he entered while she in silence held the door ajar, afraid to speak.

Only after she closed the door softly behind him did Ellen notice that there were tears streaming across his cheeks. Never had she known him to cry. "Whatever could be wrong?" Instinctively she threw her arms around him. There was nothing in his expression now to cause her to fear. Really, he looked humble and broken. He stood silent in the middle of the kitchen floor, folding her close in his embrace. Those strong arms that before seemed to know no tenderness now caressed the one they had often abused.

"Ellen," his voice trembled, "Ellen, the Lord has heard and answered your prayers today."

"Joseph! Joseph!" She clasped his hand in hers, looking searchingly into his eyes.

"Yes, Ellen, He saved my soul." Then Joseph went on to tell her how the Lord has spoken very definitely to him that morning. One after another he confessed his sins, seeking her forgiveness. Together they knelt and prayed.

"Now there is much more I will have to face," Joseph began, "but by God's grace I am going to do all He asks me to do. First I must see Jake. You know what kind of life we have lived and the sins we have been involved in together. I want to confess Christ to him and to confess my sins. Ellen, pray for me while I plead with him to surrender his life to God."

"Yes, Joseph, I will."

"Let's pray together once more before I go," he suggested. "I feel urgently that I should go right away. But I want to seek the Lord's will and pray His guidance and direction on my visit with Jake."

Before Joseph left the house there was a knock on the door.

"Why, hello, Jake. What brings you here this time of day?" his surprised voice greeted the man at the door.

"Oh, it's my day off and I decided to go fishing this afternoon. Then when I drove by and noticed your car at home I thought maybe you would want to go along."

Joseph hesitated only a moment. He glanced at Ellen. Many times she had dreaded to see him leave the house with Jake. But this time it was different. There was a smile of approval on her face. "Yes, sure I would like to go along. When are you leaving?"

"Right now. Soon as you can get ready."

"All right. Let me get into some other clothes. Come on in and sit down a few minutes." Joseph left the room.

Ellen quickly spread several pieces of bread for some cheese sandwiches and filled a small bag with some of her freshly baked cookies. She looked at the lemon custard—no, that would be better for supper. With four big, delicious apples, she finished the lunch and carried it into the living room where she met her husband. How different he looked—so unlike the Joseph she had known for years! Tenderly he kissed her "good-bye."

"God bless you, Dear. I will be praying for you," she said, squeezing his big calloused hand.

"You don't care if I go?" he asked considerately.

"No, not this time. I believe the Lord is directing in this."

"Thank you, Dear. Do pray for me all afternoon." Joseph walked on out to the kitchen with the bag in his hand. "All right, Pal. Ready to go?" Ellen waved from the back door as the two men left the house. She walked back into the kitchen. "Twelve-thirty. Joseph must have been here about an hour and a half. What a short hour it was and the happiest I have known for years." Instinctively she dropped to her knees to thank the loving Father for answered prayer, for His long extended mercy, and with a petition that Jake, too, would be touched and would surrender his life to God. "Keep Joseph true to Thee till death, at any cost," she prayed.

The children were still outside. They had no habit of running in to meet their father. She would call them and tell them it would be different now. Joseph had meant to talk to the children about the change in his heart but decided he would do that this evening since Jake came.

*　　*　　*　　*　　*　　*　　*　　*　　*　　*　　*　　*

It was eight o'clock. Ellen could hardly wait for his return. Supper had been waiting for two and a half hours. The children were getting hungry and dissatisfied. Ellen walked restlessly from one window to another. She had spent much of the after-noon on her knees praying for Jake's conversion and for grace and wisdom for her husband.

At eight-thirty she gave the children their supper and put the younger ones to bed. An hour later the two older children also went to bed. Now in the quietness of her own bedroom Ellen knelt again, committing all to the Father above. She had a calm feeling of assurance that all was well. But the question kept entering her mind, "What could be keeping the men so long?" Jake had said when they left the house that he expected to be back by five or five-thirty. She looked at the clock again. Ten o'clock! A car drove in. Ellen walked to the kitchen door. Someone knocked when she expected the door to fling open and Joseph to step in. Ellen started. "Who could be calling on her at this hour?" She wished Joseph were at home.

Slowly Ellen walked to the door. Two men stood on the porch. Ellen flipped the light switch. They were both strangers. Ellen breathed a prayer for guidance and protection and felt the presence of the Lord very near.

"Is this where Joseph Miller lives?"

"Yes," Ellen answered.

"Are you his wife?" the man questioned further.

"Yes," she answered again.

"He went fishing this afternoon with Jake Slabaugh," the man continued, then paused a moment, clearing his throat and shifting nervously from one foot to the other.

"Yes, sir." Ellen confirmed his statement.

"Sorry to have to bring you this message, Ma'am," the man said in a husky voice, "but the boat your husband was in turned over, apparently early in the afternoon. There must have been no one around. No one knows just what happened or why both men drowned, since they can both swim; but they were found this evening and the boat turned over, floating downstream." The men turned and left the house. Ellen stood staring after them, too shocked to move, too bewildered even to close the door and go inside. Joseph was gone. He would never return to their home again. He would never have the privilege to be a godly father and spiritual leader in their home. The children would never know a gentle loving father and look forward to his footsteps returning from work each evening.

Ellen looked out into the dark night. She could see only darkness ahead until at last a vision of the hour from eleven till twelve-thirty all passed vividly before her again. "Thank God," she cried with deep feeling. "We shall again be united! We are not separated forever! He is gone on before to await us there. I must bring all the children with me, and our circle will not be broken." Ellen fell to her knees. Her grief was great but did not compare with her joy that Joseph had prepared himself to meet God.

"All is well. God answers prayer and He will care for us." With this calm assurance, Ellen walked to the telephone to call her parents. A host of thoughts rushed through her mind. Joseph, her own dear Joseph, would not return and transform their home to a heaven on earth as she had expected. No, but he would be awaiting her over there. This was her only comfort and consolation now. Praise the Lord! Joseph was ready to die! What about Jake? Probably no one would ever know.

Oh, how thankful Ellen was that she had the privilege of that last hour with Joseph! He died a saved man and perhaps Jake had been convicted and yielded, too—but only God knew. "Today is the day of salvation."

"Not Ashamed of My Lord"

The evangelist stood behind the pulpit on the last night of the meetings. For a moment he silently searched the faces before him.

The radiance of heaven's joy was evident on some. On others were signs of fear and distress. Some faces seemed blank—expressionless.

Brother John's heart was touched. How could he help all these people to find the true joy and peace that Christ offers?

Possibly those who had not been moved by his messages could be reached by faithful words of testimony from the home congregation. Those who had recently yielded their lives to God would surely be happy to tell what Christ had done for them.

So, on Sunday evening, Brother John invited anyone from the audience to give a personal testimony.

"If God has been good to you, share your experience with us. Tell us what Jesus means to you," Brother John encouraged the waiting audience. "Let us all together magnify Christ's Name tonight."

A brother near the back of the church rose to his feet. He straightened his coat and stood straight and tall. His speech was quite lengthy. His words were carefully chosen. There was little real heartfelt expression. Daniel took his seat with an air of satisfaction.

"S-s-since I c-came back to the Lord," Brother James

stuttered, "He-He-ah-He has received me and g-g-given me real peace." Poor Brother James. His handicap in his speech would not keep him quiet even in such a large crowd. The radiance of joy and a deep settled peace were so evident that for the true seeker or one who truly loved the Lord, James and his handicap were not seen, but his Lord who had done so much for him.

"I-I-I s-surely want to pr-pr-praise Him and re-recommend Him to anyone who is, ah, is, lost in sin. Jesus is all you need. Jesus satisfies. Come to Him tonight," James pleaded earnestly. "Jesus is w-w-waiting to receive you."

Brother James took his seat again, bowing his head humbly, till another voice was heard.

For the second time Daniel was on his feet. Indignation and scorn covered his features. "If I were not able to testify for my Lord any better than that, I'd keep quiet!" Daniel's voice had a quite different tone from the words of the last testimony that had been given. "I'd be ashamed of myself," he muttered half under his breath, taking his seat again.

Rising to his feet again, James replied quietly, "I'm a-a-ashamed of my-s-s-self. But I'm not ashamed of my Lord!" Though he stammered and stumbled over the words, James's heart was at peace. The listeners knew that Jesus Christ was very real and precious to this young man. In his words were hope for the sinner and comfort for the saint. And many timid souls were encouraged to speak for their Lord.

The Corn Thieves

Dorcas rolled over. What was that sound? She lay still a minute listening. Surely she must have been mistaken. No, there it was again—a low crackling sound—the sound of long leaves rustling—then came the plop, plop, plop as ear after ear was dropped onto the pile. "Yes. They are at it again," she decided definitely. Quietly Dorcas raised herself up, but with no stars or moon to light the cornfield there was no possible chance for a sight of the thieves.

"Paul," Dorcas whispered, nudging her husband with her elbow. "Wake up!" She did not turn on a light. If someone was in the cornfield, she did not want to frighten him away until they had a chance to see who it was.

"Paul, I am sure I hear someone in the corn," she whispered.

Sleepily Paul opened his eyes. "Three o'clock!" he exclaimed. "Surely not at this hour!" He leaned forward to join his wife at the window. "Well! There is surely something rustling through those rows of corn. Three o'clock—and Sunday morning!"

Plop! Plop! Something was surely being steadily dropped, and the rustling, crackling sounds continued to drift to the bedroom window. Now there was a plunking sound as if a whole armload had been thrown down.

"O Paul, what will we do? We are not going to get any corn to can if this keeps up," Dorcas said in low tones. "We have hardly had any to eat. I wanted so badly to put up a lot of corn this year and it did so well. Now the patch has been stripped every time just before it was ready to pull. I just looked at it yesterday and decided there would be a nice batch to can on Monday."

Paul was quickly stepping into his trousers and jacket.

"But what can you do?" Dorcas asked. "There may be several men out there. Do you think it is safe to go out? Suppose it would be bears. You know there had been some up in Miller's corn last year."

"Yes, I know," Paul replied, "but I don't think our thieves are the four-footed kind. Remember those footprints we found last week?"

"Yes." Dorcas remembered that the footprints had been made with large shoes which had heavy tread. They could not be mistaken for bear tracks.

"I don't know what I can do," Paul answered. "I am not even going to try to frighten them. I don't know whether or not the thieves know we are nonresistant. If they don't they will likely run before I get near. They will naturally be frightened at being caught."

Paul opened the back door as quietly as possible. He slipped noiselessly around the back side of the house. Dorcas watched from the bedroom window. Her eyes were becoming accustomed to the darkness. Dimly she could see Paul's shadow creeping closer to the place where there was the constant movement of the tall stalks of corn.

Now she saw the outline of a pickup truck. "Surely they aren't planning to take a truckload," she hoped. But she remembered other times when nearly a truckload must have left the field overnight. "Oh, I did so badly want to can lots of that corn we worked so hard for." Dorcas watched breathlessly. Paul was standing not ten feet from the thieves, apparently unnoticed. Why did he not say something?

Just when the forms of two other men stepped out into the row where Paul was standing, he called a hearty "Good morning" in his friendly way.

The men stopped short. They stared a moment, completely dumbfounded. They had been caught in the act. There was no denying what they were doing, since each man had at least a dozen choice ears of corn stacked on his arm. In an instant both men turned to run, dropping every ear at the feet of their host.

"Stop!" demanded Paul in his sternest tones.

Dorcas was almost enjoying the moment when the two men obeyed as if the order had been given by a chief commander. She smiled. "If they knew Paul would do nothing more than watch them go, that is probably exactly what they would do."

The thieves waited tensely a moment before Paul spoke again. "Come back here and pick up this corn you dropped," Paul ordered. He really did sound as though he meant for them to do exactly that and they did. All the while they were casting anxious glances first toward Paul and then toward the house, as if they expected to see an officer approaching any minute.

When the corn was picked up, they faced their host again. They waited for the next order to be given.

"Where were you going with the corn?" Paul asked in a very businesslike way. He waited for an answer and followed their anxious glances in the direction of the waiting truck.

"Oh, I had not seen that." Paul looked as surprised as the men did when they first saw him. He started toward the truck, saying, "Come on. Let's unload your arms so we can go inside and visit awhile." Up to this time the men had been too shocked to speak.

"Please, sir, if you will just let us unload it all here I promise we won't be back to bother you anymore. If you just won't call an officer." The short man had spoken first.

The tall man began to plead for mercy, too. "We sure won't

come back. Just let us go now. Please don't report us. They had unloaded their corn onto the half-loaded pickup.

"Come on inside," Paul invited, as cordially as if he were speaking to his best friend. His voice no longer held the tone of a commander.

The men shifted nervously from one foot to the other. "Really, sir," the short man begged, "we won't be back, just let us go now."

"No," Paul answered firmly. "You are my guests. You have come to my home and I insist you come in and visit awhile. I only want to talk with you. I promise you will not be harmed nor reported under my roof. But do come in." He started toward the house. Reluctantly the corn thieves followed.

Dorcas glanced at the clock. "Three-fifteen. What an unusual hour to entertain guests—strangers!" The three men neared the house. Quickly Dorcas dressed. She put on a freshly ironed blue dress and was just tying an apron around her waist when Paul called, "Dorcas, are you up?"

"Yes," she replied, opening the bedroom door.

"We have guests," Paul explained matter-of-factly, as if it were an everyday occurrence to entertain at all hours. "Do you have a snack handy that we could enjoy together while we visit awhile?"

"Surely," she answered sweetly. Dorcas followed her husband to the kitchen where he had offered the men chairs at the kitchen table. While walking through the living room, Paul had picked up his well-worn Bible and took his chair opposite the short man, who was fidgeting uneasily.

Dorcas could think of nothing but the brownies she had saved for Sunday for a quick snack. There were half a dozen left. They would do fine with a cup of hot chocolate. Quickly Dorcas took out a small pan and poured about a half gallon of milk into it. To this she added some chocolate syrup she had cooked earlier. Soon

260

she set the three steaming cups of chocolate before the men with the plate of chewy, nutty brownies.

All the while the delicious food was being prepared, Paul had been talking kindly to the men about the seriousness of stealing, not because of their disadvantage, oh, no! The thief was in a serious condition because of his standing before God. This was Paul's plea. "Repent, or you have gained God's disfavor." Paul turned to verse after verse, reading and explaining the Word. When the food was brought, he laid his Bible on the back corner of the table. "You men just pull up your chairs. I want you to enjoy a snack with me before you go. We will bow our heads for prayer before we eat."

"Father, we do thank You this morning for this food," he prayed. "And now we seek Thy blessing for this day. We pray that You will be with our guests. Speak to their hearts. May they turn to Thee and find salvation through Jesus Christ. We desire Thy will on earth as it is in heaven. For Thine is the kingdom, the power, and the glory. Amen."

Paul passed the brownies first to his guests, then took one and began to visit pleasantly with the men who had not joined in the conversation. He spoke of the weather, the crops, how God had blessed them, and many other subjects to set his guests at ease. But it was plain to see they were not enjoying the chewy goodness of the brownies nor the rich, creamy hot chocolate. After offering them a second helping, which they refused, Paul rose to his feet to show his visitors that they were free to leave now if they chose to leave.

As he walked with them to the truck, Paul invited them to come back again to visit and added, "And if you are hungry for corn, come on back. We will be glad to give you enough for several meals. Just come on up to the house and ask for it. We will be happy to share with you. The Lord has bountifully blessed us with a good crop. My wife would like to can a little yet if she can."

"Tell her we sure are sorry, and we won't bother her corn anymore," were the last words the men spoke when they drove out of the corn patch just as the first streaks of dawn began to redden the sky.

Not another ear of corn was missing from the patch, and by the end of the next week Dorcas had canned a nice supply of tender sweet corn.

Opportunity Lost

"Ninety-eight, ninety-nine, one hundred; the last bottle filled," sighed Arneda, replacing the large container of pills on the shelf.

Very weary, Arneda began doing the last-minute jobs always waiting at the end of each day in the office. As she worked, her mind was not at rest; she could not forget the sad look on Mrs. Allen's face, nor the bitter words from Mr. Allen, following the shocking verdict that their son had only a few weeks to live. Arneda well knew that the Allens had been calling on God to heal their son, without submitting themselves to God's will. How could she, a busy nurse, help the grief-stricken parents?

She reviewed the day at the clinic, her mind going from one patient to another. She thought of old Mr. Dillinger; the Charles family, with four small children who did not receive the physical care they needed; and many others. With these thoughts troubling her, Arneda finished tidying the office and started back down the hall to make each patient comfortable for the night.

As she tiptoed through, the nursery was quiet and peaceful. "If only," thought Arneda, "each one of our patients were as peaceful—as innocent—my conscience would be clear." Again her conscience smote her as she thought of the many opportunities she lost each day to witness to souls who had not found peace with God. She stood for a moment, watching these innocent little sleepers. Then, moving on, she found most of her patients sleeping soundly. Mrs. Carter tossed restlessly on her bed.

"Please, Nurse," she called, "could I have another sleeping pill? I'm so miserable."

"I'm sorry, Mrs. Carter," replied Arneda, "but it has been only a short time since you took one, I can't give you another now."

"Oh, no" groaned Mrs. Carter, raising herself on her elbow. "These doctors don't know how miserable a patient can be, lying here staring at four bare walls; why can't they do something for me?"

"But, Mrs. Carter, the doctors are doing their best for you," Arneda answered softly. She was trying to calm her patient before others in the ward awoke. "Would you like to have your back rubbed?" she asked. "That might help."

"Yes," was her low-spirited reply, "but I doubt whether it will help."

As she rubbed, Arneda listened to Mrs. Carter's many troubles, appearing sympathetic but feeling condemned for not trying to lead the poor, despondent soul to Jesus, the answer to all her problems.

Mrs. Carter seemed relaxed after a lengthy outpouring of her troubles. Arneda quietly left the room with a heavy heart.

When Arneda knelt to pray before retiring, a sad picture of restless humanity crowded other things from her mind: poor wanderers stumbling through life without the help of a guide, people who needed Christ, people who needed encouragement. But what could Arneda do? Her work was important, but what was the most important?

Arneda remembered with pain the promise she had made to God after completing her training. She recalled the words she had spoken, "Lord, in my nursing career, You will always have first place. People do need physical help, but most of all they need spiritual help. By Your grace, I'll be a witness to the people I meet." Now, feeling ashamed that she had fallen far short of keeping that promise, she resolved with new determination to witness for Christ. Deep in her heart Arneda knew that she could find time to talk to many of her patients about the Lord Jesus, but she did not trust God to give her words of wisdom in her testimony.

Three o'clock the following afternoon found Arneda again at Mrs. Carter's bedside, endeavoring to make her restless patient comfortable. Mrs. Carter seemed eager to talk. Arneda, sensing her longing for peace, decided that this was the opportunity for which she had been waiting. Now again doubt arose—"How shall I approach her?"

Just then the doorbell rang, interrupting their conversation. So the afternoon wore on.

Old Mr. Dillinger did not come in for his appointment but postponed it. Arneda felt relieved; she could justify her desire to put her burden of witnessing into the future.

The day came to a close as usual. When Arneda again knelt to pray, she excused herself for not having made more effort to show Mrs. Carter her need of Jesus. Mrs. Carter had slept most of the afternoon, and she had been busy; she would approach her tomorrow.

Day after day slipped by. Mrs. Carter was discharged; other patients came and went. Weeks turned to months. Arneda thought less and less of her promise to God. Less effort was made to witness until one day she realized the seriousness of her promise and failure.

There was great excitement outside. The doorbell rang; someone called, "Come quickly, Doctor Kendel! There has been a bad accident—several people are seriously injured!"

After packing in his bag the things he would need, Arneda met Doctor Kendel at the door with it and he was off. Arneda wondered, "Who is hurt? How seriously? Will we have more patients?" She did not have long to wonder.

The ambulance soon arrived, bringing two-month-old Debbie, her father, and her six-year-old brother. All were brought in for X rays. Little Debbie, seemingly in good condition, was placed in a small crib to wait until her grandparents could come for her.

Arneda again joined Doctor Kendel, helping him dress Mr. Carter's wounds and those of his young son. At the first opportunity, she asked, "Dr. Kendel, was Mrs. Carter along? Was she hurt?"

After a moment's pause (checking to be sure his patients were out of hearing distance) Doctor Kendel answered, "Mrs. Carter was killed instantly."

Mrs. Carter killed instantly—now in the presence of God without a moment's notice! Her destiny was sealed—time was past—eternity begun!

Oh, for one more opportunity to speak to Mrs. Carter of Jesus' precious blood shed for us, of His redeeming love, and of our personal responsibility to accept it!

As these thoughts rushed through Arneda's troubled mind, it seemed more than she could bear; she wanted to cry out to everyone to accept Christ's love and pardon while there was yet time. Her tongue seemed paralyzed—she could not talk. She wanted to flee from the presence of the Carter children who had lost a mother with no hope of seeing her again. As she stared, she saw only the longing restless face of Mrs. Carter; then all was blank.

Doctor Kendel, alarmed when his nurse slumped to the floor, quickly called for an assistant, thinking that the ugly wounds of the Carter boy were more than she could bear. Arneda regained consciousness in a few minutes. Arneda realized she had lost an opportunity she would never regain.

By a few months later, each patient whose lot it was to be confined to this hospital was often gently reminded of the emptiness, the weariness, and the danger of a life not surrendered to God, through the testimony of a sympathetic, concerned nurse. This proved to be a blessing both to Arneda and her patients.

But never could Arneda erase from her memory the many lost opportunities.

The Midnight Prayer Meeting

"God bless you," John Wagler greeted Paul Sharp at the door of the church.

"God bless you," the other returned, with a warm handshake and a kiss of love.

Martin Wells joined the brethren, greeting them in the same manner.

"We surely need more of the type of message we heard this evening, don't we?" Martin remarked.

"Yes," Paul agreed. "John and I were just talking about the need of putting into practice now the things we have heard. Our ministers have faithfully brought the Word to us. What are we going to do about it now? Can we just say, 'That was a wonderful message!' and then go on, content to sit back and do nothing?"

"No," John Wagler answered. "We cannot. When we hear the Word, we react to it in one way or another. Either we reject it or we accept it. No doubt there are sinners around us. We meet them every day. Are we witnessing to them? Do we know the Lord and experience fellowship with Him? Have we told our neighbors about it?"

"Brother, those questions you've asked are truly heart-searching." Martin hung his head. "I'm afraid I for one will have to confess I've often failed in leaving a good testimony with those with whom I come in contact daily. Too often I've been satisfied that all is well with my soul and have not felt a real burden for

268

my neighbors when it is evident that they need the Lord."

The lights went out in the main building, and the three brethren realized that they were left alone in the vestibule. Only the janitor remained. Everyone else had gone home and the janitor was leaving now by the side door.

Paul looked at his watch. "We have stood here an hour discussing this," he exclaimed. "Prayer meeting dismissed at nine o'clock. I would like to suggest that we three do something more definitely about the matter of concern for other souls, beginning right now."

The other two brethren waited for his suggestion.

"Why don't we just continue our prayer meeting right here now, bringing our concerns to the Father?"

The brethren were agreeable to this suggestion. Kneeling together there in the vestibule, they poured out their hearts to God, first confessing their own carelessness in the matter of seeking lost souls. There were many burdens expressed for members in the church and for the lost about them. The Spirit's presence could be felt as they united their hearts together in fervent intercession. It seemed that the Lord had laid on the hearts of all three brethren the concern for one family in particular. Over and over again the Woods family was mentioned. The burden just was not lifted. There was a need. Something must be done!

At twelve o'clock the three brethren arose from their knees, tears streaming across their faces.

"The Lord has spoken to us about a need in our own congregation," Martin reminded the brethren. "What are we going to do about it?"

"Yes, we have prayed, but I wonder if the Lord isn't asking us to go a step farther. When there is a need we are also responsible to see what can be done about correcting it."

"What are you suggesting?" John asked.

"I hardly know," Martin Wells began slowly. "But I feel

strongly that something should be done for the Woods."

"Perhaps since we hardly know how to proceed it might be well to speak to our ministers about this before going any further. We do want to be faithful to the Lord. But on the other hand, we don't want to run ahead of the Lord. Why don't we wait until we can speak with Brother Mast and Brother Tice?" Paul cautioned.

"But, brethren, the Lord has spoken. You believe that, don't you? He laid the burden on the heart of each of us."

The other two nodded. They felt definitely that this was true.

"Then how long are you suggesting we wait?" Martin questioned. "The Lord gave us the burden tonight. Why didn't He just wait till our help was needed to lay the burden on our hearts? I propose we seek His leading and proceed now. There is no question that they need help. The Lord has laid this burden heavily on us without question. Are we willing to be used of Him?"

The brethren waited, solemnly weighing the possibilities of trying to help the Woods.

"Would you two be willing to go with me to Brother Mast's home now?" Martin pushed for action. "We could simply go and explain our burden and ask his advice. I will be content then to leave the decision with him as to how to proceed. But I cannot be content until something is done toward obedience to the call we have all felt."

After some discussion this plan was agreed upon. At twelve-thirty Brother Mast was surprised by a persistent knocking on his door.

"Come right in, Brethren," he invited, greeting each one warmly as they entered the room. "Come in and sit down."

There was a moment's silence before Brother Wells spoke. "Brother Mast, we have come to you for help. We want you to know we appreciate the ministry here and your faithful service to us. We three have been together since prayer meeting dismissed, praying for the lost about us and for needs in our own congregation. It seems the Lord has especially laid one need on the hearts of us all. This is the Wood family."

Brother Mast sat quietly for some time, in deep thought.

"The Lord has so definitely spoken to us about a need here that I cannot rest until something is done for them," Martin continued.

"I will look into it soon," Brother Mast promised. "I believe the Lord has spoken to you and I'm glad you have taken the burden seriously."

"Then you will go over and speak to them now?" Martin Wells surprised the minister by his urgency.

Brother Mast looked thoughtful. "It's one o'clock. Don't you suppose the Woods are all in bed sleeping?"

"Well, maybe they are," Martin replied. "That may well be. But what if they are? The Lord might come before morning! Then what? If God spoke to our hearts at midnight, He can speak to theirs at one o'clock. We'd better mind the Lord and go see if we can help them now, it seems to me."

Brother Mast walked slowly across the room. "I don't know about getting people out of bed to talk to them about the Lord. And yet, I hesitate to wait since you brethren have spent the night praying and the Lord has given you this burden."

"Brother Mast, why don't we pray once more and seek definite guidance in this matter?" John suggested.

"Yes," Martin agreed. "After prayer, I will consent to leave the decision with you." The four men knelt in silent prayer for several minutes before leading out one by one in earnest desire for help and guidance.

When they arose from their knees, Brother Mast walked out into the dining room, picked up the telephone receiver, and dialed a number.

271

"Good morning, Brother Tice."

"Yes, this is Simon Mast."

"I want to counsel with you on a problem that confronts me now."

Brother Mast went on to explain the situation.

"Yes," he agreed after several minutes. "If you will come, I will consent to go now."

After hanging up the receiver, he returned to the men waiting in the living room.

"Would you brethren be satisfied if Brother Tice and I would go alone and see how the Lord directs us further?"

"Yes, we certainly would. And we will remain in prayer for you until you return," Martin offered readily.

"Yes," Paul agreed. "I feel this is of the Lord and we will be happy to continue in prayer for guidance for you brethren in this contact."

John also expressed his satisfaction with this plan.

"God bless and direct you," Martin encouraged the ministers as they left the house.

The three brethren continued in fervent prayer for two more hours.

Soon after they arose from their knees, the minister's car returned.

*   *   *   *   *   *   *   *   *   *   *   *

"Brother Tice, this is an unusual call we are making tonight. I do definitely feel the Lord is leading in this, but I don't quite understand," Brother Mast began soon after they left the house at one-thirty. "I've never before called on a member after midnight."

"Yes, this is unusual," Brother Tice agreed. "But somehow I can't doubt the sincerity of the brethren who were praying. There

272

is a definite need in the Wood home. It seems up to this time we haven't been able to put our finger on anything, and yet we know the need exists. Perhaps by carefully following the Lord's leading now, we can accomplish something toward better attitudes and deeper spirituality there."

"Look," Brother Mast exclaimed suddenly. "The house is lit up as if it were early evening."

"Sure," Brother Tice sounded as if there were nothing unusual about lights at one-thirty. "You didn't expect the Lord to bring us over to talk to a sleeping family, did you? Why, the Lord knew all the time when we'd get here," he finished expectantly.

Together the brethren walked across the lawn, wondering how to explain this unusual visit, but they did not have long time for such contemplations. When the first sound of their knocking was heard, there were hurried steps on the stairway. The door was flung wide open. The loud talking and commotion in the kitchen stopped.

A young girl stood in the doorway. Her eyes were red and swollen. Her distressed expression gave the ministers new assurance that they were certainly called of the Lord to make this visit at this hour.

"Oh, I knew someone would come soon," she cried. "I've prayed all night that God would send us help. It seemed you'd never come!"

"What is the trouble?" Brother Mast asked. "What can we do for you?"

"Mama and Papa have been fighting and fussing ever since we got home from prayer meeting. I can't stand it any longer!" The opening of the door brought Brother and Sister Wood to the front room.

After her sudden outburst, their daughter turned and fled back upstairs, leaving the two ministers standing in the open doorway facing her parents, each too baffled to speak.

There was an awkward pause. The ministers felt that their presence needed to be explained and the Woods were unable to explain their quarreling.

"We felt led of the Lord to visit you folks tonight. Is there anything we can do to help?" Brother Mast asked with concern.

"We need help," Brother Wood admitted, hanging his head in shame. "Come inside, please."

The four were seated in the living room. "We do not wish to pry into family affairs," Brother Mast explained, "only to be of help if we can be."

Brother Tice went on to explain their reason for being there and the burden that was felt by the interceding brethren.

The Woods were deeply touched and were open to be helped. They saw their need and surrendered. Together they discussed and prayed over their problems.

After a little tip-toeing around upstairs, all was quiet. Evidently the young daughter could now lie down and sleep.

The Woods' responsiveness to the Word greatly encouraged the ministers. In a short while it seemed that the problems were all ironed out. The four knelt together to seek forgiveness and grace to go on, faithful to the Lord.

"We thank you for coming." Brother Wood gripped the hand of his pastor. Embracing one another, the brethren wept together, marveling at the way God answered prayer.

Did It Just Happen?

Uncle Harry drove slowly along the country road, enjoying the lovely spring scenery. Everything seemed refreshed by the rain that had fallen the evening before. Now the sun glistened on the wet grass. The two-hour drive to the new home he was building in Sunnyslope was a pleasure on these early spring mornings.

Nearing Sunnyslope, Uncle Harry noticed an old, bent man walking slowly along the road ahead. He was not in the habit of picking up hitchhikers, but this was different. "Who knows? He may be my neighbor some day." Uncle Harry chuckled pleasantly and pulled to a stop. "Would you like a ride?" he called.

"Yes, if you're going toward town," the man answered, obviously thankful for a lift.

Uncle Harry thought quickly. He had not planned to go on into town this morning. And the road into Sunnyslope turned off just about a hundred feet ahead. "Why not run on into town for those nails right away this morning," he decided. "I would need them by this afternoon anyway."

"Yes," he answered, "I will be going to Southern Hardware. You are welcome to ride along."

"Sure would be glad to," the old man answered, pulling himself into the door Harry opened for him. "I used to easily walk these few miles into town, but it's not easy anymore."

"A few years makes a difference, doesn't it?" Harry chuckled.

"Nice morning though, isn't it?"

"Yes, it sure is. Makes a fellow feel good to walk, too. Where are you from?" The man changed the subject, looking at Harry as if he were not used to seeing strangers in these parts.

"I'm from over on Eastern Shore, about a hundred miles from here," Uncle Harry replied. "I am in the process of building a house in Sunnyslope—expect to move down here in about two months."

"I see." The older man seemed pleased. "Do you like it here?"

"Yes, indeed, I do. This is nice country. A whole group of our people are settling in the Sunnyslope area. There will be a half dozen families at least," Uncle Harry explained.

The man looked a little doubtful. "A whole group." This was unusual. Neighbors had not changed much here for years. "What do you represent? What are you coming here for?" he questioned like one who belonged and had a right to know.

"We are a church group. We are here only to represent our Father and His Son, our Savior."

The man listened with interest, nodding slightly every now and then.

"We are Mennonites," Harry explained further. "Our people do not like living in the crowded areas near large cities, so we are moving out here in the country. We want to get our children on farms. Most of us have large families."

The native of this community now seemed at ease, and even pleased to have these strange people a part of their quiet community. "What do you believe and practice in your religion?" he wondered next.

Uncle Harry gave a brief statement of what the faith and practice of their church had been and of their intention as a group to hold to these things to the end, though many are departing from them these days. "Here," he finished, "is a little booklet, *What We Believe.* Take it with you and read it," he offered.

"Thank you." He accepted the booklet, scanning its pages as they entered the small town of Bells Mill. When Uncle Harry pulled up in front of Southern Hardware, his visitor reached for the door handle. Then, looking back over his shoulder, he said, "Will you pray for me, Sir? I know I need the Lord." With that he stepped out of the car and hurried down the street.

"What a strange and abrupt way to end our first visit!" Harry exclaimed. He sat still for a minute, almost expecting the man to return to talk some more. He watched him until he disappeared in the doorway of a small shop.

Uncle Harry purchased his nails. He came out and looked all around. "I wonder if Mr.—what is his name? I do believe I forgot to ask him. Well, I do wonder who he is and where he went. I would be glad if he would ride along back with me." Uncle Harry started down the only street in this small town. There were no more than half a dozen small stores and shops on either side of the road, but his search was fruitless. After spending a half hour, Uncle Harry decided to go on out to Sunnyslope alone. "If I don't soon get started, I won't get much done today."

Harry's mind turned again and again to the man who had seemed much interested in his beliefs and even felt enough concern for his soul to request prayer. He had admitted that he was away from the Lord. "Why, oh, why didn't I get his name and address—at least his name? Maybe I could find him then. I have no idea where he lives. How will I ever find the man? And he seemed to be such an honest seeker."

Uncle Harry went about the task of building his house day after day. Some days he thought much about the man and always looked for him when he went to Bells Mill, but after not seeing him for weeks and weeks, the old man was less and less in his thoughts. Harry had often prayed for him, hoping that some day he would have another opportunity to speak to him and help him. He was often sorry he had not said more that day concerning salvation.

Uncle Harry finished his house and was soon settled in Sunnyslope. Within a year six Mennonite families were living there. They were being watched by curious neighbors who had not known of Mennonites before.

Uncle Harry's nephew was the last to move into the new community. Samuel Mann had come with his six children and was now living next door to Uncle Harry. The children loved the country and were interested a great deal in the farm. Six-year-old Johnny was eager to get eggs set in his little incubator. He could hardly wait to have some chicks hatch out.

"Uncle Harry doesn't have chickens anymore like he did in Eastern Shore," his father explained. "So we will have to wait until we get to town to get you some setting eggs."

On Friday evening when his father was ready to go for groceries, Johnny asked, "May I go with you?"

"Yes, you may go along, Son. Why do you want to go along?" he asked, noticing the boy's eagerness.

"Well, Papa, I thought maybe we could get some eggs for my incubator," Johnny grinned.

"I see. Well, perhaps we can. We will see what we can do."

In the grocery store Johnny waited patiently while Papa filled the cart. But when he passed the egg counter without getting any eggs, he asked, "Weren't we going to get eggs?"

"We can't get them here, Son. These eggs have been in cold storage. We want fresh eggs for your incubator."

"Where will we get them?" Johnny asked, keeping his eyes on the pretty white eggs.

"We will see if we can find a farm on the way home where they have chickens. Then we will stop and see if we can buy some eggs."

As they left town Johnny sat forward on the seat, helping to watch for a chicken farm.

"Here, Papa, here! They have lots and lots of chickens. Let's stop!" Johnny was excited. Samuel slowed down, but when he noticed they had already passed the driveway, he kept rolling on. "There are other farms. I guess we won't turn around. Try to watch for the next one a little quicker."

Soon Johnny called again. "O Papa. They had chicken houses, too, but I didn't notice till we were past." This happened a number of times. Most everyone had chickens, but it seemed no place seemed the right place to stop.

"There—up ahead—see, Papa, they have a chicken house and there are the chickens all over the yard."

Samuel stopped in the driveway. The house was all closed up and the blinds all drawn. There were no signs of anyone around. No car was in the open garage. "I don't believe anyone is at home here. Let's go on and look for another," Papa suggested. But Johnny was very disappointed.

"We are almost home. Maybe no one else has chickens."

They drove on and on. Johnny was just beginning to think he was not going to have any eggs for his incubator when Papa suddenly pulled to a stop and backed in a driveway to a small house. Yes, there was a chicken house and about half a dozen chickens in the fenced yard. A large rooster sat proudly on a post near the yard gate.

Johnny bounced up and down with joy. There was someone at home here. An old, bent man was coming up the path, holding three or four fresh eggs he had just gathered.

"Good evening," Samuel called. "I am Samuel Mann from the Sunnyslope area. You wouldn't sell a few eggs, would you?"

"Well, sir, I don't sell eggs, but I might let you have a few if you need them," the old man answered.

Samuel explained about the boy's incubator. "Sure. He is

welcome to these eggs. No, no, I don't want anything for them," he hurriedly added when Samuel reached for his billfold.

"Be glad to pay you," Samuel offered, sorting through his change.

"No indeed," the man replied, handing him the three warm eggs. "Say your name is Samuel Mann?"

"Yes, sir. And yours?"

"I'm Dan Collins. I've lived here all my life. My wife died last fall. I've been alone since then and mighty lonesome. The grandchildren come over once in a while and spend a day or so. I'd be glad if you and the boy would stay awhile."

"Really, we need to be getting home this evening. Maybe we could come another time and get better acquainted."

"You are not related to the Harry Mann who was going to live out in the Sunnyslope area about a year ago, are you?"

"Yes. He's my uncle," Samuel replied.

"I've often wondered about that man and wished to see him again. He picked me up one day on his way into Bells Mill. Has your church gotten settled out there yet?"

"Yes, we are all getting pretty well settled. We have lots of building to do yet till we get our church and school both finished. Come out to church sometime."

"I'd like to. But I don't have a car and don't get around much," the old man replied. "Tell Mr. Mann to stop by and see me sometime."

"I will," Samuel Mann promised. "Come, Johnny. We must go. Mama will be looking for us."

After supper Samuel Mann with his wife and children went down to visit Uncle Harry and his family.

"Say, Uncle Harry, you don't happen to remember an old man hitchhiking into Bells Mill one day last spring, do you?"

Uncle Harry started to shake his head. Then suddenly he exclaimed, "Why, yes. I certainly do remember an old man I picked up one day. Did you find him? Where does he live? Who is he?"

"Just a minute, Uncle Harry. Now what is so exciting about finding your hitchhiker?"

"Why, I've wished for a year or more for an opportunity to meet him again and have been praying for the man. He seemed real interested in our church and expressed a concern for his own soul. Now what is the man's name?" Uncle Harry began again.

"He is Dan Collins. He lives out here on Route 249 about a mile before you turn in on Sunnyslope Road toward Bells Mill."

"Well, well! I was afraid I would never meet him again. Dan Collins, you say?" Uncle Harry repeated, pulling a note pad out of his shirt pocket. "I must go see him."

"Yes, you surely must," his nephew agreed heartily. "He asked us to bring you that message. His wife died in the fall and he is alone. He gets very lonesome and doesn't get around much."

"Yes, I want to go and see him right away," Uncle Harry decided.

The following morning about ten o'clock found Dan and Uncle Harry visiting like old friends.

"Sure am glad your nephew happened to stop here for eggs," Dan remarked. "I have been hoping to get in touch with you folks somehow."

"Did it just happen?" Uncle Harry asked himself on the way home. "No, God surely has directed in this contact."

"Father, continue to direct," he prayed, "as other contacts are made with this man who seems to be an honest seeker. May we be faithful in helping him to find the way."

At prayer meeting that evening Uncle Harry told the others about the man out on Route 249 who would like a group to come and have a cottage meeting in his home.

"Here is an opportunity. Let us be faithful to answer the call."

The Last Opportunity

Samuel Horst picked up his toolbox as he walked through the garage. Hurriedly he flung it onto the back of the truck. A few long strides brought him to the door. Pulling himself up onto the seat of the truck, Samuel turned the switch. He was in a hurry this morning, but already he was later than usual getting started. He hoped this was no indication of the way the day would go.

Samuel looked at his watch again as he pulled out of the driveway. "Seven-thirty." He spoke to no one but himself. Samuel was alone this morning to hang the garage door on the last house in Sharon Heights. Ray and John were not working today. "I surely hope I can finish by noon." Samuel pushed the watch back into his pocket. "I should be able to if I don't have any trouble."

Samuel had only about six miles to this job. That was to his advantage.

At noon Verda would have herself and the children ready. They would eat a quick lunch and then start for the fellowship meeting. That would give them time to reach Roxbury before the evening meeting started. But there would be no time to waste.

Samuel pulled into the driveway of the last brick house on Camelia Street. He set to work immediately. Things were going well. "I can easily finish till noon," he decided at ten o'clock.

"Good morning, Mr. Horst," a friendly voice greeted the busy man. He had not noticed Mr. Carter approaching.

"Oh, good morning, Mr. Carter," Samuel returned the friendly greeting.

"How are you today?" Samuel continued, tightening bolts and fastening springs. He just did not have time to come down and visit this morning.

"I reckon I'm all right," Mr. Carter answered halfheartedly. "I don't know. It seems I've been having a funny feeling in here the last several days," Mr. Carter answered, holding his hand across his chest. "I think I'll go to have a checkup one of these days. Lots of people are having heart trouble these days, you know."

"Yes," Samuel answered without taking his eyes off his work.

Mr. Carter had been a regular visitor for the past months while the Horst group hung all the garage doors in Sharon Heights. On a number of occasions Samuel had had good talks with him. Through these visits he had discovered that Mr. Carter considered himself a good moral man but did not profess to have experienced the New Birth. At times he had seemed interested and had been quite free and open to discuss this subject with Samuel. Always Samuel had taken time to simply stop and visit when the middle-aged Mr. Carter appeared on the job.

This morning he was pushed for time. This job must be finished today. The meeting two hundred miles away would begin at seven-thirty. There just was not a minute to spare. Samuel picked up another wrench and went on tightening bolts.

"I sometimes get a feeling I won't be here much longer," Mr Carter went on, still rubbing his chest as if in discomfort.

Now Samuel paused. "Mr. Carter," he spoke earnestly, "how about your soul? Have you done anything about making sure that all is well?" Looking searchingly at the man, he waited for an answer.

"Well, Mr. Horst, I just don't know. I have never been a bad man, but I'm just not sure that all is well," Mr. Carter answered with frankness and honesty.

"Mr. Carter." Samuel came down the ladder a few steps. "Mr. Carter, won't you come in here and let me pray with you, or is there something I can explain to you? I will be happy to study the Word with you awhile and pray with you. The Lord has offered us salvation. We can accept or reject it. All eternity will depend on this decision. It is important that you make sure."

"No, no, Mr. Horst, not right now. I'll think about it. In fact, I've been thinking seriously about it. But I'm not ready to make a decision just yet. There are things I don't understand."

"I will be happy to help you find your answers in the Word for these things," Samuel offered. He picked up a few more bolts.

"No, not right now." Mr. Carter slowly started to walk away.

Samuel breathed a prayer for the man and went on to finish the job. As if reluctant to leave, Mr. Carter paused several times as he was going out the driveway and watched Mr. Horst at his work.

"Possibly I should go down and urge him to make a decision now. Or maybe if I'd offer to come over to his home some evening we could have a better talk. But we will be away at the fellowship meetings for about a week now. I'll find him when I come back," Samuel decided. "He surely does look old this morning."

Soon the job was finished. Samuel hurried home where Verda and the children were waiting and ready for dinner. In less than an hour they were on their way.

After enjoying rich blessings in fellowship with hundreds of others of like precious faith, the Horsts returned home on Saturday.

Not once had Mr. Carter been in his thoughts the entire weekend. Early on Monday Samuel drove to Sharon Heights to pick up the toolbox he had forgotten last Wednesday in his haste.

When he arrived, one of the bricklayers was already on the job.

"Say, Mr. Horst," he called from his perch high on the scaffold. "Do you remember that Mr. Carter you talked to last Wednesday morning?"

"Yes, sir," Samuel answered.

"They buried him Saturday afternoon," the bricklayer stated.

"Saturday afternoon," Samuel repeated.

"Yes, he left here Wednesday morning, went home, and told his wife he's not feeling well. She didn't think of anything serious, though he just sat in the house all afternoon and went to bed early that evening.

"On Thursday morning he did not awaken at the usual time. When she went to call him, he was dead."

Samuel's thoughts went back to the Wednesday morning visit. "Should I have pressed him for a decision? If only I hadn't been so busy, perhaps he would have visited longer. I had no idea this was my last visit with Mr. Carter. By God's help I want to be more faithful to witness at times when the door is open." He felt a deep sense of remorse for having lost his opportunity.

For Your Protection

Ruth and Sarah sat waiting for the 4:30 train. The large depot was crowded. Like the crowd of people around them, they watched the tracks, listening for the next announcement, and carried purses and tickets.

But in appearance they were quite different. Their dresses were noticeably longer. There was no outward display on their clothing or shoes. On their heads were neat black bonnets, sufficiently covering their head and ears for adequate protection against the strong gusts of wind outside. Their hair was simply fixed, covered in back by the bonnet and showing only enough in front to reveal that it was well kept and neatly drawn back over the head.

Sarah and Ruth had been the object of considerable attention since they entered the depot.

The girls talked quietly between themselves and were no part of the noise and confusion about them. There was the general hustle and bustle of those coming in at the last minute. Some were nervous and irritated. Some were loud and using every means to draw attention. There were shrill whistles and loud laughter as the crowd passed by them.

Suddenly the train pulled into the station. The name of the city to which Ruth and Sarah were headed was called over the loudspeaker. Quickly they gathered up their things and walked out to the train.

While waiting to enter, Ruth placed her heavy suitcase on the platform. Just then two young boys came rushing up, nearly upsetting the baggage. The crowd pressed close to the entrance. The boys pushed closer. Ruth could feel their breath on her neck. In this position it was impossible not to hear the sneers and remarks of the boys.

Using a number of vile words, the tall boy called the attention of the other to the "queer girls" in front of them. Both boys laughed loudly. The language of the second boy was no cleaner than that of the first. Ruth and Sarah edged closer together, moving with the crowd toward the entrance.

Inside the train, they walked near the back of the car before being seated.

"I hope they're not on this car," Ruth whispered.

"Yes," Sarah agreed. "I don't mind being mocked and laughed at for my modesty and simplicity. My Savior was mocked and jeered at, too. But I certainly don't like those boys so close."

"They followed us all the way across the platform," Ruth confided in undertones. "I surely hope they won't come in here."

Suddenly a very familiar whistle sounded from the front of the car. Both girls kept their heads lowered. They did not need to look up to know that they were still being followed.

"I believe we should breathe a silent prayer that we might be a real witness for Christ on this trip and might in no way, by our actions or speech, bring reproach to Christ's Name," Sarah suggested.

"Yes," Ruth agreed almost inaudibly. "I believe it would be well to ask for our protection, too."

Both girls remained silent for some time.

"You know, Ruth," Sarah spoke softly as the train rolled along, leaving the station far in the distance, "at times like this I wonder how some girls can so easily leave off the Christian Woman's Veiling. You never know when such a situation will arise. God has provided this veiling for a sign of our submission to His order and plan for mankind, showing the headship of Christ in the Christian church and the headship of man under Christ in the home and the church. We certainly should be a witness at all times and be able to come to Him with our present needs. I surely feel that the covering was intended to be worn at all times."

"Yes, indeed," Ruth agreed. "We really have much to be thankful for. We've been privileged to have been taught these things from our youth."

By this time the boys had come up the aisle and stood less than six feet from Ruth and Sarah.

With a cynical smile the tall boy stopped shortly, as if his attention had suddenly been arrested by some most unusual appearance. For a full half minute he stared, his expression never changing until the other boy said, "Here, the seat right behind them is empty. Be seated before you pass clear out." In mock gesture of half fainting the tall boy dropped into the seat and burst into a most derisive laughter. Loud and long both boys laughed, amidst many cruel and insulting remarks about the "queer girls" in the seat in front of them. Their shoes, hose, dresses, and black bonnets all were discussed at length and each ridiculed in turn.

The girls remained silent most of the time, except for an occasional remark about some lovely countryside scenery.

The air became stuffy and warm. To be more comfortable, Ruth and Sarah removed their bonnets. This seemingly gave occasion for one more outburst of ridicule from the mocking boys. With vile words the tall boy began expressing his feelings about that "ridiculous white thing" on the girls' heads, referring of course to the veiling.

"Why, it's enough to scare the devil!" he remarked sarcastically.

"That's exactly why we're wearing them," Ruth said in a quiet and earnest voice as she turned and faced their tormentors. She looked squarely into his eyes for only a moment, then turned her back again and remained silent.

So far each torment had been met by complete silence on the part of the girls. Now the meek and quiet answer that Ruth had very simply given seemed to stop completely the mouths of the two who before knew only ridicule and abuse for anything sacred and pure.

The boys left their seat, never to be seen by the girls again.

Ruth and Sarah thanked God that He had made every provision for the Christian's testimony to be effective in a sinful world and for their protection.

"Have You Kept That Vow?"

Janet's Disappointment

"Uncle Harry, I will carry in the wood for you this evening," Janet offered. "Mama said I may stay ten minutes." Janet felt sorry for Uncle Harry when she saw that it hurt him to walk. He was using his cane more and more.

"But you wanted to see the new pictures Aunt Jane got yesterday, didn't you?"

"Yes, but I can see them any time," Janet suggested. "The wood has to be carried in now. Maybe I can hurry fast enough for both," she offered cheerfully, starting toward the little woodpile.

Uncle Harry slipped back out of his blue denim jacket, grateful that he would not need to get out in the cold with his aching limbs. Ten minutes later Janet waved good-bye with a satisfied feeling, though she was a bit disappointed about not getting to see the pictures.

"Janet," Uncle Harry called from his seat by the cozy fire in the front room. "Your birthday is next week, isn't it?"

"Yes," she answered.

"I am going to see that you have a nice surprise. Thanks for bringing in the wood."

Janet looked forward to this birthday more than any before. What would Uncle Harry's surprise be? Her birthday came and went. She waited expectantly. Days passed. She never said a word but kept hoping. When months and years passed, Janet stopped looking for the surprise, but she could never forget the sad disappointment this experience had been in her childhood. It nearly broke her heart.

Sara's Applesause

"Good morning, Sister Anna," Sara greeted her neighbor. "Come on in."

"No, I don't have time to sit down," Anna replied when Sara pulled out a chair for her. "Our trees were so loaded with apples that I have been making sauce nearly every day for two weeks."

"Oh, what a blessing to have so much good fruit!" Sara answered wistfully, remembering her one lone jar of applesauce on the bare pantry shelf. Even it would not be there if she would not have set it aside to open sometime when there was company.

"Could you use some apples?" Anna asked.

"Oh, I surely could!" Sara's face lit up hopefully.

"They are not very nice this year. But if you would want to bother with them I will be glad to send you several bushels."

"That is very kind of you. But I have no jars. Perhaps I could not handle that many," Sara replied, embarrassed. There was no money for buying jars now. But how she would have loved to have those apples!

"I have about a hundred jars in the attic since we have the new freezer," Anna offered. "You are welcome to them."

"Oh, I do thank you." Tears came to Sara's eyes. "God bless you for your kindness."

"The boys will bring the jars along over when they bring the apples," Anna offered generously. "I know you don't have any way to get around, with John in the hospital."

Days passed. Sara waited. The apples and jars were never mentioned again. The lone jar of applesause was opened that winter with a pang as Sara remembered the unkept promise.

Aunt Susie's Niece

"Aunt Susie, it is so good to see you again," Laura cried, throwing her arms around the invalid. It had been ten years and Aunt Susie was quite changed from the bustling, busy woman in the kitchen that Laura had always known her from childhood.

Tears came to Aunt Susie's eyes. "I am so glad you could come. The days get so long since I cannot leave my bed. It seems so few people ever stop by."

"I see you have a nice scrapbook here," Laura said, leafing through the well-worn pages.

"Yes, it is one I got about five years ago and I still enjoy it as much as the day I got it. I suppose I have read some of those pieces a hundred times and more."

"Aunt Susie, do you know what I am going to do as soon as I get home?" Laura asked the day she was leaving. "I am going to sit right down and make you a new scrapbook."

"Oh, you dear, dear niece!" the older woman cried, so pleased at the prospect. "You were always such a thoughtful child." She hugged her over and over, telling her what a blessing it was to have her here a few days again and what a pleasure it would be to look forward to a new book to read! "Thank you so much for your kindness. I will watch the mail eagerly every day till my scrapbook comes," she added.

It had only been about a week since Laura returned to her family, but already Aunt Susie watched eagerly each day for the package. "Laura is busy," she said. Perhaps it will come next week."

The long winter days passed slowly. Aunt Susie spent hours with the cherished old book. But each day brought new disappointment when the promised book did not come.

Two years later Aunt Susie went to be with the Lord, nevermore to know a disappointment.

"I had planned to make her a scrapbook," Laura said

casually to a friend, "but I never got it done."

The Vows You Made

You stood before the church and in the presence of God and solemnly vowed to be faithful to Him. You promised to renounce the sins of the world, your own carnal will, and desired to be true to the church and help, encourage, and uphold the sound doctrine you believe. You promised to keep your life pure and free from sin. Have you kept that vow? Are you breaking someone's heart? A promise not kept may cause deepest grief. Our Father yearns over His children, longingly, patiently waiting for each to keep his vows. Have you kept that vow?

The Price Is High

It was time for prayer meeting to begin. Lena glanced around. Most everyone was there—everyone but Bill, and no one expected to see him at prayer meeting. It had been months since he had attended any regular services. Quick tears came to her eyes as she saw all the other young sisters with their husbands and families around them. She always had to come alone, with a few of the children she could induce to leave the television that long. Recently the older ones almost always stayed home with their father.

That television! It had wrecked their home. Bill had stopped attending church—and then one by one the children did, too. There were no more enjoyable evenings with the family together. They were too wrapped up in that TV. And what a problem it was now to get any of them to leave it long enough to eat a meal or even go to bed! The Benders seldom all ate together at the table anymore. Someone had a favorite show to watch, no matter what time she served a meal.

With a heavy heart, Lena knelt with the group of believers that evening. For months she had been praying about their problem. This evening, at last, she had shared her concern with the rest of the church. Lena was ashamed that a television set had entered their home. She had pleaded with Bill not to get it. But he wanted it and brought it in. There was nothing she could do. Now she decided to commit it to the Lord. Only He could get it out of their home before it damned the souls of her dear children. What a change had come over their happy home in these past months since that evil influence had come in! Something must be done soon or she could not expect her children to grow up to be serious, sober-minded Christian young people.

Several had led out in prayer, each one remembering the need in the Bender home. They prayed for Bill's salvation and for Lena in the problem she faced of raising her children alone since Bill no longer encouraged the children in spiritual things.

There was a long pause, then Lena prayed. "Lord, somehow remove that television from our home at any price!" These words were not uttered thoughtlessly, nor without counting the cost. No, Lena did not know how the Lord would do this. But she knew He was not pleased that any instrument of the devil should rob her family of pure minds, planting all kinds of evil thoughts and intentions in their young hearts. The Lord was able to remove this influence somehow. What would the price be? Lena did not know, but she was willing to pay any price to save her family.

After the service Lena started home. The burden was heavy. Yet there was an assurance that God would somehow remove the television and its evil influence from their home. Had He not promised that if we ask according to His will our request would be granted? Claiming this promise, she left the problem with the Lord to solve and work out in His own good way. Whatever that way would be, she was ready to submit to it.

Arriving home, she noticed the car was gone. The boys and Carol were alone in the dimly-lighted living room. There was not another sound in the house but the noise coming from the corner where all eyes were glued, watching with breathless interest a wild western show.

"Where is your father?" Lena spoke, walking directly to the television set and turning the knob.

"O Mama, you scared me!" Carol screamed. "I didn't know you were here."

"Please, Mama," the boys begged in unison. "Just a few more minutes would finish that program." John rushed to the TV, trying to reach the knob over which she continued to hold her hand firmly.

"No," she said firmly. "It is bedtime and this is not fit to see. I wish you would not. . ."

"Mama!" Don raced across the floor. "Please, just a few more minutes. I just have to know what is going to happen to that Indian." Both boys fought for the knob.

"Boys, no," their mother repeated firmly. "No more tonight—nor ever—if I can help it!" She looked at them pleadingly. Why should such temptations be set before children too young to know the dangers? Her heart bled for them.

"Go over there and sit down." John and Don turned and sullenly obeyed. Where was the cheerful obedience she used to get from both boys? The TV had surely changed many things.

"Where did your father go?" Lena again turned to the boys. Twelve-year-old Don shrugged his shoulders and looked away, showing plainly he did not want to answer. "John, do you know where your father went?" She looked straight at her oldest son who hung his head for a moment. Then, seeing she was waiting for an answer, he replied, "Over to the poolroom with Mr. White."

"Boys, I am sorry to have to tell you this, but I hope you will not follow your father's example. The path he is following will not lead to joy, peace, and heaven— only heartache and disappointment. I wish you would go to church with me regularly as we used to do."

Both boys hung their heads. Ten-year-old Carol fidgeted uneasily under her mother's searching, pleading gaze. Until only a few months ago they had all attended church regularly. But

Father stayed home—so why shouldn't they?

"Let's go to bed, children," Mama spoke tenderly. "We will talk more about this in the morning." Without a word of protest the three oldest children walked to their rooms while Lena tucked the babies in.

"If only Bill would come back to the Lord. What a difference it would make in our home!" Lena remembered how it used to be before Bill started running around with Mr. White and his gang. How their family had worked together and enjoyed good times together!

"Father," Lena breathed a silent prayer as she settled the children, "speak to Bill tonight. Draw him back into the fold. And somehow save my children. Lord, use me as it pleases you. And, Father, remove this evil influence from our home at any cost!"

There was no use to wait for Bill if he was out with Mr. White, so Lena went to bed. The house was quiet. The night was long. Sometime toward morning Lena fell asleep, resting assured that God would work things out for her family somehow. She did not know that the next morning the TV would be moved out of her living room, never to return, without a word of protest from anyone. Nor did she know that even this very night the very one who had brought this evil influence into their home had left the house never to return.

Shortly after Bill left the house that Wednesday evening, he was involved in a fatal accident—hurled instantly into eternity!

"What Would You Do?"

John stood in line, restlessly awaiting his turn. There would have to be a big crowd here today to register. John had not counted on spending the whole afternoon in the office, trying to register as a conscientious objector. He certainly was glad for this loophole to escape the army, but it surely was a trying experience to waste the whole afternoon trying to register as a conscientious objector. The draft had been calling more and more young men from his community. John knew his turn would come sooner or later. He may as well get it over.

John had noticed several of his acquaintances in the line ahead of him. It appeared that some of them were having a hard time convincing the officer to fix up their papers for service in the conscientious-objector camps.

Suddenly his attention was drawn to the desk, where Paul was explaining his firm convictions concerning war to the apparently interested officer. In his clear unwavering voice, Paul's testimony rang out through the building. A solemn hush suddenly seemed to change the atmosphere there.

"Maybe by the time I get there this question of conscientious-objectors' camp will be more settled," John thought wistfully. "I never could speak up as Paul does."

"Very well," the officer was saying, "you are free to choose—"

"Good afternoon, young man," a voice broke in, as a friendly hand was laid across John's shoulder.

John looked up, expecting to see an old friend. To his surprise the voice was from a total stranger.

John searched his face, hoping to recognize him if he were someone he should know.

"My name is Jim Davis," the stranger went on. "I've been waiting here a long time and was looking for someone to talk to."

"Yes, this is getting tiresome," John agreed. "I had hoped to get home in time to go fishing a while this evening. Looks as though we might be here half the night."

"Yes, I don't know why it should take so long to register. Some of those fellows up there have wasted more time than it would take for a dozen of us to enlist in the armed service," the stranger added. "I tried to get here earlier this morning, but everything went wrong. First thing, the neighbor's pigs got into my wife's garden. It's her pride and joy. They practically ruined it. I worked an hour or so driving them all out and fixing up the garden fence they tore down."

"That's a shame when people allow their animals to run over other people's things like that," John put in with fervor. "I'd make them pay double for everything they destroyed."

"I don't know what to do," Mr. Davis went on. "The worst of it is that it happens every year. I've told them and begged them and threatened them but nothing does any good. They are pretty good neighbors, but they won't keep their animals in. I hate to start trouble, but I can't have them disturbing my wife's garden like this."

"Well, you certainly can't," John exclaimed emphatically. "I surely would not stand for it. Next time the pigs come over, I'd send a few of them to the butcher shop and stock my freezer," he finished with a hearty laugh.

"Then what would you do when Mr. Smith came over and held his fist under your nose?" Mr. Davis inquired.

"I'd show him mine so fast that he'd forget what he came

for," John laughed.

"Next," the officer called.

John looked up. He was next in line. The crowd had cleared some. John stepped over to the desk.

"Be seated, young man," the officer smiled. "Have you been called or are you enlisting voluntarily?" he asked in a very businesslike tone.

"Voluntarily," John answered stiffly, hoping he could get through this without having to answer too many questions.

"Army or Navy?" the officer went on without looking up.

"Conscientious objector," John answered.

The officer looked up. "Why?"

"Religious beliefs," John answered shortly.

"I don't believe we will need to go into that in detail," the officer began. "There have been a number of—"

"Just a minute," a familiar voice broke in. Jim Davis stood before the officer, unbuttoning his coat. He reached inside, and, facing John, pulled out a badge.

John became uneasy. Apparently the pretended Jim Davis was an officer.

"What is it?" the man behind the desk asked impatiently.

"This young man is not a conscientious objector," Mr. Davis answered firmly.

"How can you judge so hastily?" the other officer asked.

Looking straight into John's eyes, Mr. Davis asked pointedly, "What would you do if the neighbor's pigs got into your garden?"

John hung his head in shame. In his heart he knew the answer.

For a half hour the restless boys in the line waited.

John begged and pleaded for the privilege to go to the conscientious-objectors' camp. He did not believe in war. Others were granted this privilege.

John was not. And he knew the reason why.

At half-past six John walked out of the register hall with his papers in his pocket. They read: "John Miller, enlisted in U.S. Armed Forces."